COMPLEX NUMBERS AND FUNCTIONS

COMPLEX NUMBERS AND FUNCTIONS

by

T. ESTERMANN

UNIVERSITY OF LONDON
THE ATHLONE PRESS
1962

Published by
THE ATHLONE PRESS
UNIVERSITY OF LONDON
at 2 Gower Street London WC1
Distributed by Constable & Co. Ltd
12 *Orange Street London* WC2

Canada
University of Toronto Press

U.S.A.
Oxford University Press Inc
New York

© *T. Estermann*, 1962

Printed in Great Britain by
WILLIAM CLOWES AND SONS LIMITED
London and Beccles

PREFACE

This book is meant to be used in connection with university courses on the theory of functions of a complex variable. It also deals with certain more elementary matters needed for an understanding of that theory, but the reader is supposed to be familiar with the elements of the theory of real functions of real variables.

I have aimed at a high degree of rigour, and have avoided any appeal to geometrical intuition. I have tried to give full explanations of fundamental ideas rather than a large number of complicated theorems, but, to the best of my knowledge, the book contains all the important theorems on functions of a complex variable needed for Honours degree courses in Mathematics. The usual proofs of a fair number of standard theorems have been revised with a view to greater clarity, accuracy, or simplicity.

An asterisk at the beginning of a section or chapter indicates that the contents of that section or chapter are at present outside the normal syllabus for a first degree.

University College, London   T. E.

CONTENTS

CHAPTER 1

COMPLEX NUMBERS

1.1. The system of the *natural numbers*—let us call it S_1—is extended, by the introduction of 0 and the *negative integers*, to the system S_2 of the *integers*. S_2 is extended, by the introduction of the *fractions* (i.e. all those numbers which are not integers but can be expressed as vulgar fractions), to the system S_3 of the *rational numbers*. S_3 is extended, by the introduction of the *irrational numbers*, to the system S_4 of the *real numbers*.

1.2. A number system S is called a *field* if and only if it has the following six properties:

(i) The numbers 0 and 1 are members of S.

(ii) Addition and multiplication are defined in S. This means that, with every pair of members a, b of S, there are associated a number $a+b$ (their sum) and a number ab (their product). These are members of S, and are uniquely determined by a and b.

(iii) Addition and multiplication are *commutative* $(a+b=b+a,\ ab=ba)$, *associative* $[a+(b+c)=(a+b)+c,\ a(bc)=(ab)c]$ and *distributive* $[a(b+c)=ab+ac]$.

(iv) For every member a of S, $a+0=a\times1=a$.

(v) Subtraction is always possible in S. This means that, for every pair of members a, b of S, there is one and only one member z of S such that $z+b=a$.

(vi) Division by numbers other than 0 is always possible in S. This means that, for every pair of members a, b of S, such that $b\neq0$, there is one and only one member w of S such that $wb=a$.

S_1 and S_2 are not fields, but S_3 and S_4 are. In fact, the purpose of the first two extensions mentioned in §1.1 is to obtain a field.

1.3. The immediate purpose of the next extension—that of S_4 to the system of the complex numbers—is to extend S_4 to a field in which the equation $z^2+1=0$ is soluble. Incidentally, however, the complex numbers have many other uses.

I begin by creating a new number, calling it i, and defining $i \times i$ as -1. A field which contains the real numbers and the number i must, however, contain other numbers as well. In fact, by §1.2(ii), corresponding to every pair of real numbers† x, y, the field must contain a number equal to $x + iy$, and it will soon be shown that, in general, this is a number still to be created.

1.4. Let us assume that there is such a field (or that it is possible to construct one). Then, by §1.2, we must have $i \times 1 = 0 + i = i$ and $i \times 0 + i = i \times 0 + i \times 1 = i(0 + 1) = i \times 1 = i$. As there is only one number z in the field such that $z + i = i$, it follows that $i \times 0 = 0$. (In the same way it can be proved that $a \times 0 = 0$ for any member a of any field.) Hence, if $y = 0$, then $x + iy$ is the real number x, and if $x = 0$ and $y = 1$, then $x + iy$ is the number i. We shall see that, in all other cases, $x + iy$ is different from all the numbers introduced so far.

Suppose

$$x + iy = x' + iy'.$$

Then, by §1.2, $(x - x') + (x + iy) = (x - x') + (x' + iy') = (x - x' + x') + iy' = x + iy'$ and $i(y' - y) + (x + iy) = i(y' - y) + (iy + x) = \{i(y' - y) + iy\} + x = i(y' - y + y) + x = iy' + x = x + iy'$. As there is only one number z in the field such that $z + (x + iy) = x + iy'$, it follows that $x - x' = i(y' - y)$. Squaring each side of this equation (i.e. multiplying it by itself), and using §1.2(iii) and §1.3, we obtain $(x - x')^2 = -(y' - y)^2$. Since the square of any real number other than 0 is positive, it follows that $x - x' = y' - y = 0$, which means that $x = x'$ and $y = y'$. Thus, to *different* pairs of real numbers x, y correspond *different* numbers $x + iy$.

Now suppose that $x + iy$ is a real number x', say. Then $x + iy = x' + i \times 0$, and hence, by what has just been proved, $y = 0$. Similarly, if $x + iy = i$, then $x + iy = 0 + i \times 1$ and hence $x = 0$ and $y = 1$. Thus the only cases in which $x + iy$ is a real number or i are those mentioned above.

It follows from §1.2(iii) and §1.3 that

$$(x + iy) + (u + iv) = (x + u) + i(y + v) \tag{1}$$

---

† From now on, the letters x, y, u, and v, with or without suffixes, accents and the like, will denote real numbers throughout.

and
$$(x+iy)(u+iv) = (xu-yv)+i(xv+yu).\qquad(2)$$

1.5. I shall now *construct* a field which contains the real numbers and the number i.

Corresponding to every pair of real numbers x, y, except the pairs $x, 0$ and $0, 1$, I create† a new number, which I shall temporarily denote by $[x, y]$. It is to be understood that $[x, y]=[u, v]$ only if $x=u$ and $y=v$. The purpose of this creation is to supply the numbers $x+iy$ of §1.3 and §1.4.

The real numbers, the number i and the numbers just created are called the *complex numbers*. I have to define the sum and product of any two complex numbers, not both real, except the product $i \times i$, which has already been defined by the equation
$$i \times i = -1.\qquad(3)$$

To obtain a uniform notation, which will simplify these definitions, I attach a meaning to the expression $[x, y]$ also in the case $y=0$ and in the case $x=0, y=1$, putting

$$[x, 0] = x\qquad(4)$$

and

$$[0, 1] = i.\qquad(5)$$

Now every complex number can be expressed in the form $[x, y]$, and in only one way. It is therefore sufficient to define $[x, y]+[u, v]$ and $[x, y] \times [u, v]$. I do this by putting

$$[x, y]+[u, v] = [x+u, y+v]\qquad(6)$$

and

$$[x, y] \times [u, v] = [xu-yv, xv+yu],\qquad(7)$$

except in the case $y=v=0$ and, as far as (7) is concerned, in the case $x=u=0, y=v=1$. In these cases (6) and (7) are true too, but are not definitions. The reason why I give the above values (that is to say, those stated on the right-hand sides of

† If the reader objects to the 'creation' of numbers, he may, instead, *define* the new numbers as pairs of real numbers. The number i is then to be defined as the pair $0, 1$.

(6) and (7)) to $[x, y] + [u, v]$ and $[x, y] \times [u, v]$ is that I want the formula

$$x + iy = [x, y] \tag{8}$$

to hold, and the system of the complex numbers to be a field. It follows from (1) and (2) that none but these values are consistent with these objects. It will be proved in the next section that these objects have been achieved.

1.6. By (4), (5), (6) and (7),

$$
\begin{aligned}
x + iy &= [x, 0] + [0, 1] \times [y, 0] = [x, 0] + [0 \times y - 1 \times 0, \\
& \qquad\qquad\qquad\qquad\qquad\qquad\qquad 0 \times 0 + 1 \times y] \\
&= [x, 0] + [0, y] = [x + 0, 0 + y] = [x, y].
\end{aligned}
$$

This proves (8).

To prove that the system of the complex numbers is a field, as defined in §1.2, I note that 0 and 1 are complex numbers, and that addition and multiplication have been defined in the system. It is trivial that this addition is commutative and associative, and that this multiplication is commutative. Also

$$
\begin{aligned}
[x_1, y_1]([x_2, y_2][x_3, y_3]) \\
&= [x_1, y_1][x_2 x_3 - y_2 y_3, x_2 y_3 + y_2 x_3] \\
&= [x_1(x_2 x_3 - y_2 y_3) - y_1(x_2 y_3 + y_2 x_3), \\
& \qquad x_1(x_2 y_3 + y_2 x_3) + y_1(x_2 x_3 - y_2 y_3)] \\
&= [(x_1 x_2 - y_1 y_2)x_3 - (x_1 y_2 + y_1 x_2)y_3, \\
& \qquad (x_1 x_2 - y_1 y_2)y_3 + (x_1 y_2 + y_1 x_2)x_3] \\
&= [x_1 x_2 - y_1 y_2, x_1 y_2 + y_1 x_2][x_3, y_3] \\
&= ([x_1, y_1][x_2, y_2])[x_3, y_3]
\end{aligned}
$$

and

$$
\begin{aligned}
[x_1, y_1]([x_2, y_2] + [x_3, y_3]) \\
&= [x_1, y_1][x_2 + x_3, y_2 + y_3] \\
&= [x_1(x_2 + x_3) - y_1(y_2 + y_3), \quad x_1(y_2 + y_3) + y_1(x_2 + x_3)] \\
&= [x_1 x_2 - y_1 y_2, x_1 y_2 + y_1 x_2] + [x_1 x_3 - y_1 y_3, x_1 y_3 + y_1 x_3] \\
&= [x_1, y_1][x_2, y_2] + [x_1, y_1][x_3, y_3].
\end{aligned}
$$

Thus the system has property (iii) of §1.2.

It is trivial that it has property (iv).

Let z denote a complex number. Then it is trivial that $z+[u, v]=[x, y]$ if and only if $z=[x-u, y-v]$. Also, if $[u, v]\neq 0$, it is easily seen that $w[u, v]=[x, y]$ if and only if

$$w = \left[\frac{xu+yv}{u^2+v^2}, \frac{-xv+yu}{u^2+v^2}\right].$$

Thus the system has properties (v) and (vi) of §1.2, which completes the proof that it is a field.

1.7. I now abandon the temporary notation $[x, y]$, and write $x+iy$ instead, which is customary, and is permissible in virtue of (8). One may, of course, also use a single letter, such as z or w, to denote a complex number. Remember, however, that in this book the letters u, v, x and y are reserved for *real* numbers.

Corresponding to any complex number z, there is one and only one pair of real numbers x, y such that $z=x+iy$. I denote these numbers x and y by re z and im z respectively. This is the notation adopted by the Oxford University Press, but several other notations are in use. re z is called the *real part*, im z the *imaginary part* of z. A complex number which is not real is called an *imaginary number*. A number of the form iy, where $y\neq 0$, is called a *purely imaginary* number. Note that the imaginary part of a complex number is not an imaginary number, but a real number.

1.8. It is known that, if a and b are real numbers, then $a-b$ is the number z for which $z+b=a$. If, moreover, $b\neq 0$, then a/b is the number w for which $wb=a$. I define $a-b$ and a/b for complex numbers a and b, not both real, in the same way. Alternative notations for a/b are $\dfrac{a}{b}$ and $a\div b$. For any imaginary number a, I define $-a$ as $0-a$. I may now write $x-iy$ for $x+i(-y)$ and $-iy$ for $i(-y)$.

The following six formulae follow at once from these definitions:

$$a-b+b=a, \qquad (a/b)b = a \quad (b\neq 0), \qquad a-0=a,$$
$$a/1 = a, \qquad a-a = 0, \qquad a/a = 1 \quad (a\neq 0).$$

1.9. The following formulae can now be proved for complex numbers in the same way as they are usually proved for real numbers:

$$a+(b-c) = a+b-c, \qquad a-(b+c) = a-b-c,$$
$$a-(b-c) = a-b+c, \qquad a(b/c) = (ab)/c \quad (c \neq 0),$$
$$a/(bc) = (a/b)/c \quad (b \neq 0, c \neq 0),$$
$$a/(b/c) = (a/b)c \quad (b \neq 0, c \neq 0),$$
$$a(b-c) = ab-ac, \qquad \frac{a+b}{c} = \frac{a}{c} + \frac{b}{c} \quad (c \neq 0),$$
$$\frac{a-b}{c} = \frac{a}{c} - \frac{b}{c} \quad (c \neq 0), \qquad \frac{ac}{bc} = \frac{a}{b} \quad (b \neq 0, c \neq 0).$$

It follows from these formulae, (3), §1.6 and §1.8 that, if $u+iv \neq 0$, then

$$\frac{x+iy}{u+iv} = \frac{(x+iy)(u-iv)}{(u+iv)(u-iv)} = \frac{xu+yv+i(-xv+yu)}{u^2+v^2}$$
$$= \frac{xu+yv}{u^2+v^2} + i\,\frac{-xv+yu}{u^2+v^2}$$

This agrees with the last formula in §1.6.

1.10. I shall now prove that the product of two complex numbers cannot be 0 unless at least one of these numbers is 0. This will follow from the fact that the system of the complex numbers is a field.

It is sufficient to prove that, if $ab=0$ and $b \neq 0$, then $a=0$. Suppose, therefore, that $ab=0$ and $b \neq 0$. Then $0 \times b = 0$, and there is only one number w such that $wb=0$. Hence $a=0$.

1.11. The number $x-iy$ is called the *conjugate complex number* to $x+iy$, or, when there is no risk of ambiguity, the *conjugate* of $x+iy$. Let us denote the conjugate of z by $\bar{z}$. It is trivial that $\bar{z}=z$ if and only if z is real, and that $\bar{z}=-z$ if and only if z is 0 or purely imaginary. It may be left to the reader to prove that the conjugates of $z+w$, $z-w$, zw and (if $w \neq 0$) z/w are $\bar{z}+\bar{w}$, $\bar{z}-\bar{w}$, $\overline{zw}$ and $\bar{z}/\bar{w}$ respectively. It follows that, if in an expression consisting only of complex numbers and the symbols of addition, subtraction, multiplication and division every complex number is replaced by its conjugate, then the value of the expression so obtained is the conjugate of that of the original expression.

1.12. For any imaginary number z, I define $|z|$ (the *modulus* or *absolute value* of z) as $\sqrt{(z\bar{z})}$, it being understood that $\sqrt{c}$ denotes the *positive* square root of c if c is positive. It should be noted that the formula $|z| = \sqrt{(z\bar{z})}$ holds also if z is real.

It follows that $|x+iy| = \sqrt{(x^2+y^2)}$ and $|zw| = \sqrt{\{(zw)\overline{zw}\}}$ $= \sqrt{\{(zw)(\bar{z}\bar{w})\}} = \sqrt{\{(z\bar{z})(w\bar{w})\}} = \sqrt{(z\bar{z})}\sqrt{(w\bar{w})} = |z||w|$. The reader will easily deduce that, if $w \neq 0$, then $|z/w| = |z|/|w|$.

1.13. Of any two distinct real numbers, one is always the greater, the other the lesser. This property of the real numbers is not extended to imaginary numbers. An imaginary number is neither greater nor less than any other complex number, real or imaginary. Thus the statement $|z| \geqslant z$ is false unless z is real. It is, however, always true (and trivial) that $|z| \geqslant \mathrm{re}\, z$.

I shall now prove that

$$|z+w| \leqslant |z| + |w|. \tag{9}$$

This is trivial if $z+w = 0$. Suppose, therefore, that $z+w \neq 0$. Then

$$\frac{|z|+|w|}{|z+w|} = \frac{|z|}{|z+w|} + \frac{|w|}{|z+w|}$$

$$= \left|\frac{z}{z+w}\right| + \left|\frac{w}{z+w}\right| \geqslant \mathrm{re}\,\frac{z}{z+w} + \mathrm{re}\,\frac{w}{z+w}$$

$$= \mathrm{re}\left(\frac{z}{z+w} + \frac{w}{z+w}\right) = \mathrm{re}\,1 = 1,$$

and (9) follows.

To prove that

$$|z-w| \geqslant |z| - |w|, \tag{10}$$

replace z in (9) by $z-w$. This gives $|z| \leqslant |z-w| + |w|$, and (10) follows.

It may now be left to the reader to prove the inequalities $\big|\,|z|-|w|\,\big| \leqslant |z-w| \leqslant |z|+|w|$ and $\big|\,|z|-|w|\,\big| \leqslant |z+w|$.

1.14. In this section, let m and n denote integers.

For imaginary numbers z, I define z^n (as for real numbers z, other than 0) by the formulae $z^0 = 1$, $z^n = z^{n-1}z$ $(n = 1, 2, 3, \ldots)$ and $z^n = 1/z^{|n|}$ $(n < 0)$.

It may be left to the reader to prove that, for all complex numbers z, other than 0, we have $z^{m+n} = z^m z^n$, $z^{m-n} = z^m/z^n$ and $z^{mn} = (z^m)^n$, and that, if $\bar{z}$ is conjugate to z, then $\bar{z}^n$ is conjugate to z^n. It is also easily proved that $(zw)^n = z^n w^n$ unless $zw = 0$ and $n < 0$.

1.15. It is customary to represent complex numbers by points in a plane. For this purpose, I choose a plane and in it a system of rectangular cartesian coordinates, and consider the complex number $x + iy$ as represented by the point with co-ordinates x, y. In this way I obtain a one-one correspondence between the complex numbers and the points of the plane. If the complex number z corresponds in this way to the point P of the plane, then z is sometimes called the *affix* of P. In this book, however, I shall treat a point and the corresponding complex number as if they were the same thing. This is often done, and does not lead to misunderstandings. Accordingly, the *real axis* is the set of the real numbers, the *imaginary axis* the set of the purely imaginary numbers and the number 0, the *upper half-plane* the set of those complex numbers z for which im $z > 0$, the *fourth quadrant* the set of those for which re $z > 0 >$ im z, the *unit circle* the set of those for which $|z| = 1$, the *unit disc* the set of those for which $|z| < 1$, and so on.

It is customary to extend the plane by the creation of a point corresponding to ∞, a point which I shall simply call 'the point ∞'. The points other than ∞ are then called the *finite points*. This extension of the plane is convenient for some purposes, but inconvenient for others. I shall, therefore, sometimes include and sometimes exclude the point ∞. Though ∞ is a point, it is not a number, and must not be substituted for any letter. Thus a point z is a finite point.

1.16. The last section suggests that we may consider, together with the complex number $z = x + iy$, the polar coordinates r, θ of the point (x, y), referred to the origin as pole and the positive x-axis as initial line. Then

$$x = r \cos \theta, \qquad y = r \sin \theta, \tag{11}$$

and it follows from §1.12 that $r = |z|$.

Corresponding to any complex number $z = x + iy$, there are infinitely many real numbers θ for which $x = |z| \cos \theta$ and

$y = |z| \sin \theta$. If $z \neq 0$, and θ_0 is one of these numbers θ, then all are given by the formula $\theta = \theta_0 + 2k\pi$, where k is an arbitrary integer. These numbers θ are called *the values of the amplitude of z*, and that one for which $-\pi < \theta \leqslant \pi$ is called *the principal value of the amplitude of z*, or, briefly, *the principal amplitude of z*. I denote the principal value of the amplitude of z (and *nothing else*) by am z, though many mathematicians use this notation for any value of the amplitude. Some use the word 'argument' for 'amplitude', and 'arg z' for 'am z'. In Hardy*, on the other hand, 'argument' is used for 'affix'.

Note that am z is defined only if $z \neq 0$, and that am $(x+iy)$ is not the same as $\tan^{-1}(y/x)$. If, by $\tan^{-1} u$, we mean that number v for which $\tan v = u$ and $-\tfrac{1}{2}\pi < v < \tfrac{1}{2}\pi$, then

$$\mathrm{am}(x+iy) = \begin{cases} \tan^{-1}(y/x) & (x > 0) \\ \tan^{-1}(y/x) + \pi & (x < 0,\, y > 0) \\ \tan^{-1}(y/x) - \pi & (x < 0,\, y < 0) \\ \tfrac{1}{2}\pi & (x = 0,\, y > 0) \\ -\tfrac{1}{2}\pi & (x = 0,\, y < 0) \\ \pi & (x < 0,\, y = 0). \end{cases}$$

1.17. If θ and ϕ are real numbers, then

$(\cos \theta + i \sin \theta)(\cos \phi + i \sin \phi)$

$\quad = \cos \theta \cos \phi - \sin \theta \sin \phi + i (\sin \theta \cos \phi + \cos \theta \sin \phi) \quad (12)$

$\quad = \cos (\theta + \phi) + i \sin (\theta + \phi)$

and

$$\frac{\cos \theta + i \sin \theta}{\cos \phi + i \sin \phi} = \cos (\theta - \phi) + i \sin (\theta - \phi). \quad (13)$$

Now let z and w be any complex numbers, other than 0, and put am $z = \theta$, am $w = \phi$. Then, by §1.12, §1.16 and (12),

$zw = |z|(\cos \theta + i \sin \theta)|w|(\cos \phi + i \sin \phi)$

$\qquad\qquad = |zw|\{\cos(\theta + \phi) + i \sin (\theta + \phi)\}.$

Hence $\theta + \phi$ is one of the values of the amplitude of zw. It

---

* See the bibliography at the end of the book.

2—C.N.F.

is not necessarily the principal value, that is to say, am (zw) — am z — am w is not necessarily 0, but it is easily seen that

$$\text{am } (zw) - \text{am } z - \text{am } w = \begin{cases} 0 & (-\pi < \text{am } z + \text{am } w \leqslant \pi) \\ -2\pi & (\text{am } z + \text{am } w > \pi) \\ 2\pi & (\text{am } z + \text{am } w \leqslant -\pi). \end{cases} \tag{14}$$

The formula

$$\text{am } z - \text{am } (-z) = \begin{cases} \pi & (\text{im } z > 0) \\ -\pi & (\text{im } z < 0) \end{cases} \tag{15}$$

is also easily proved.

1.18. It follows from (12) by induction that

$$(\cos \theta + i \sin \theta)^n = \cos n\theta + i \sin n\theta \tag{16}$$

for every natural number n. (16) is trivial for $n = 0$. If n is a negative integer, we have, by §1.14 and what has just been proved,

$(\cos \theta + i \sin \theta)^n$
$$= 1/(\cos \theta + i \sin \theta)^{|n|} = 1/(\cos|n|\theta + i \sin|n|\theta)$$
$$= \cos|n|\theta - i \sin|n|\theta = \cos n\theta + i \sin n\theta.$$

Thus (16) holds for all integers n. This is De Moivre's theorem.

1.19. The above way of introducing the imaginary numbers is the one which seems most satisfactory to me. For alternative ways see Hardy and Landau (1).

EXERCISES

1.1. Prove that each of the following two sets of conditions is sufficient for the formula am $(zw) = \text{am } z + \text{am } w$ to hold:

    (i) re $z > 0$,   re $w \geqslant 0$, $w \neq 0$;

    (ii) im $z < 0 \leqslant$ im w, $w \neq 0$.

1.2. Prove that, if im z and im w are both positive, then am $(zw) -$ am $z -$ am w is equal to 0 or -2π according as im $(zw) \geqslant 0$ or im $(zw) < 0$.

1.3. Prove that, if im z and im w are both negative, then am $(zw) -$ am $z -$ am w is equal to 0 or 2π according as im $(zw) < 0$ or im $(zw) \geqslant 0$.

1.4. Prove that $|z+i|^2 + |z-i|^2 = 2(|z|^2 + 1)$.

1.5. Prove that $(|z+i|^2 - 2)(|z-i|^2 - 2) = |z^2 + 1|^2 - 4|z|^2$.

CHAPTER 2

SEQUENCES AND SERIES OF COMPLEX NUMBERS

2.1. The definition of the limit of a sequence of complex numbers is formally the same as that of the limit of a sequence of real numbers. The sequence

$$z_1, z_2, z_3, \ldots \tag{1}$$

is said to tend to ζ if and only if, for every positive number ϵ, there is a natural number μ, such that, for every natural number $n \geqslant \mu$, we have $|z_n - \zeta| < \epsilon$.

It follows from this definition that a sequence cannot tend to more than one number, though it may tend to none. The number, if any, to which it tends, is called its *limit*. The limit of the above sequence is denoted by $\lim\limits_{n \to \infty} z_n$.

If this sequence does not tend to any number, we say that $\lim\limits_{n \to \infty} z_n$ does not exist.

A sequence is said to be *convergent*, or to *converge*, if and only if it tends to a number. *Divergent* means 'not convergent'.

2.2. The following four theorems follow at once from the last section:

THEOREM 2.1. $\lim\limits_{n \to \infty} (x_n + iy_n)$ *exists if and only if both* $\lim\limits_{n \to \infty} x_n$ *and* $\lim\limits_{n \to \infty} y_n$ *exist, and then*

$$\lim_{n \to \infty} (x_n + iy_n) = \lim_{n \to \infty} x_n + i \lim_{n \to \infty} y_n.$$

THEOREM 2.2. $\lim\limits_{n \to \infty} z_n = \zeta$ *if and only if* $\lim\limits_{n \to \infty} (z_n - \zeta) = 0$.

THEOREM 2.3. $\lim\limits_{n \to \infty} z_n = 0$ *if and only if* $\lim\limits_{n \to \infty} |z_n| = 0$.

THEOREM 2.4. *If*

(i) *there is a natural number v, such that, for every natural number $n \geqslant v$, we have $|z_n| \leqslant a_n$, and*

(ii) $\lim\limits_{n\to\infty} a_n = 0,$

then

(iii) $\lim\limits_{n\to\infty} z_n = 0.$

2.3. The sequence

$$w_1, w_2, w_3, \ldots \tag{2}$$

is called a *sub-sequence* of the sequence (1) if and only if there is a strictly increasing sequence of natural numbers

$$n_1, n_2, n_3, \ldots,$$

such that, for every natural number m, we have $w_m = z_{n_m}$.

If the second of three sequences is a sub-sequence of the first, and the third a sub-sequence of the second, then the third is also a sub-sequence of the first. This is trivial, and so is the following theorem:

THEOREM 2.5. *Any sub-sequence of a convergent sequence has the same limit as that sequence.*

2.4. The sequence (1) is said to be *bounded* if and only if there is a number c, such that, for every natural number n, $|z_n| < c$.

It follows that every convergent sequence is bounded, and that the sequence

$$x_1 + iy_1, x_2 + iy_2, x_3 + iy_3, \ldots$$

is bounded if and only if the sequences $x_1, x_2, x_3, \ldots$ and $y_1, y_2, y_3, \ldots$ are both bounded.

2.5. The following theorem is assumed here:

THEOREM 2.6. *Every bounded sequence of real numbers has a convergent sub-sequence.*

To extend this to complex numbers, I first establish two lemmas.

LEMMA 1. *Every bounded sequence of complex numbers $z_1, z_2, z_3, \ldots$ has a sub-sequence $w_1, w_2, w_3, \ldots$ such that $\lim\limits_{n\to\infty} \operatorname{re} w_n$ exists.*

Proof. Let $z_n = x_n + iy_n$. Then $x_1, x_2, x_3, \ldots$ is a bounded sequence of real numbers. Hence, by Theorem 2.6, there is a strictly increasing sequence of natural numbers $m_1, m_2, m_3, \ldots$

such that $\lim\limits_{n\to\infty} x_{m_n}$ exists.   Putting $w_n = z_{m_n}$, we obtain the result stated.

LEMMA 2.   *Every bounded sequence of complex numbers* $w_1, w_2, w_3, \ldots$ *has a sub-sequence* $\zeta_1, \zeta_2, \zeta_3, \ldots$ *such that* $\lim\limits_{n\to\infty} \mathrm{im}\, \zeta_n$ *exists.*

This can be proved in the same way as Lemma 1.

THEOREM 2.7.   *Every bounded sequence of complex numbers has a convergent sub-sequence.*

Proof.   Let $z_1, z_2, z_3, \ldots$ be a bounded sequence of complex numbers.   Then, by Lemma 1, it has a sub-sequence $w_1, w_2, w_3, \ldots$ such that $\lim\limits_{n\to\infty} \mathrm{re}\, w_n$ exists.   By Lemma 2, the sequence $w_1, w_2, w_3, \ldots$ has a sub-sequence $\zeta_1, \zeta_2, \zeta_3, \ldots$ such that $\lim\limits_{n\to\infty} \mathrm{im}\, \zeta_n$ exists.   Now the sequence $\mathrm{re}\, \zeta_1, \mathrm{re}\, \zeta_2, \mathrm{re}\, \zeta_3, \ldots$ is a sub-sequence of $\mathrm{re}\, w_1, \mathrm{re}\, w_2, \mathrm{re}\, w_3, \ldots$.   Hence, by Theorem 2.5, $\lim\limits_{n\to\infty} \mathrm{re}\, \zeta_n = \lim\limits_{n\to\infty} \mathrm{re}\, w_n$, which implies that $\lim\limits_{n\to\infty} \mathrm{re}\, \zeta_n$ exists. It therefore follows from Theorem 2.1 that the sequence $\zeta_1, \zeta_2, \zeta_3, \ldots$ converges, which proves Theorem 2.7.

2.6. The series of complex numbers $a_0 + a_1 + a_2 + \ldots$, or

$$\sum_{n=0}^{\infty} a_n, \tag{3}$$

is said to *converge* if and only if $\lim\limits_{m=\infty} \sum\limits_{n=0}^{m} a_n$ exists, and the sum of the series is then defined as this limit.   The series is said to converge *absolutely* if and only if $\sum\limits_{n=0}^{\infty} |a_n|$ converges.

It may be left to the reader to prove the following theorem:

THEOREM 2.8.   *The series (3) converges if and only if the two series*

$$\sum_{n=0}^{\infty} \mathrm{re}\, a_n \tag{4}$$

and

$$\sum_{n=0}^{\infty} \mathrm{im}\, a_n \tag{5}$$

converge, and then

$$\sum_{n=0}^{\infty} a_n = \sum_{n=0}^{\infty} \operatorname{re} a_n + i \sum_{n=0}^{\infty} \operatorname{im} a_n.$$

The series (3) *converges absolutely if and only if* (4) *and* (5) *converge absolutely.*

COROLLARY. *If a series of complex numbers converges absolutely then it converges.*

2.7. I assume the following theorem:

THEOREM 2.9. *Let* $\sum a_n$ *and* $\sum b_n$ *be two absolutely convergent series of real numbers, and let*

$$c_n = \sum_{m=0}^{n} a_m b_{n-m} \quad (n = 0, 1, 2, \ldots).$$

Then

$$\sum_{n=0}^{\infty} c_n = \sum_{n=0}^{\infty} a_n \cdot \sum_{n=0}^{\infty} b_n.$$

I shall now prove

THEOREM 2.10. *Let* $\displaystyle\sum_{n=0}^{\infty} a_n$ *and* $\displaystyle\sum_{n=0}^{\infty} b_n$ *be two absolutely convergent series of complex numbers, and let*

$$c_n = \sum_{m=0}^{n} a_m b_{n-m} \quad (n = 0, 1, 2, \ldots). \tag{6}$$

Then

$$\sum_{n=0}^{\infty} c_n = \sum_{n=0}^{\infty} a_n \cdot \sum_{n=0}^{\infty} b_n.$$

Proof. Let

$$a_n = a_n' + i a_n'', \qquad b_n = b_n' + i b_n'', \tag{7}$$

where the letters with accents denote real numbers. Then, by Theorem 2.8, the four series

$$\sum_{n=0}^{\infty} a_n', \qquad \sum_{n=0}^{\infty} a_n'', \qquad \sum_{n=0}^{\infty} b_n', \qquad \sum_{n=0}^{\infty} b_n''$$

converge absolutely. Let us denote their sums by s, t, u, v respectively. Then

$$\sum_{n=0}^{\infty} a_n = s + it, \qquad \sum_{n=0}^{\infty} b_n = u + iv. \tag{8}$$

Now let

$$c_{1,n} = \sum_{m=0}^{n} a'_m b'_{n-m}, \qquad c_{2,n} = \sum_{m=0}^{n} a'_m b''_{n-m},$$

$$c_{3,n} = \sum_{m=0}^{n} a''_m b'_{n-m}, \qquad c_{4,n} = \sum_{m=0}^{n} a''_m b''_{n-m}. \tag{9}$$

Then, by Theorem 2.9,

$$\sum_{n=0}^{\infty} c_{1,n} = su, \quad \sum_{n=0}^{\infty} c_{2,n} = sv, \quad \sum_{n=0}^{\infty} c_{3,n} = tu, \quad \sum_{n=0}^{\infty} c_{4,n} = tv. \tag{10}$$

Also, by (7),

$$a_m b_{n-m} = (a'_m + i a''_m)(b'_{n-m} + i b''_{n-m})$$
$$= a'_m b'_{n-m} - a''_m b''_{n-m} + i(a'_m b''_{n-m} + a''_m b'_{n-m}).$$

Hence, by (6) and (9),

$$c_n = c_{1,n} - c_{4,n} + i(c_{2,n} + c_{3,n}).$$

From this and (10) and (8) it follows that

$$\sum_{n=0}^{\infty} c_n = su - tv + i(sv + tu) = (s+it)(u+iv) = \sum_{n=0}^{\infty} a_n \cdot \sum_{n=0}^{\infty} b_n,$$

which was to be proved.

EXERCISE

2.1. Prove that, if $|a_n| \leqslant b_n$ $(n = 0, 1, 2, \ldots)$, and the series $b_0 + b_1 + b_2 + \ldots$ converges, then so does the series $a_0 + a_1 + a_2 + \ldots$.

CHAPTER 3

SETS OF POINTS

3.1. By a *point* I mean a point of the plane in which the complex numbers are represented. In this chapter, the point ∞ is excluded. As explained in §1.15, I do not distinguish between a point and its affix. The word 'point' may therefore be interpreted as meaning 'complex number'.

Following Hardy, §18, I define an *aggregate* or *set* of points as a system of points, defined in any way whatever. As this definition is essentially Hardy's, I have no doubt that it will be generally accepted. Those readers who do not feel enlightened by it are not necessarily in *good* company, but certainly in mine. Seriously speaking, the notion of an aggregate or set—these two terms are used synonymously—is one of those fundamental notions which mathematicians have to accept without definition. The objects of which an aggregate or set consists are called its *members* or *elements*. An aggregate, notwithstanding the etymology of the word, need not have more than one element, and it is an accepted convention to postulate the existence of an aggregate which has no element at all. This is called the *empty aggregate*.

3.2. Let S and T denote sets of points. The statement '$z \in S$' (read 'z is in S') means that z is a member or element of S. The statement '$S \subset T$' (read 'S is contained in T' or 'S is a sub-set or sub-aggregate of T') means that every member of S is a member of T. This is taken to imply that the empty set is contained in any set; for, by modern mathematical logic (as distinct from Aristotelian logic), the statement 'every A is B' is true if no A exists.

The statement '$S \supset T$' (read 'S contains T') means the same as '$T \subset S$'. The statement '$S = T$' is equivalent to '$S \subset T$ and $T \subset S$'.

3.3. It is convenient to use the term *disc* for the interior of a circle. The disc about z_0 with radius r is then the set of those points z for which $|z - z_0| < r$. The point z_0 is said to be *interior* to the set S (or an *interior point* of S) if and only if there is a disc about z_0 contained in S. It is called a *limit point* of S if and only if there is, in every disc about z_0, a point of S other than z_0. Whether z_0 itself is a point of S is irrelevant in this connection; a limit point of S may or may not be a point of S.

3.4. A set S is said to be *open* if and only if every point of S is interior to S; it is said to be *closed* if and only if every limit point of S is a point of S. 'Closed' does not mean 'not open'. The empty set and the whole plane are both open and closed, and there are infinitely many sets which are neither open nor closed.

A set is said to be *finite* or *infinite* according as it has only a finite number of members or infinitely many; it is said to be *bounded* or *unbounded* according as there is or is not a disc which contains it.

For any set of points S, the set of those points which are not in S is called the *complement* of S.

The *distance* of a point z from a non-empty set S is defined as the lower bound of $|w-z|$ for all points w in S. The *distance* between two non-empty sets S and T is defined as the lower bound of $|w-z|$ for all pairs of points w, z for which $w \in S$ and $z \in T$.

3.5. The proof of the next two theorems may be left to the reader.

THEOREM 3.1. *Let S be a closed set, and let $z_1, z_2, z_3, \ldots$ be a sequence of points of S, tending to ζ. Then $\zeta \in S$.*

THEOREM 3.2. *The complement of any open set is closed, and the complement of any closed set is open.*

I shall prove the next three theorems, the first of which is due to Weierstrass.

THEOREM 3.3. *Any bounded infinite set of points has at least one limit point.*

Proof. Let S be a bounded infinite set. Choose any point z_1 of S. Then choose a point z_2 of S, different from z_1. Then choose a point z_3 of S, different from z_1 and z_2, and so on, that is to say, for any natural number n, choose a point z_n of S not previously chosen. This is possible, since S, being infinite, does not consist of $z_1, z_2, \ldots, z_{n-1}$ only. That it is permissible to make the infinitely many choices corresponding to all natural numbers n follows from an axiom which most mathematicians accept. We thus obtain a sequence $z_1, z_2, z_3, \ldots$ of distinct points of S. This sequence is bounded since S is bounded. Hence, by Theorem 2.7, it has a convergent subsequence. The latter is obviously also a sequence of distinct points of S. From this it easily follows that its limit is a limit point of S. This proves the theorem.

The limit point need not, of course, be a point of S.

THEOREM 3.4. *Suppose that S and T are non-empty closed sets of points, having no point in common, and that S is bounded. Then the distance between S and T is positive.*

Proof. It is trivial that the distance is either positive or 0. Suppose, if possible, that it is 0. Then, corresponding to every natural number n, there are points z_n and w_n, such that $z_n \in S$, $w_n \in T$ and $|w_n - z_n| < 1/n$. From this and Theorem 2.4 it follows that

$$\lim_{n \to \infty} (w_n - z_n) = 0. \tag{1}$$

Now, since S is bounded, so is the sequence $z_1, z_2, z_3, \ldots.$. It has, therefore, by Theorem 2.7, a convergent sub-sequence $z_{n_1}, z_{n_2}, z_{n_3}, \ldots$, say. Let

$$\lim_{m \to \infty} z_{n_m} = \zeta. \tag{2}$$

Now, by (1) and Theorem 2.5, $\lim_{m \to \infty} (w_{n_m} - z_{n_m}) = 0$. Hence, by (2),

$$\lim_{m \to \infty} w_{n_m} = \zeta. \tag{3}$$

From (2), (3) and Theorem 3.1 it follows that the sets S and T have the point ζ in common. This is a contradiction, and so the theorem is proved.

THEOREM 3.5. *Let $S_1, S_2, S_3, \ldots$ be a sequence of non-empty closed bounded sets, each containing the next. Then these sets have at least one point in common.*

Proof. Choose a point z_1 from S_1, a point z_2 from S_2, and so on. Then all members of the sequence $z_1, z_2, z_3, \ldots$ are points of S_1. Hence this sequence is bounded, and so, by

Theorem 2.7, it has a convergent sub-sequence $z_{n_1}, z_{n_2}, z_{n_3}, \ldots$, say.   Let

$$\lim_{m \to \infty} z_{n_m} = w.$$

Then, for every natural number m, w is the limit of the sequence $z_{n_m}, z_{n_{m+1}}, z_{n_{m+2}}, \ldots$, and it is easily seen that all members of this sequence are points of S_m.   Hence, by Theorem 3.1, $w \in S_m$.   Thus the said sets have the point w in common.

3.6. Let S and T be any sets of points.   Then $S \cap T$ (read 'S cap T'), the *intersection* of S and T, is defined as the set of the points common to S and T; and $S \cup T$ (read 'S cup T'), the *union* of S and T, is defined as the set of those points which are in at least one of the sets S, T.   The meaning of $S_1 \cap S_2 \cap \ldots \cap S_k$ and $S_1 \cup S_2 \cup \ldots \cup S_k$ (the intersection and the union of the sets $S_1, S_2, \ldots, S_k$) is now obvious.

Now let α be an aggregate (not necessarily finite) of sets of points.   Then the intersection and the union of the members of α are respectively defined as the set of the points common to all members of α and the set of those points which are in at least one member of α.   In other words, the intersection of the members of α is the set I such that $z \in I$ if and only if $z \in S$ for every member S of α, and the union of the members of α is the set U such that $z \in U$ if and only if there is a set S for which $z \in S$ and $S \in \alpha$.

EXERCISES

3.1. Prove that a union of open sets is always open, and that an intersection of closed sets is always closed.

3.2. Prove that the intersection of a finite number of open sets is always open, and that the intersection of infinitely many open sets is sometimes open, but not always.

3.3. Prove that the union of a finite number of closed sets is always closed, and that the union of infinitely many closed sets is sometimes closed, but not always.

3.4. Show by an example that the distance between two unbounded closed sets, which have no point in common, can be 0.

3.5. Show that, if z is a limit point of S and an interior point of T, then z is a limit point of $S \cap T$.

3.6. Show that, if z is a limit point of S, then every disc about z contains infinitely many points of S.

3.7. Show that, if the distance of the point z from the set S is 0, then z is a point of S or a limit point of S or both.

3.8. Show that a set of points S is closed if and only if the limit of every convergent sequence of points of S is a point of S.

3.9. Show that the limit of a convergent sequence of points of a set S is not always a limit point of S.

3.10. Show that, if the distance of the point z from the closed set S is d, then there is a point w in S such that $|z - w| = d$.

3.11. S and T are closed sets, S is bounded, and the distance between S and T is d. Show that there are points z, w such that $z \in S$, $w \in T$, and $|z - w| = d$.

CHAPTER 4

FUNCTIONS

4.1. When we speak of *ordered pairs of numbers*, we mean that we consider the pair (a, b) as different from (b, a) (unless $a = b$). For convenience, I call the first member of a pair its *abscissa*, the second its *ordinate*. I define a *function* (of one variable) as a non-empty aggregate of ordered pairs of numbers, such that no two members of the aggregate have the same abscissa. Let f be a function (i.e. such an aggregate). Then the set of the abscissae of the members of f is called the *region of existence* of f. Let it be denoted by S. Then, corresponding to any member z of S, there is one and only one number w such that $(z, w) \in f$. This number w is denoted by $f(z)$. Of any number z which is not in S, we say that $f(z)$ does not exist. Thus the region of existence of f is the set of those numbers z for which $f(z)$ exists. A number w is called *a value assumed by f* if and only if there is a number z such that $f(z) = w$. If (and only if) every value assumed by f is a real number, then f is called a *real function*. Strictly speaking, every function (including the real functions) is a *complex function*, since every number is a complex number, but when we speak of complex functions, we mean to indicate that the functions considered are not necessarily real functions. A function f, such that every value assumed by f is a rational number, is not called a rational function; nor is a function f, such that every value assumed by f is an integer, called an integral function. For the meaning of the term *rational function* see Hardy, §24. The term 'integral function' will be defined later in this book. If the region of existence of f consists entirely of real numbers, then f is called a *function of a real variable* (Hardy, Chapter II); if it consists entirely of positive integers, then f is called a *function of a positive integral variable* (Hardy, §50). One might assume, by analogy, that every function (of one variable) is a function of a complex variable, and that, when we speak of functions of a complex variable, we mean to indicate that the functions considered are not necessarily functions of a real variable. According to Hardy, §227, however, it is futile to use the term 'function of a complex variable' in this sense. It is, therefore, not done.

4.2. If f is a function, then $f(z)$ (or any expression with the same meaning as $f(z)$) is called a *function of z*. Thus $1/z$ is a function of z; for we may take f to be the aggregate of those pairs of numbers (z, w) for which $w = 1/z$. This ambiguity in the use of the word 'function' is not likely to lead to misunderstandings. When we say 'the function f is defined by $f(z) = 1/z$', we mean that f is the aggregate just mentioned.

The reader may have noticed that my definition of a function excludes the so-called *many-valued functions*. This is because I have no use for them, and hold the view that they have no place in rigorous mathematics. I shall, however, deal in due course with the multiform functions, which are often mistakenly called 'many-valued functions'. My definition, by the way, agrees with Landau 2, Definition 19, and Courant, Chapter I, §2, though it disagrees with Hardy, §20.

4.3. The statement

$$f(z) \to l \quad \text{as} \quad z \to a \tag{1}$$

means that, for every positive number ϵ, there is a positive number δ, such that, for every (complex) number z for which $0 < |z - a| < \delta$, we have $|f(z) - l| < \epsilon$.

The statement

$$f(x) \to l \quad \text{as} \quad x \to a, \tag{2}$$

on the other hand, in virtue of §1.3, footnote, means that, for every positive number ϵ, there is a positive number δ, such that, for every *real* number x for which $0 < |x - a| < \delta$, we have $|f(x) - l| < \epsilon$. Clearly (1) always implies (2), but not vice versa.

A similar difference between the meanings of '$\phi(x) \to l$ as $x \to \infty$' and '$\phi(n) \to l$ as $n \to \infty$' is explained in Hardy, §90.

The definitions of '$f(x) \to l$ as $x \to a+$' and '$f(x) \to l$ as $x \to a-$' are obtained from that of (2) by substituting '$x - a$' and '$a - x$' respectively for '$|x - a|$'.

It is trivial that, corresponding to any function f and any number a, there is at most one number l such that (1) holds.

If there is such a number l, it is denoted by $\lim\limits_{z\to a} f(z)$; otherwise we say that $\lim\limits_{z\to a} f(z)$ does not exist.   There is a similar relation between (2) and $\lim\limits_{x\to a} f(x)$ if a is real.   If a is not real, then $\lim\limits_{x\to a} f(x)$ does not exist.   It is trivial that, if $\lim\limits_{z\to a} f(z)$ and $\lim\limits_{x\to a} f(x)$ both exist, then they are equal.

It may be left to the reader to define $\lim\limits_{x\to a+} f(x)$ and $\lim\limits_{x\to a-} f(x)$.

4.4. The statement 'f is *continuous* at a' may mean either $\lim\limits_{z\to a} f(z)=f(a)$ or $\lim\limits_{x\to a} f(x)=f(a)$.   Where necessary to avoid ambiguity, I shall indicate the former meaning by the phrase *fully continuous*, the latter by the phrase *continuous relative to the real axis*.   The statement 'f is continuous in S' (where S denotes a set of points) is not ambiguous.   It means that, for every point z of S and every positive number ϵ, there is a positive number δ, such that, for every point w of S for which $|w-z|<\delta$, we have $|f(w)-f(z)|<\epsilon$.

The statements 'f is *continuous to the right* at a' and 'f is *continuous to the left* at a' mean $\lim\limits_{x\to a+} f(x)=f(a)$ and $\lim\limits_{x\to a-} f(x)=f(a)$ respectively.

The statement 'f is *bounded* in S' means that there is a number c, such that, for every point z of S, we have $|f(z)|<c$.

EXERCISE

4.1. Prove that the function f defined by $f(z)=\operatorname{am} z$ is fully continuous at all points other than 0 and the negative real numbers.

4.5. What has just been said of continuity applies also to differentiability.   The statement 'f is *differentiable* at a' may indicate the existence of either

$$\lim_{z\to a}\frac{f(z)-f(a)}{z-a} \tag{3}$$

or

$$\lim_{x\to a}\frac{f(x)-f(a)}{x-a},$$

either of which is usually denoted by $f'(a)$.   Ambiguity can again be avoided by the use of phrases like 'fully' and 'relative to the real axis'. The statement 'f' is a *derivative in the full sense*' is meant to imply that $f'(a)$ exists only for those points a at which f is fully differentiable, i.e. that $f'(a)$ is defined as (3).

4.6. The formulae which express the derivatives of the sum, difference, product and quotient of two functions in terms of these two functions and their derivatives, well known from the calculus for derivatives relative to the real axis, can be similarly proved for derivatives in the full sense. Corresponding to the theorem of the calculus on differentiating a function of a function, one can similarly prove the following two:

THEOREM 4.1. *Suppose that the function f is fully differentiable at z_0, that the function g is fully differentiable at $f(z_0)$, and that the function h is defined by the equation $h(z) = g\{f(z)\}$. Then h is fully differentiable at z_0, and $h'(z_0) = g'\{f(z_0)\}f'(z_0)$.*

THEOREM 4.2. *Suppose that the function f is differentiable relative to the real axis at x_0, that the function g is fully differentiable at $f(x_0)$, and that the function h is defined by the equation $h(z) = g\{f(z)\}$. Then h is differentiable relative to the real axis at x_0, and $h'(x_0) = g'\{f(x_0)\}f'(x_0)$.*

4.7. The next theorem may be known to the reader, in a slightly different form, as a result of the theory of real functions of two real variables. It is, in fact, a generalisation of Hardy, §103, Theorem 2. It is included here for the sake of some of its applications.

THEOREM 4.3. *Let S be a non-empty closed bounded set of points, and let f be a real function continuous in S. Then there are points z_1, z_2 in S such that $f(z_1) \leqslant f(z) \leqslant f(z_2)$ for every point z of S.*

Proof. If f is not bounded above in S (for I have not yet proved that this is impossible), let

$$a_n = n \quad (n = 1, 2, 3, \ldots). \tag{4}$$

If f is bounded above in S, let M be its upper bound there, and let

$$a_n = M - 1/n \quad (n = 1, 2, 3, \ldots). \tag{5}$$

In either case there is, corresponding to every natural number n, a point w_n in S such that $f(w_n) > a_n$. Since S is bounded, so is the sequence $w_1, w_2, w_3, \ldots$. It therefore has, by Theorem

2.7, a convergent sub-sequence $w_{n_1}, w_{n_2}, w_{n_3}, \ldots$, say, where $n_1, n_2, n_3, \ldots$ is a strictly increasing sequence of natural numbers. Let

$$\lim_{m \to \infty} w_{n_m} = z_2. \tag{6}$$

Then, by Theorem 3.1, $z_2 \in S$. From this and (6) and the hypothesis that f is continuous in S it follows that

$$\lim_{m \to \infty} f(w_{n_m}) = f(z_2). \tag{7}$$

Now

$$f(w_{n_m}) > a_{n_m} \geqslant a_m. \tag{8}$$

Hence it is impossible that (4) holds. Thus f must have the upper bound M in S, and (5) holds. It therefore follows from (7) and (8) that

$$f(z_2) \geqslant \lim_{m \to \infty} a_m = M \geqslant f(z)$$

for every point z of S. Similarly there is a point z_1 in S such that $f(z_1) \leqslant f(z)$ for every point z in S.

COROLLARY. *Any (complex) function ϕ continuous in a closed bounded set S is bounded in S.*

This follows from Theorem 4.3 with $f(z) = |\phi(z)|$.

*4.8. The last theorem may be used in order to prove the *fundamental theorem of algebra*, which states that every algebraic equation has a root. An *algebraic equation* is an equation of the form $p(z) = 0$, where $p(z)$ is a non-constant polynomial. A *polynomial* is an expression of the form

$$\sum_{m=0}^{n} a_m z^m,$$

where z is a variable, and $a_0, a_1, a_2, \ldots, a_n$ are constants. The polynomial may itself be constant, namely if $n = 0$, and also if $n > 0$ and $a_1 = a_2 = \ldots = a_n = 0$. The fundamental theorem of algebra will follow immediately from the next two theorems.

THEOREM 4.4. *Let $p(z)$ be a polynomial. Then there is a number z_0 such that $|p(z_0)| \leqslant |p(z)|$ for every number z.*

Proof. If $p(z)$ is constant, there is nothing to prove. Suppose, therefore, that $p(z)$ is not constant. Then

$$p(z) = \sum_{m=0}^{n} a_m z^m,$$

say, where $n \geqslant 1$ and $a_n \neq 0$. Choose the positive number r so large that

$$|a_0| + \sum_{m=0}^{n-1} |a_m| r^m < |a_n| r^n,$$

for instance

$$r = 1 + |a_n|^{-1}(|a_0| + \sum_{m=0}^{n-1} |a_m|).$$

Then, for every number z for which $|z| \geqslant r$, we have

$$|p(z)| \geqslant |z|^n(|a_n| - \sum_{m=0}^{n-1} |a_m| \, |z|^{m-n}) \geqslant r^n(|a_n| - \sum_{m=0}^{n-1} |a_m| r^{m-n})$$

$$= |a_n| r^n - \sum_{m=0}^{n-1} |a_m| r^m > |a_0|.$$

Thus

$$|p(z)| > |p(0)| \quad (|z| \geqslant r). \tag{9}$$

Now let S be the set of those points z for which $|z| \leqslant r$, and let $f(z) = |p(z)|$. Then S is closed and bounded, and f is continuous in S. Hence, by Theorem 4.3, there is a point z_0 in S such that $f(z_0) \leqslant f(z)$, that is to say

$$|p(z_0)| \leqslant |p(z)|, \tag{10}$$

for every point z in S. In particular, $|p(z_0)| \leqslant |p(0)|$. From this and (9) it follows that (10) holds also for those points z which are not in S.

THEOREM 4.5. *Let $p(z)$ be a non-constant polynomial, and let $p(z_0) \neq 0$. Then there is a number z_1 such that $|p(z_1)| < |p(z_0)|$.*

Proof. We have

$$\frac{p(z_0 + w)}{p(z_0)} = \sum_{m=0}^{n} b_m w^m, \tag{11}$$

say, where the numbers $b_0, b_1, \ldots, b_n$ are independent of w, and the numbers $b_1, b_2, \ldots, b_n$ are not all 0. Putting $w = 0$, we obtain $b_0 = 1$. Let k be the least positive integer m such that $b_m \neq 0$. Then, by (11),

$$\frac{p(z_0 + w)}{p(z_0)} = 1 + \sum_{m=k}^{n} b_m w^m. \tag{12}$$

Now let am $b_k = \theta$, so that $b_k = |b_k|(\cos\theta + i\sin\theta)$, let $\phi = (\pi - \theta)/k$, so that $\theta + k\phi = \pi$, and let $w = t(\cos\phi + i\sin\phi)$, where t is positive and so small that

$$\sum_{m=k+1}^{n} |b_m|t^m < |b_k|t^k \leqslant 1,$$

for instance

$$t = (|b_k| + |b_k|^{-1}\sum_{m=k}^{n}|b_m|)^{-1}.$$

Then, by (12) and Chapter 1, (16) and (12),

$$\frac{|p(z_0+w)|}{|p(z_0)|} \leqslant |1 + b_k w^k| + \sum_{m=k+1}^{n}|b_m|\,|w|^m$$

$$= 1 - |b_k|t^k + \sum_{m=k+1}^{n}|b_m|t^m < 1.$$

Hence, putting $z_0 + w = z_1$, we have $|p(z_1)| < |p(z_0)|$. This proves Theorem 4.5, and so completes the proof of the fundamental theorem of algebra.

4.9. If $a < b$, then the *closed interval* $[a, b]$ and the *open interval* (a, b) are defined as the sets of those points x for which $a \leqslant x \leqslant b$ and $a < x < b$ respectively. Note that an open interval is not an open set.

If the function f is not a real function, I define the integral of f over $[a, b]$, following Hardy, §170, by the formula

$$\int_a^b f(x)dx = \int_a^b \mathrm{re}\,f(x)dx + i\int_a^b \mathrm{im}\,f(x)dx.$$

EXERCISE

4.2. Prove formula (1) of Hardy, §170, by the method used in this book to prove formula (9) of §1.13.

4.10. The next theorem is trivial.

THEOREM 4.6. *Let* $\lim_{x \to x_0} f(x) = l$. *Then* $\lim_{x \to x_0} \mathrm{re}\,f(x) = \mathrm{re}\,l$ *and* $\lim_{x \to x_0} \mathrm{im}\,f(x) = \mathrm{im}\,l$.

This remains true if the letter x is replaced by z throughout.

In the remainder of this chapter, I shall distinguish pedantically between the derivatives of any function f in the full sense and relative to the real axis, denoting the former by f', the latter by f'_R.

THEOREM 4.7.   *Let $F'_R(x_0)$ exist, and let the functions g and h be defined by $g(z) = \mathrm{re}\, F(z)$, $h(z) = \mathrm{im}\, F(z)$. Then $g'_R(x_0) = \mathrm{re}\, F'_R(x_0)$, $h^R(x_0) = \mathrm{im}\, F'_R(x_0)$.*

This follows from Theorem 4.6 with

$$f(x) = \{F(x) - F(x_0)\}/(x - x_0) \quad \text{and} \quad l = F'_R(x_0).$$

Notwithstanding the remark following Theorem 4.6, Theorem 4.7 becomes false if the suffix R is omitted. Its proof becomes false because the real part of $\{F(z) - F(x_0)\}/(z - x_0)$ is not, in general, equal to $\{\mathrm{re}\, F(z) - \mathrm{re}\, F(x_0)\}/(z - x_0)$. That the theorem itself becomes false will be clear later, when we shall see that a real function cannot have a derivative in the full sense except where this derivative is 0.

The next theorem is known from the elementary calculus.

THEOREM 4.8.   *Let $f(x)$ be real for every number x in the closed interval $[a, b]$, and let f'_R be continuous in $[a, b]$.   Then*

$$\int_a^b f'_R(x)dx = f(b) - f(a).$$

THEOREM 4.9.   *Let f'_R be continuous in $[a, b]$.   Then*

$$\int_a^b f'_R(x)dx = f(b) - f(a).$$

Proof.   Let $g(x) = \mathrm{re}\, f(x)$ and $h(x) = \mathrm{im}\, f(x)$.   Then,   by Theorem 4.7,

$$g'_R(x) = \mathrm{re}\, f'_R(x), \qquad h'_R(x) = \mathrm{im}\, f'_R(x) \quad (a \leqslant x \leqslant b).$$

From this and the hypothesis it follows that g'_R and h'_R are continuous in $[a, b]$.   Hence, by Theorem 4.8,

$$\int_a^b g'_R(x)dx = g(b) - g(a), \qquad \int_a^b h'_R(x)dx = h(b) - h(a).$$

From this and §4.9 we obtain the result stated.

4.11. If the (complex) function g is bounded in the interval $[a, b]$, then the *oscillation* of g in $[a, b]$ is defined as the upper bound of $|g(t) - g(t')|$ for all pairs of points t, t' of $[a, b]$.

EXERCISES

4.3. Prove that this definition is consistent with that of the oscillation of a real function (Hardy, §104).

4.4. Prove that, if a complex function is bounded in an interval, then its oscillation in that interval is less than or equal to the sum of those of its real and imaginary parts.

THEOREM 4.10. *Let the (complex) function g be continuous in the interval $[a, b]$, and let δ be any positive number. Then $[a, b]$ can be divided into a finite number of sub-intervals, in each of which the oscillation of g is less than δ.*

This can be proved in the same way as Hardy, §107, Theorem I, of which it is the extension to complex functions. It can also be deduced from that theorem.

4.12. The statement 'f is *uniformly continuous* in S' (where S denotes a set of points) means that, for every positive number ϵ, there is a positive number δ, such that, for every pair of points z, w of S, for which $|w - z| < \delta$, we have $|f(w) - f(z)| < \epsilon$.

THEOREM 4.11. *Let S be a closed bounded set of points, and let the function f be continuous in S. Then f is uniformly continuous in S.*

Proof. Suppose this is not so. Then there is a positive number ϵ_0, such that, for every positive number δ, there are numbers z, w in S, for which $|w - z| < \delta$ and $|f(w) - f(z)| \geqslant \epsilon_0$. Choose ϵ_0 accordingly, take δ successively equal to 1, $\frac{1}{2}$, $\frac{1}{3}$, . . ., choose z and w in each case as indicated above, and denote the values of z and w corresponding to $\delta = 1/n$ by z_n and w_n. Then we obtain two sequences $z_1, z_2, \ldots$ and $w_1, w_2, \ldots$, such that, for every natural number n,

$$z_n \in S, \qquad w_n \in S, \qquad |w_n - z_n| < 1/n, \qquad |f(w_n) - f(z_n)| \geqslant \epsilon_0. \tag{13}$$

Since S is bounded, so is the sequence $z_1, z_2, \ldots$. Hence, by Theorem 2.7, it has a convergent sub-sequence $z_{n_1}, z_{n_2}, \ldots$, say, where $n_1, n_2, \ldots$ are natural numbers, and $n_1 < n_2 < \ldots$. Let

$$\lim_{m \to \infty} z_{n_m} = \xi. \tag{14}$$

Then, by Theorem 3.1, $\xi \in S$. Hence, for every positive number ϵ, there is a positive number δ, such that, for every point

z in S for which $|z-\xi| < \delta$, we have $|f(z)-f(\xi)| < \epsilon$. Take $\epsilon = \frac{1}{2}\epsilon_0$, and choose δ accordingly. Now, by (14), there is a natural number m_0, such that, for every integer $m \geqslant m_0$, we have $|z_{n_m}-\xi| < \frac{1}{2}\delta$. Take $m = \max(m_0, [2/\delta]+1)$. Then $|w_{n_m}-z_{n_m}| < 1/n_m \leqslant 1/m < \frac{1}{2}\delta$ and $|z_{n_m}-\xi| < \frac{1}{2}\delta$, so that $|w_{n_m}-\xi| < \delta$ and $|z_{n_m}-\xi| < \delta$. It follows that $|f(w_{n_m})-f(\xi)| < \epsilon = \frac{1}{2}\epsilon_0$ and $|f(z_{n_m})-f(\xi)| < \frac{1}{2}\epsilon_0$, which implies that $|f(w_{n_m})-f(z_{n_m})| < \epsilon_0$. On the other hand, by (13), $|f(w_{n_m})-f(z_{n_m})| \geqslant \epsilon_0$. This is a contradiction, and so the theorem is proved.

EXERCISES

4.5. Deduce Theorem 4.10 from Theorem 4.11.

4.6. The functions h_1, h_2, h_3, h_4 are defined by

$$h_1(z) = f(z) + g(z), \quad h_2(z) = f(z) - g(z), \quad h_3(z) = f(z)g(z), \quad h_4(z) = f(z)/g(z).$$

Prove that h_1, h_2 and h_3 are continuous at any point, and in any set, at or in which f and g are continuous. Prove the same for h_4 on the assumption that g does not assume the value 0 at the point or in the set in question.

CHAPTER 5

EXPONENTIAL, LOGARITHMIC AND CIRCULAR FUNCTIONS OF A COMPLEX VARIABLE

5.1. The formula

$$\exp z = \sum_{n=0}^{\infty} \frac{z^n}{n!},$$

known to hold if z is real (in which case $\exp z$ is an alternative notation for e^z), may be taken as the definition of $\exp z$ for imaginary numbers z. Note that the series involved converges absolutely for every number z.

THEOREM 5.1. $\exp(z+w) = \exp z \cdot \exp w.$

Proof. Using Theorem 2.10 with $a_n = z^n/n!$, $b_n = w^n/n!$ and the corresponding value of c_n, we obtain

$$\exp z \cdot \exp w = \sum_{n=0}^{\infty} c_n.$$

Now

$$c_n = \sum_{m=0}^{n} \frac{z^m}{m!} \cdot \frac{w^{n-m}}{(n-m)!} = \frac{1}{n!} \sum_{m=0}^{n} \binom{n}{m} z^m w^{n-m} = \frac{(z+w)^n}{n!}.$$

Hence $\sum c_n = \exp(z+w)$, and the result follows.

THEOREM 5.2. $\exp(iy) = \cos y + i \sin y.$

Proof. We have $\exp(iy) = \sum i^n y^n/n!$. Noting that the even powers of i are alternately 1 and -1, while the odd powers of i are alternately i and $-i$, we obtain

$$\mathrm{re}\,\exp(iy) = 1 - y^2/2! + y^4/4! - \ldots = \cos y$$

and

$$\mathrm{im}\,\exp(iy) = y - y^3/3! + y^5/5! - \ldots = \sin y,$$

and the result follows.

THEOREM 5.3. $\exp(x+iy) = e^x(\cos y + i \sin y).$

This follows from Theorems 5.1 and 5.2.

COROLLARY. $|\exp z| = e^{\mathrm{re}\,z}$.

EXERCISES

5.1. Using Theorem 5.1 with $w = -z$, or otherwise, prove that $\exp z$ is never 0.

5.2. Prove that $\exp(nz) = (\exp z)^n$ for every complex number z and every integer n.

5.2. Any number w such that

$$\exp w = z \tag{1}$$

may be called *a value of the logarithm of z*. If $z = 0$, there are, by Exercise 5.1, no such numbers w. Suppose, therefore, that $z \neq 0$. Then it follows from Theorem 5.3 that, for any integer k, the number

$$w = \log|z| + i(\mathrm{am}\,z + 2k\pi) \tag{2}$$

satisfies equation (1), and is thus a value of the logarithm of z. The number $\log|z| + i\,\mathrm{am}\,z$, where $\mathrm{am}\,z$ is the principal amplitude of z (see §1.16), is called the *principal value* of the logarithm of z, and is denoted by $\log z$. This agrees with the meaning of 'log z' for positive real numbers z, with which the reader is already familiar. According to Hardy, any value of the logarithm of z may be denoted by Log z. Some mathematicians write 'log z' for 'Log z', but this will be avoided here.

EXERCISE

5.3. Show that *all* values of the logarithm of z are given by formula (2).

5.3. If $z \neq 0$, then any number which may be denoted by $\exp(w\,\mathrm{Log}\,z)$ may be called a value of the wth power of z. The principal value of this power is defined as $\exp(w \log z)$, and this is what most mathematicians mean by z^w on most occasions, especially if z is real and positive, and still more especially if $z = e$. It seems that, by e^w, most mathematicians mean $\exp w$ on all occasions, and all mathematicians on most occasions. One of the rare exceptions is Hardy, Chapter X. Disregarding these exceptions, and following the common practice, I shall use 'e^w' in this book only in the sense of $\exp w$.

The nth root of z is the $(1/n)$th power of z, and the principal value of the former is that of the latter.

EXERCISES

5.4. Prove that, if $z \neq 0$, and n is an integer, then the only value of the nth power of z is z^n as defined in §1.14.

5.5. Assuming that all the powers involved have their principal values, and that neither z nor z_1 is 0, prove that, of the following three formulae, only the first is always true:

1. $z^{w+w_1} = z^w z^{w_1}$.
2. $(z^w)^{w_1} = z^{ww_1}$.
3. $(zz_1)^w = z^w z_1^w$.

5.4. It follows from Theorem 5.2 that, if z is real, then

$$\cos z = \tfrac{1}{2}(e^{iz}+e^{-iz}), \qquad \sin z = -\tfrac{1}{2}i(e^{iz}-e^{-iz}). \qquad (3)$$

For imaginary numbers z, (3) may be taken as the definition of $\cos z$ and $\sin z$, and the remaining circular functions are defined by the formulae $\tan z = \sin z/\cos z$, $\cot z = \cos z/\sin z$, $\sec z = 1/\cos z$, $\operatorname{cosec} z = 1/\sin z$, which are known to hold also for real numbers z.

The hyperbolic functions are defined for imaginary numbers z in the same way as for real numbers, namely by the formulae $\cosh z = \tfrac{1}{2}(e^z+e^{-z})$, $\sinh z = \tfrac{1}{2}(e^z-e^{-z})$, $\tanh z = \sinh z/\cosh z$, $\coth z = \cosh z/\sinh z$, $\operatorname{sech} z = 1/\cosh z$, $\operatorname{cosech} z = 1/\sinh z$.

EXERCISES

5.6. Prove the formulae $\cos iz = \cosh z$ and $\sin iz = i \sinh z$.

5.7. Prove the formulae $\sin(z+w) = \sin z \cos w + \cos z \sin w$ and $\cos(z+w) = \cos z \cos w - \sin z \sin w$.

5.8. Prove that $|\sin(x+iy)|^2 = \sin^2 x + \sinh^2 y$.
Using the trivial results $0 \leqslant |x+iy| - |x| \leqslant |y|$ and $|\sin a| \leqslant \sinh b (0 \leqslant a \leqslant b)$, prove that, if n is an integer and $|z| = (n+\tfrac{1}{2})\pi$, then $|\sin z| \geqslant 1$ and $|\cot z| \leqslant \sqrt{2}$.

5.9. Prove that $|\sinh y| \leqslant |\sin(x+iy)| \leqslant \cosh y$ and

$$|\sinh y| \leqslant |\cos(x+iy)| \leqslant \cosh y.$$

5.10. Prove that, if n is a positive integer, and z lies on any of the sides of the square with corners at the four points $(n-\tfrac{1}{2})\pi(\pm 1 \pm i)$, then $|\sin z| \geqslant 1$ and $|\cot z| \leqslant \sqrt{2}$.

5.11. State and prove the results corresponding to Exercises 1.1–1.3 with 'log' instead of 'am'.

5.12. Prove that each of the following four sets of conditions is sufficient for the formula $z^a w^a = (zw)^a$ to hold:

(i) re $z > 0$, re $w \geqslant 0$, $w \neq 0$;

(ii) im $z < 0 \leqslant$ im w, $w \neq 0$;

(iii) im $(zw) > 0$, im $w \geqslant 0$;

(iv) im $(zw) < 0$, im $w < 0$.

5.13. Prove that

$$\log z - \log(-z) = \begin{cases} \pi i & (\text{im } z > 0) \\ -\pi i & (\text{im } z < 0). \end{cases}$$

CHAPTER 6

THE CAUCHY-RIEMANN EQUATIONS. REGULARITY

6.1. Before stating the next theorem, I remind the reader of the footnote to §1.3. Accordingly, in what follows, the partial derivatives with respect to x and y are derivatives relative to the real axis (see §4.5).

THEOREM 6.1. *Let* $w = u + iv = f(x + iy)$. *Then, at any point* $x + iy$ *at which f is fully differentiable,*

$$\frac{\partial u}{\partial x} = \frac{\partial v}{\partial y}, \qquad \frac{\partial v}{\partial x} = -\frac{\partial u}{\partial y} \tag{1}$$

and

$$f'(x + iy) = \frac{\partial u}{\partial x} + i \frac{\partial v}{\partial x}. \tag{2}$$

Proof. By Theorem 4.2, $\partial w / \partial x = f'(x + iy)$, $\partial w / \partial y = i f'(x + iy)$. Also, by Theorem 4.7, $\partial w / \partial x = (\partial u / \partial x) + i(\partial v / \partial x)$, $\partial w / \partial y = (\partial u / \partial y) + i(\partial v / \partial y)$. The results now easily follow.

Equations (1) are called the *Cauchy-Riemann equations.* Theorem 6.1 shows that they are implied in the full differentiability of f. To show that they do not by themselves imply it, take $f(z) = 0$ everywhere on the two axes, and $f(z) = 1$ everywhere else. Then the Cauchy-Riemann equations hold at the origin, but f is not fully continuous there, let alone fully differentiable. The Cauchy-Riemann equations, together with the continuity of the derivatives involved in them, do imply the full differentiability of f. This will be shown in the next theorem.

THEOREM 6.2. *In the notation of Theorem 6.1, the function f is fully differentiable, and satisfies (2), at any point $x + iy$ at which $\partial u / \partial x$, $\partial u / \partial y$, $\partial v / \partial x$ and $\partial v / \partial y$ are continuous functions of (x, y) and satisfy the Cauchy-Riemann equations.*

Proof. By a well-known theorem on real functions of two real variables (see, for instance, Hardy, §159), in the usual notation,

$$\lim_{(\delta x,\,\delta y)\to(0,\,0)} \frac{\delta u - (\partial u/\partial x)\delta x - (\partial u/\partial y)\delta y}{|\delta x| + |\delta y|} = 0,$$

which is equivalent to

$$\lim_{\delta z\to 0} \frac{\delta u - (\partial u/\partial x)\delta x - (\partial u/\partial y)\delta y}{\delta z} = 0,$$

where $z = x + iy$. Hence, by the Cauchy-Riemann equations,

$$\lim_{\delta z\to 0} \frac{\delta u - (\partial u/\partial x)\delta x + (\partial v/\partial x)\delta y}{\delta z} = 0.$$

Similarly

$$\lim_{\delta z\to 0} \frac{\delta v - (\partial v/\partial x)\delta x - (\partial u/\partial x)\delta y}{\delta z} = 0.$$

It follows that

$$\lim_{\delta z\to 0} \frac{\delta u + i\,\delta v - \{(\partial u/\partial x) + i(\partial v/\partial x)\}(\delta x + i\,\delta y)}{\delta z} = 0,$$

which is equivalent to $\lim_{\delta z\to 0} (\delta w/\delta z) = (\partial u/\partial x) + i(\partial v/\partial x)$, i.e. $f'(z) = (\partial u/\partial x) + i(\partial v/\partial x)$, where f' is a derivative in the full sense (see §4.5). This proves the theorem.

6.2. *Examples.* (i) Let $f(z) = e^z$. Then $u = e^x \cos y$ and $v = e^x \sin y$. Hence $\partial u/\partial x = e^x \cos y = \partial v/\partial y$ and $\partial v/\partial x = e^x \sin y = -\partial u/\partial y$. From this and Theorem 6.2 it follows that f is fully differentiable everywhere, and that $f'(z) = e^z$ for every complex number z.

(ii) Let $f(z) = \log z$. Then $u = \frac{1}{2} \log (x^2 + y^2)$ and $v = \operatorname{am} (x + iy)$, $(z \neq 0)$. Hence $\partial u/\partial x = x/(x^2 + y^2)$ and $\partial u/\partial y = y/(x^2 + y^2)$, $(z \neq 0)$. Also, by the formula at the end of §1.16, $\partial v/\partial x = (\partial/\partial x) \tan^{-1} (y/x) = -y/(x^2 + y^2)$, $(x \neq 0)$, and $\partial v/\partial y = (\partial/\partial y) \tan^{-1} (y/x) = x/(x^2 + y^2)$ unless either $x = 0$ or $x < 0 = y$. If, however, $x = 0 < y$, then

$$\frac{\partial v}{\partial x} = \lim_{x' \to 0} \frac{\text{am}\,(x' + iy) - \frac{1}{2}\pi}{x'} = -\lim_{x' \to 0} \left(\frac{1}{x'} \tan^{-1} \frac{x'}{y} \right)$$

$$= -\frac{1}{y} = -\frac{y}{x^2 + y^2}$$

and $\partial v/\partial y = 0 = x/(x^2 + y^2)$. Similarly, if $x = 0 > y$, then also $\partial v/\partial x = -y/(x^2 + y^2)$ and $\partial v/\partial y = x/(x^2 + y^2)$. Hence, by Theorem 6.2, f is fully differentiable at all (finite) points other than 0 and the negative real numbers, that is to say, at all points at which f is fully continuous, and $f'(z) = (x - iy)/(x^2 + y^2) = 1/z$ at all these points.

6.3. *Regular at z_0* means 'fully differentiable at z_0 and at all points sufficiently near z_0', i.e. 'fully differentiable at all points of some disc about z_0'.

The phrase *regular in S* (where S is a set of points) means 'regular at all points of S'. The meaning of such sentences as '$f(z)$ is regular for $|z| \leqslant 1$' is now obvious.

It follows from these definitions that, if D is an open set, then the phrase 'regular in D' means the same as 'fully differentiable at all points of D'.

The term 'regular' is sometimes used by mathematicians in meanings inconsistent with the above, but this will not be done here.

6.4. The next two theorems follow from §4.6.

THEOREM 6.3.   *Let the functions f and g be regular at z_0. Then so are the functions $f(z) + g(z)$, $f(z) - g(z)$, $f(z)g(z)$ and, if $g(z_0) \neq 0$, $f(z)/g(z)$.*

THEOREM 6.4.   *Suppose that the function f is regular at z_0, that the function g is regular at $f(z_0)$, and that the function h is defined by the equation $h(z) = g\{f(z)\}$. Then h is regular at z_0.*

6.5. The term 'regular at ∞' will be defined later. An *integral function* is a function regular at all finite points.

EXERCISES

6.1. If f is any function, and S the set of those points at which f is regular, prove that S is open.

6.2. Show that the continuity of the four partial derivatives occurring in the Cauchy-Riemann equations is not a necessary condition for the full differentiability of a function at a point. (It will be seen later that it is a necessary condition for the full differentiability of a function at all points of an open set.)

6.3. Show that, if $f(z) = |z|^2$, then f is fully differentiable at 0, but nowhere else.

6.4. Show that, if $f(0) = 0$ and $f(z) = e^{-z^{-4}}$, $(z \neq 0)$, then the Cauchy-Riemann equations hold at the origin (and, in fact, everywhere else), but f is not fully differentiable there.

6.5. Show that, if the function g is regular in the open set S, and $f(z) = g(z)$ for every point z of S, then f is regular in S.

Show also that the open sets are the only sets of points for which this is always true.

6.6. Prove the following theorem:

Let α be an aggregate of open sets of points, U the union of the members of α, f a function, and suppose that, for every member D of α, there is a function g, regular in D, such that, for every point z of D, we have $f(z) = g(z)$. Then f is regular in U.

Show that this theorem becomes false if the word 'open' is omitted.

6.7. Show that, if $f(z)$ is regular for $|z| \leqslant r$, then there is a number $R > r$ such that $f(z)$ is regular for $|z| < R$.

6.6. *Example.* The function $f(z)$ is defined for all complex numbers z satisfying $|z| \leqslant 1$, and is such that its imaginary part is always zero. Show that the function cannot have a non-zero derivative for any value of z in the circle. [London, 1949.]

Solution. By Theorem 6.1, at any point $x + iy$ at which f is fully differentiable,

$$f'(x+iy) = \frac{\partial v}{\partial y} + i\,\frac{\partial v}{\partial x}.$$

By hypothesis, v is always 0. Hence f cannot have a non-zero derivative (in the full sense) at any point. The references to the unit circle are irrelevant.

CHAPTER 7

TRANSFORMATIONS

7.1. In this chapter, the point ∞ is excluded.

With any function f, there is associated the *transformation* $w = f(z)$ (or, more briefly, the transformation f), which transforms any sub-set S of the region of existence of f into the set T for which $w \in T$ if and only if there is a point z in S such that $f(z) = w$. A transformation may also be called a *representation* or a *mapping*. I shall sometimes denote the set into which the transformation f transforms S by $f(S)$. The term *mapped on* is sometimes used for 'transformed into', and the term *mapped into* for 'transformed into a sub-set of'.

The next three sections deal with examples.

7.2. Let S be the intersection of the discs of radius $\sqrt{2}$ about the points i and $-i$, and let U be the unit disc (see §1.15). Then the transformation $w = 2z/(1 + z^2)$ transforms S into U.

Proof. We have to prove the following two statements:

(i) If $z \in S$, then $2z/(1 + z^2) \in U$.

(ii) For every point w of U, there is a point z in S such that $2z/(1 + z^2) = w$.

Proof of (i). Let $z \in S$. Then $|z - i| < \sqrt{2}$ and $|z + i| < \sqrt{2}$. Hence $(|z + i|^2 - 2)(|z - i|^2 - 2) > 0$. Now, by Exercise 1.5,

$$(|z + i|^2 - 2)(|z - i|^2 - 2) = |z^2 + 1|^2 - 4|z|^2. \tag{1}$$

Hence $|z^2 + 1|^2 - 4|z|^2 > 0$, i.e. $|2z/(1 + z^2)| = 2|z|/|z^2 + 1| < 1$, which means that $2z/(1 + z^2) \in U$.

Proof of (ii). Let $w \in U$. If $w = 0$, take $z = 0$, and the result follows. Suppose, therefore, that $w \neq 0$. Then the equation $z^2 - (2/w)z + 1 = 0$ has roots z_1, z_2, say, where $|z_1| \leqslant |z_2|$. Now $z_1 z_2 = 1$, so that $|z_1||z_2| = 1$, and hence

$$|z_1| \leqslant 1. \tag{2}$$

Also $z_1^2 - (2/w)z_1 + 1 = 0$, which implies that

$$2z_1/(1 + z_1^2) = w. \tag{3}$$

Now $|w| < 1$. Hence, by (3), $|z_1^2 + 1|^2 - 4|z_1|^2 > 0$. From this and (1) it follows that $(|z_1 + i|^2 - 2)(|z_1 - i|^2 - 2) > 0$, which means that either

$$|z_1 + i| > \sqrt{2}, \qquad |z_1 - i| > \sqrt{2} \tag{4}$$

or

$$z_1 \in S. \tag{5}$$

Now, by (2) and Exercise 1.4, $|z_1 + i|^2 + |z_1 - i|^2 = 2(|z_1|^2 + 1) \leqslant 4$, which is inconsistent with (4). Hence (5) must hold. Thus, for every point w of U, other than $w = 0$, there is a point z_1 which satisfies (5) and (3). This completes the proof.

7.3. Let S be the whole plane, T the set of all points other than the origin. Then the transformation $w = e^z$ transforms S into T.

Proof. By Exercise 5.1, $e^z \in T$ for any z. Now let w be any point of T, i.e. $w \neq 0$. Then, taking $z = \log w$, we have $z \in S$ and $e^z = w$.

7.4. Let S be the *right-hand half-plane* (i.e. the set of those points whose real parts are positive), T the *plane cut along the negative real axis* (i.e. the set of all points other than 0 and the negative real numbers). Then the transformation $w = z^2$ transforms S into T.

Proof. (i) Let $z = x + iy \in S$. Then $x > 0$, and $z^2 = x^2 - y^2 + 2ixy$. Hence $z^2 \in T$; for otherwise we should have $x > 0$, $xy = 0$ and $x^2 - y^2 \leqslant 0$, which is impossible.

(ii) Let $w = u + iv \in T$. Then, if $v = 0$, we have $u > 0$. In this case, let $z = \sqrt{u}$ (taking the positive square root). If $v > 0$, let $z = \sqrt{\{\frac{1}{2}u + \frac{1}{2}\sqrt{(u^2 + v^2)}\}} + i\sqrt{\{-\frac{1}{2}u + \frac{1}{2}\sqrt{(u^2 + v^2)}\}}$, and if $v < 0$, let $z = \sqrt{\{\frac{1}{2}u + \frac{1}{2}\sqrt{(u^2 + v^2)}\}} - i\sqrt{\{-\frac{1}{2}u + \frac{1}{2}\sqrt{(u^2 + v^2)}\}}$. Then, in all cases, $z \in S$ and $z^2 = w$.

7.5. The function f is said to be *simple* in the set S if and only if (i) $f(z)$ exists for every point z of S, and (ii) $f(z_1) \neq f(z_2)$ for every pair of distinct points z_1, z_2 of S. A *simple function* is a function which is simple in its region of existence. A transformation associated with a simple function is called a *one-one transformation*.

The *inverse function* of a simple function f is the aggregate of those ordered pairs of numbers (see §4.1) (w, z) for which $(z, w) \in f$. In other words, if S is the region of existence of f, then the inverse function of f is the function g with region of existence $f(S)$ (see §7.1) such that, for every w in $f(S)$, $g(w)$ is the number z for which $f(z) = w$.

Having defined a function as an aggregate of pairs of numbers, I define a *sub-function* of a function f as a non-empty sub-aggregate of f. Thus g is a sub-function of f if and only if $g(z) = f(z)$ for every z for which $g(z)$ exists.

The next theorem is trivial.

THEOREM 7. *Let the function f be simple in S, let g be the sub-function of f with region of existence S, h the inverse function of g, and $T \subset S$. Then $f(T)$ is the set of those points w for which $h(w) \in T$.*

EXERCISES

7.1. Prove that, if a is a constant, then the transformation $w = e^{az}$ transforms the real axis into (i) the set of the positive numbers if a is real and not 0, (ii) the set consisting of the single point 1 if $a = 0$, (iii) the unit circle if a is purely imaginary, (iv) an equiangular spiral otherwise.

7.2. Prove that the transformation $w = z^2$ transforms the line re $z = 1$ into a parabola.

7.3. The function f is continuous in the set S, the function g is continuous in $f(S)$, and the function h is defined by $h(z) = g\{f(z)\}$. Prove that h is continuous in S.

7.4. S is the set of those points z for which $|z - i| > \sqrt{2}$ and $|z + i| > \sqrt{2}$. Prove that the transformation $w = 2z/(1 + z^2)$ transforms S into the set of those points w for which $0 < |w| < 1$.

CHAPTER 8

BILINEAR TRANSFORMATIONS

8.1. In this chapter, the point ∞ is included in the plane. A *bilinear transformation* is a transformation

$$w = (az + b)/(cz + d), \qquad (1)$$

where a, b, c, d are constants, and

$$ad \neq bc. \qquad (2)$$

The following conventions are adopted in connection with this transformation: If $c = 0$, then ∞ is transformed into itself. If $c \neq 0$, then ∞ is transformed into a/c, and $-d/c$ into ∞.

8.2. A *linear transformation* is a transformation $w = az + b$, where $a \neq 0$, with the convention that ∞ is transformed into itself. It is trivial that every linear transformation is bilinear, and that [subject to (2)] the transformation (1) is linear if $c = 0$. It is also trivial that every bilinear transformation is a one-one transformation of the whole plane into itself.

8.3. A *straight line* may be defined as a set S with the property that there are numbers z_0 and w, such that $w \neq 0$, and that S consists of ∞ and those points z for which im $\{(z - z_0)w\} = 0$. This definition agrees with the meaning of the term 'straight line' in coordinate geometry except for the inclusion of the point ∞.

8.4. THEOREM 8.1. *Let z_1 and z_2 be any two distinct finite points, and let the set S consist of ∞ and those points z for which*

$$|z - z_1| = |z - z_2|. \qquad (3)$$

Then S is a straight line.

Proof. (3) is equivalent to each of the following formulae, as can be seen by comparing each of them with the preceding one ($\bar{z}$ being the conjugate of z):

$$(z - z_1)(\bar{z} - \bar{z}_1) - (z - z_2)(\bar{z} - \bar{z}_2) = 0,$$

$$\{z - \tfrac{1}{2}(z_1 + z_2)\}(\bar{z} - \bar{z}_1) - \{z - \tfrac{1}{2}(z_1 + z_2)\}(\bar{z} - \bar{z}_2)$$

$$- \tfrac{1}{2}(z_1 - z_2)(\bar{z} - \bar{z}_1) - \tfrac{1}{2}(z_1 - z_2)(\bar{z} - \bar{z}_2) = 0,$$

$$\{z - \tfrac{1}{2}(z_1 + z_2)\}(\bar{z}_2 - \bar{z}_1) + \{\bar{z} - \tfrac{1}{2}(\bar{z}_1 + \bar{z}_2)\}(z_2 - z_1) = 0,$$

and

$$\mathrm{im}\,\{(z - z_0)w\} = 0, \tag{4}$$

where $z_0 = \tfrac{1}{2}(z_1 + z_2)$ and $w = i(\bar{z}_2 - \bar{z}_1)$. The result therefore follows from §8.3.

THEOREM 8.2. *Let S be a straight line. Then there are two distinct finite points z_1, z_2, such that S consists of ∞ and those points z for which (3) holds.*

Proof. Choose z_0 and w in accordance with §8.3, take $z_1 = z_0 - \tfrac{1}{2}i\bar{w}$, $z_2 = z_0 + \tfrac{1}{2}i\bar{w}$, and use the equivalence of (3) and (4).

THEOREM 8.3. *Let $z_1 \neq z_2$, $k > 0$ and $k \neq 1$. Then the set of those points z for which*

$$|z - z_1| = k|z - z_2| \tag{5}$$

is a circle.

Proof. (5) is equivalent to each of the following formulae:

$$(z - z_1)(\bar{z} - \bar{z}_1) - k^2(z - z_2)(\bar{z} - \bar{z}_2) = 0,$$

$$(1 - k^2)z\bar{z} - z(\bar{z}_1 - k^2\bar{z}_2) - \bar{z}(z_1 - k^2 z_2) + |z_1|^2 - k^2|z_2|^2 = 0,$$

and

$$z\bar{z} - z\bar{a} - \bar{z}a + b = 0,$$

where $a = (z_1 - k^2 z_2)/(1 - k^2)$ and $b = (|z_1|^2 - k^2|z_2|^2)/(1 - k^2)$. Thus (5) is equivalent to $(z - a)(\bar{z} - \bar{a}) = |a|^2 - b$, and a straightforward calculation shows that $|a|^2 - b = k^2|z_1 - z_2|^2(1 - k^2)^{-2}$. Hence the set in question is the circle with centre a and radius $k|z_1 - z_2|/|1 - k^2|$.

8.5. THEOREM 8.4. *Any bilinear transformation transforms any straight line into a circle or a straight line.*

Proof. Let the transformation be (1), and the straight line S. The case $c = 0$ is trivial. Suppose, then, that $c \neq 0$. Let S_0 be the set of all finite points other than $-d/c$, and T_0 the set of all finite points other than a/c. Let the functions f and h be defined by

$$f(z) = (az + b)/(cz + d), \qquad h(w) = (dw - b)/(-cw + a). \tag{6}$$

Then f and h are simple (see §7.5), their regions of existence are S_0 and T_0 respectively, $f(S_0) = T_0$ (see §7.1), and h is the inverse function of f. Hence, by Theorem 7, $f(S_0 \cap S)$ is the set of those points w for which

$$h(w) \in S_0 \cap S. \tag{7}$$

Now choose z_1 and z_2 in accordance with Theorem 8.2. This can be done in infinitely many ways, and it is easily seen that it can be done in such a way that neither z_1 nor z_2 is equal to $-d/c$.

Suppose, therefore,

$$z_1 \neq -d/c, \qquad z_2 \neq -d/c. \tag{8}$$

Then S consists of ∞ and those points z for which (3) holds. Consider first the case in which $-d/c$ is not a point of S. Then $S_0 \cap S$ consists of those points z for which (3) holds. In virtue of this and (6), the formula (7) is equivalent to

$$\left| \frac{dw-b}{-cw+a} - z_1 \right| = \left| \frac{dw-b}{-cw+a} - z_2 \right|, \tag{9}$$

and this is equivalent to the statement '$w \neq a/c$ and

$$|dw - b + cz_1 w - az_1| = |dw - b + cz_2 w - az_2|'. \tag{10}$$

Hence $f(S_0 \cap S)$ is the set of those points w, other than $w = a/c$, for which (10) holds. Since S consists of ∞ and $S_0 \cap S$, and ∞ is transformed into a/c, it follows that S is transformed into the set of those points w for which (10) holds. Now (10) is, in virtue of (8), equivalent to

$$\left| w - \frac{az_1+b}{cz_1+d} \right| = \left| \frac{cz_2+d}{cz_1+d} \right| \left| w - \frac{az_2+b}{cz_2+d} \right|. \tag{11}$$

Also, since $-d/c$ is not a point of S, the number $z = -d/c$ does not satisfy (3). This implies that $|(cz_2+d)/(cz_1+d)| \neq 1$. It therefore follows from Theorem 8.3 that S is transformed into a circle.

Now consider the case in which

$$-\frac{d}{c} \in S. \tag{12}$$

Then $S_0 \cap S$ consists of those points z, other than $z = -d/c$, for which (3) holds. Since $(dw-b)/(-cw+a) \neq -d/c$ for any point w, it follows that (7) is again equivalent to (9). From this we obtain, by the same argument as before, that $f(S_0 \cap S)$ is again the set of those points w, other than $w = a/c$, for which (10) holds. This time, however, there are *two* points in S which are not in S_0, namely ∞ and $-d/c$, and they are transformed into a/c and ∞. Hence S is now transformed into the set consisting of ∞ and those points w for which (10) holds. (10) is again equivalent to (11) and it follows from (12) that the number $z = -d/c$ now does satisfy (3). Hence (11) is now equivalent to

$$\left| w - \frac{az_1+b}{cz_1+d} \right| = \left| w - \frac{az_2+b}{cz_2+d} \right|, \tag{13}$$

and it follows from Theorem 8.1 that the set consisting of ∞ and those points w for which (13) holds is a straight line. Thus S is now transformed into a straight line.

THEOREM 8.5.   *Any bilinear transformation transforms any circle into a circle or a straight line.*

Proof. Let the transformation again be (1), and the circle S. The case $c = 0$ is again trivial. So suppose again that $c \neq 0$. Let the centre and radius of S be z_0 and r respectively. Then S consists of those points z for which

$$|z - z_0| = r. \tag{14}$$

Arguing as in the proof of Theorem 8.4, we deduce that, if $-d/c$ is not a point of S, i.e. if

$$|-d/c - z_0| \neq r, \tag{15}$$

then S is transformed into the set of those points w for which

$$\left| \frac{dw-b}{-cw+a} - z_0 \right| = r. \tag{16}$$

If, however, $-d/c \in S$, i.e. if

$$|-d/c - z_0| = r, \tag{17}$$

then S is transformed into the set consisting of ∞ and those points w for which (16) holds. Now (16) is equivalent to

$$|(cz_0+d)w - (az_0+b)| = r|cw-a|. \tag{18}$$

If $z_0 = -d/c$, then (18) is equivalent to $|w - a/c| = |az_0 + b|/(r|c|)$. In this case, therefore, S is transformed into the circle with centre a/c and radius $|az_0 + b|/(r|c|)$. Now suppose $z_0 \neq -d/c$. Then (18) is equivalent to

$$\left| w - \frac{az_0 + b}{cz_0 + d} \right| = \frac{r|c|}{|cz_0 + d|} \left| w - \frac{a}{c} \right|.$$

Hence, if (15) holds, i.e. if $r|c|/|cz_0 + d| \neq 1$, then, by Theorem 8.3, S is transformed into a circle. If, however, (17) holds, i.e. if $r|c|/|cz_0 + d| = 1$, then, by Theorem 8.1, S is transformed into a straight line.

8.6. THEOREM 8.6. *Let* $|a| < 1$. *Then the transformation*

$$w = (z - a)/(\bar{a}z - 1) \tag{19}$$

transforms the unit disc into itself.

Proof. Let the function f be defined by $f(z) = (z - a)/(\bar{a}z - 1)$. Then f is simple, its region of existence contains the unit disc, and the inverse function of f is f itself. Hence, by Theorem 7 (with $f = g = h$), the unit disc is transformed into the set of those points w for which $|(w - a)/(\bar{a}w - 1)| < 1$. This inequality is equivalent to each of the following: $|w - a| < |\bar{a}w - 1|$, $(w - a)(\bar{w} - \bar{a}) < (\bar{a}w - 1)(a\bar{w} - 1)$, $|w|^2 + |a|^2 < |a|^2|w|^2 + 1$, $(1 - |a|^2)(1 - |w|^2) > 0$, and $|w| < 1$. This proves the theorem.

EXERCISES

8.1. Prove that, if $|a| \neq 1$, then (19) transforms the unit circle into itself.

8.2. Prove that, if $|a| > 1$, then (19) transforms the unit disc into the exterior of the unit circle, and vice versa.

Note. The point ∞ is supposed to be exterior to any circle.

8.3. Prove that, if $ad - bc \neq 0$, the transformation $w = (az + b)/(cz + d)$ transforms a circle in the z-plane into a circle or straight line in the w-plane.

Show that (i) through any given point in the z-plane there pass an infinity of circles which are transformed into straight lines, and (ii) these circles form a coaxal system. [London, 1952.]

Note. The last statement is incorrect, for if the point is $-d/c$, then every circle through it is transformed into a straight line. In (i) it is apparently tacitly assumed that $c \neq 0$.

8.7. *Example.* For the transformation $w = (z - \alpha)/(z - \bar{\alpha})$, where α is some given complex number, find what regions in the w-plane correspond to (i) the interior of a circle with centre $z = \bar{a}$ and radius ρ, (ii) the upper half of the z-plane.   [London, 1950.]

Note.   Here the word 'complex' apparently means 'imaginary', i.e. non-real.

Solution.   The inverse transformation is $z = (\bar{a}w - \alpha)/(w - 1)$.

(i) The disc in question is transformed into the set consisting of ∞ and those points w for which $|(\bar{a}w - \alpha)/(w - 1) - \bar{a}| < \rho$. This inequality is equivalent to $|-\alpha + \bar{a}| < \rho|w - 1|$, i.e. $|w - 1| > 2\rho^{-1}|\text{im } \alpha|$. Thus the answer is: the exterior of the circle with centre 1 and radius $2\rho^{-1}|\text{im } \alpha|$.

(ii) Let S be the upper half-plane, and T the set into which S is transformed. Let the functions f and h be defined by $f(z) = (z - \alpha)/(z - \bar{\alpha})$ and $h(w) = (\bar{a}w - \alpha)/(w - 1)$ (so that h is the inverse function of f).

Suppose, first, im $\alpha > 0$. Then S consists of those points z for which $|z - \alpha| < |z - \bar{\alpha}|$, i.e. $|z - \alpha|/|z - \bar{\alpha}| < 1$, i.e. $|f(z)| < 1$. Hence T consists of those points w for which $|f\{h(w)\}| < 1$, i.e. $|w| < 1$. Thus T is the unit disc.

Now suppose im $\alpha < 0$. Then S consists of those points z for which $|z - \alpha| > |z - \bar{\alpha}|$, i.e. the point $z = \bar{\alpha}$, which is transformed into ∞, and those points z for which $|f(z)| > 1$. Hence T consists of ∞ and those points w for which $|f\{h(w)\}| > 1$, i.e. $|w| > 1$. Thus T is the exterior of the unit circle.

The case im $\alpha = 0$ does not occur.

CHAPTER 9

CURVES

9.1. A *curve*, in the sense in which this word will be used here, is always obtained from a closed interval $[a, b]$ (see §4.9) and a (complex) function g, continuous in $[a, b]$ (see §4.4). These determine the curve C described by the point $z = g(t)$ as t increases from a to b. I call C 'the curve represented by $z = g(t)$, $a \leqslant t \leqslant b$', or '$\mathscr{C}\{t; g(t), a, b\}$', or '$\mathscr{C}(g, a, b)$'. The first and second of these representations are said to be *parametric*, the letter t being called the *parameter*. It may, of course, be replaced by another letter. Also $g(t)$ may be replaced by any expression which is equal to $g(t)$ for every number t in $[a, b]$. Thus we may speak of the curve represented by $z = e^{it}$, $0 \leqslant t \leqslant 1$, and denote it by $\mathscr{C}(t; e^{it}, 0, 1)$. A point z is said to be *on* the curve $C = \mathscr{C}(g, a, b)$ (or to be a point of that curve) if and only if there is a number t in $[a, b]$ such that $z = g(t)$. Thus z is on $\mathscr{C}(t; e^{it}, 0, 2\pi)$ if and only if $|z| = 1$. A curve, however, is not to be confused with the set of its points. The curve has something which this set has not, namely an *orientation*, which roughly means an indication which of any two points of the curve comes before the other. I say 'roughly' because the same point may occur on the curve more than once, and so one point may come both before and after another. On the curve $C = \mathscr{C}(g, a, b)$, the point $g(t_1)$ is said to come before $g(t_2)$ if $a \leqslant t_1 < t_2 \leqslant b$. Accordingly $g(a)$ and $g(b)$ are respectively called the *first* and the *last point* of C. Both together are called the *end points* of C.

Two curves are considered identical if and only if they have the same points and the same orientation. More precisely, $\mathscr{C}(g_1, a_1, b_1)$ and $\mathscr{C}(g_2, a_2, b_2)$ are the same curve if and only if there is a (real) function ϕ, continuous and strictly increasing in $[a_1, b_1]$, such that $\phi(a_1) = a_2$, $\phi(b_1) = b_2$, and $g_2\{\phi(t)\} = g_1(t)$ for every number t in $[a_1, b_1]$.

EXERCISE

9.1. If $C_1 = \mathscr{C}(t; e^{it}, -\tfrac{1}{2}\pi, \tfrac{1}{2}\pi)$, $C_2 = \mathscr{C}(t; e^{-it}, -\tfrac{1}{2}\pi, \tfrac{1}{2}\pi)$, and $C_3 = \mathscr{C}\{y; \sqrt{(1-y^2)} + iy, -1, 1\}$, prove that $C_1 = C_3$, and that C_1 and C_2 have the same points, but are different curves.

In the next section I give a formal definition of the term 'curve' as used here.

9.2. I define a *curve representation* as an expression (g, a, b), where $a < b$, and g is a function continuous in the closed interval $[a, b]$. I shall write 'representation' for 'curve representation' where there is no risk of misunderstanding.

The representation (g_1, a_1, b_1) is said to be *equivalent* to the representation (g_2, a_2, b_2) if and only if there is a (real) function ϕ, continuous and strictly increasing in $[a_1, b_1]$, such that $\phi(a_1) = a_2$, $\phi(b_1) = b_2$, and $g_2\{\phi(t)\} = g_1(t)$ for every number t in $[a_1, b_1]$. The symbol ' $\sim$ ' means 'is equivalent to'. This equivalence is *reflexive*, i.e. every representation is equivalent to itself. It is also *symmetrical*, i.e. if R_1 and R_2 are representations, and $R_1 \sim R_2$, then $R_2 \sim R_1$. It is also *transitive*, i.e. if $R_1 \sim R_2$ and $R_2 \sim R_3$, then $R_1 \sim R_3$. It may be left to the reader to prove these statements.

I now define a *curve* as a *class of equivalent representations*, i.e. a non-empty set of representations with the following two properties:

(i) Any two members of the set are equivalent.

(ii) If one of two equivalent representations is in the set, so is the other.

Since the equivalence is reflexive, symmetrical and transitive, any representation (g, a, b) belongs to one and only one class of equivalent representations, namely the set of all representations equivalent to (g, a, b). This class is the curve represented by (g, a, b).

9.3. I denote the set of the points of the curve C (see §9.1) by $|C|$. Thus, in the notation of §7.1, $|\mathscr{C}(g, a, b)| = g([a, b])$. It is trivial that $|C|$, though defined in terms of a representation of C, is determined by C alone, i.e. independent of the choice of that representation. The phrase 'on C' means the same as 'in $|C|$'. The sentence 'C is contained in S' means '$|C| \subset S$'.

Corresponding to any curve C, I define the curve C^* (C *described backward*) as follows: if $C = \mathscr{C}(g, a, b)$, then $C^* = \mathscr{C}\{t; g(-t), -b, -a\}$. It is easily seen that C^*, like $|C|$, is determined by C alone, and that $|C^*| = |C|$.

The *distance* of a point from a curve C is defined as its distance from $|C|$ (see §3.4).

THEOREM 9.1. *Let C be any curve, w any point. Then there is a point z_0 on C such that the distance of w from C is $|z_0 - w|$.*

Proof. Let $C = \mathscr{C}(g, a, b)$ and $h(t) = |g(t) - w|$ $(a \leqslant t \leqslant b)$. Then, by Hardy, §103, Theorem 2, h assumes its lower bound in $[a, b]$. This means that there is a number t_0 in $[a, b]$ such that $h(t_0) \leqslant h(t)$ for every number t in $[a, b]$. Let $z_0 = g(t_0)$. Then z_0 is on C. Now let z be any point of C. Then there is a number t in $[a, b]$ such that $z = g(t)$. Hence

$$|z_0 - w| = |g(t_0) - w| = h(t_0) \leqslant h(t) = |g(t) - w| = |z - w|.$$

Thus $|z_0 - w|$ is the least of the values assumed by $|z - w|$ for points z of C, and is, therefore, the distance of w from C.

COROLLARY. *If w is not on C, then the distance of w from C is positive, and w is, therefore, not a limit point of $|C|$.*

THEOREM 9.2. *The set of the points of any curve is closed.* This follows at once from the corollary.

EXERCISE

9.2. (i) Prove that the set of the points of any curve is bounded.
(ii) Prove that any function continuous on a curve C is bounded on C.

9.4. A curve C' is called an *arc* of a curve C if and only if there are numbers a, b, a', b' and a function g such that $a \leqslant a' < b' \leqslant b$, $C = \mathscr{C}(g, a, b)$, and $C' = \mathscr{C}(g, a', b')$. It is easily seen that, if C' is an arc of C, then, corresponding to *every* representation (g, a, b) of C, there are numbers a', b' such that $a \leqslant a' < b' \leqslant b$ and $C' = \mathscr{C}(g, a', b')$.

An ordered pair of curves C_1, C_2 is called a *dissection* of a curve C into two arcs if and only if there are numbers a, b, c and a function g such that $a < b < c$, $C_1 = \mathscr{C}(g, a, b)$, $C_2 = \mathscr{C}(g, b, c)$ and $C = \mathscr{C}(g, a, c)$. A dissection of a curve into k arcs, where k is any integer greater than 2, is similarly defined. By a dissection of a curve into one arc we mean the curve itself.

If the last point of a curve C_1 coincides with the first point of a curve C_2, I define $C_1 + C_2$, roughly, as the curve described by a point which first describes C_1 and then C_2. A precise definition will be given in the next section.

*9.5. THEOREM 9.3. *Let C_1 and C_2 be any curves such that the last point of C_1 coincides with the first point of C_2. Then there is one and only one curve C such that C_1, C_2 is a dissection of C into two arcs.*

Proof. Let (g_1, a_1, b_1) and (g_2, a_2, b_2) be representations of C_1 and C_2 respectively. Then, by hypothesis,

$$g_1(b_1) = g_2(a_2). \tag{1}$$

Now let $c_1 = b_1 + b_2 - a_2$ and $g_3(t) = g_2(t + a_2 - b_1)$ $(b_1 \leqslant t \leqslant c_1)$. Then, by §9.2, $(g_3, b_1, c_1) \sim (g_2, a_2, b_2)$, and hence $C_2 = \mathscr{C}(g_3, b_1, c_1)$. Now let

$$g_4(t) = \begin{cases} g_1(t) & (a_1 \leqslant t \leqslant b_1) \\ g_3(t) & (b_1 < t \leqslant c_1). \end{cases} \tag{2}$$

Then, by (1), $g_4(b_1) = g_3(b_1)$, so that $g_4(t) = g_3(t)$ for every number t in $[b_1, c_1]$. From this and (2) it follows that

$$(g_4, a_1, b_1) \sim (g_1, a_1, b_1), \qquad (g_4, b_1, c_1) \sim (g_3, b_1, c_1),$$

and that g_4 is continuous in $[a_1, c_1]$. Hence

$$C_1 = \mathscr{C}(g_4, a_1, b_1), \qquad C_2 = \mathscr{C}(g_4, b_1, c_1), \tag{3}$$

and (g_4, a_1, c_1) is a curve representation. Let C be the curve represented by it:

$$C = \mathscr{C}(g_4, a_1, c_1). \tag{4}$$

Then, by (3) and §9.4, C_1, C_2 is a dissection of C into two arcs.

Now let C' be any curve such that C_1, C_2 is a dissection of C' into two arcs. Then there are numbers a, b, c and a function g such $a < b < c$, $C_1 = \mathscr{C}(g, a, b)$, $C_2 = \mathscr{C}(g, b, c)$ and

$$C' = \mathscr{C}(g, a, c). \tag{5}$$

From this and (3) it follows that

$$(g_4, a_1, b_1) \sim (g, a, b), \qquad (g_4, b_1, c_1) \sim (g, b, c).$$

This means that there are functions ϕ_1 and ϕ_2, continuous and strictly increasing in $[a_1, b_1]$ and $[b_1, c_1]$ respectively, such that

$\phi_1(a_1) = a, \phi_1(b_1) = b = \phi_2(b_1), \phi_2(c_1) = c, g\{\phi_1(t)\} = g_4(t), (a_1 \leqslant t \leqslant b_1)$
and $g\{\phi_2(t)\} = g_4(t), (b_1 \leqslant t \leqslant c_1).$ Let

$$\phi(t) = \begin{cases} \phi_1(t) & (a_1 \leqslant t \leqslant b_1) \\ \phi_2(t) & (b_1 < t \leqslant c_1). \end{cases}$$

Then {since $\phi_1(b_1) = \phi_2(b_1)$} ϕ is continuous and strictly increasing in $[a_1, c_1]$, and $g\{\phi(t)\} = g_4(t)$ for every number t in $[a_1, c_1]$. Also $\phi(a_1) = a$ and $\phi(c_1) = c$.   Hence $(g_4, a_1, c_1) \sim (g, a, c)$, and hence, by (5) and (4), $C' = C$.   This shows that C is the only curve of which C_1, C_2 is a dissection into two arcs, and so completes the proof.

I now define $C_1 + C_2$ as the curve of which C_1, C_2 is a dissection into two arcs.

EXERCISE

9.3. (i) Prove that, if $C_1 + C_2 = \mathscr{C}(g_1, a_1, c_1)$, then there is a number b_1 such that $a_1 < b_1 < c_1$, $C_1 = \mathscr{C}(g_1, a_1, b_1)$, and $C_2 = \mathscr{C}(g_1, b_1, c_1)$.

(ii) Prove that, if $\mathscr{C}(g, a, b) = C_1 + C_2 + \ldots + C_k$, then there are numbers $t_0, t_1, \ldots, t_k$ such that $a = t_0 < t_1 < \ldots < t_k = b$ and $C_m = \mathscr{C}(g, t_{m-1}, t_m)$, $(m = 1, 2, \ldots, k)$.

9.6. If $z_1 \neq z_2$, the *line segment* $\{z_1, z_2\}$ is defined as the curve represented by $z = z_1 + t(z_2 - z_1)$, $0 \leqslant t \leqslant 1$.

EXERCISE

9.4. Prove that, if $a < b$, then $\{a, b\} = \mathscr{C}(t; t, a, b)$.

If k is any natural number, and the numbers $z_0, z_1, \ldots, z_k$ are such that $z_{n-1} \neq z_n$ $(n = 1, 2, \ldots, k)$, then the *broken line* $\{z_0, z_1, \ldots, z_k\}$ is defined as $\{z_0, z_1\} + \{z_1, z_2\} + \ldots + \{z_{k-1}, z_k\}$. For the sake of convenience, the case $k = 1$ is included, i.e. a line segment is also called a broken line.

EXERCISE

9.5. Prove that the broken line $\{z_0, z_1, \ldots, z_k\}$ is the curve represented by $z = g(t)$, $0 \leqslant t \leqslant k$, where $g(t) = z_{[t]} + (t - [t])(z_{[t]+1} - z_{[t]})$ $(0 \leqslant t < k)$, $g(k) = z_k$, and $[t]$ denotes the greatest integer less than or equal to t.

9.7. A *closed curve* is defined as a curve whose end points (see §9.1) coincide.   Thus a curve $\mathscr{C}(g, a, b)$ is closed if and only if $g(a) = g(b)$.

A curve representation (g, a, b) is said to be simple if and only if the function g is simple in the closed interval $[a, b]$ (see §7.5). It is trivial that, if *one* representation of a curve C is simple, then so are *all* representations of C. Then, and only then, C is called a *simple curve*. A simple curve may be defined less formally as a curve on which no point occurs more than once. A *simple closed curve* is defined as a curve with a representation (g, a, b), such that (i) $g(a) = g(b)$, and (ii) g is simple in the set of those points t for which $a \leqslant t < b$. It is trivial that, if *one* representation of a curve C has these two properties, then *every* representation of C has them. A simple closed curve may be defined less formally as a curve on which one point occurs exactly twice, namely as the first and last point; and otherwise no point occurs more than once.

A *polygon* is defined as a broken line which is a closed curve, a *simple polygon* as one which is a simple closed curve. Note that a simple closed curve is not a simple curve. To avoid contradictions in terms, it is safest to use the word 'simple', when applied to curves, only attributively.

9.8. Two closed curves, for instance $\mathscr{C}(t; e^{it}, 0, 2\pi)$ and $\mathscr{C}(t; e^{it}, -\pi, \pi)$, may be different according to §§9.1 and 9.2 and yet interchangeable for most purposes. They differ, as it were, only in their starting points. I call such curves equivalent, and define this term precisely as follows:

Two closed curves C_1 and C_2 are said to be *equivalent* ($C_1 \sim C_2$) if and only if either (i) $C_1 = C_2$, or (ii) there are curves C_3, C_4 such that $C_1 = C_3 + C_4$ and $C_2 = C_4 + C_3$.

EXERCISE

9.6. Prove that $\mathscr{C}(t; e^{it}, 0, 2\pi) \sim \mathscr{C}(t; e^{it}, -\pi, \pi)$.

This equivalence of closed curves is, of course, not to be confused with the equivalence of curve representations considered in §9.2.

*9.9. The equivalence just defined is obviously reflexive and symmetrical (see §9.2). I shall show that it is also transitive. Let C_1, C_2, C_3 be any closed curves such that $C_1 \sim C_2$ and $C_2 \sim C_3$. Then I have to show that $C_1 \sim C_3$. This is trivial if

$C_1 = C_2$ or $C_2 = C_3$. Suppose, therefore, $C_1 \neq C_2$ and $C_2 \neq C_3$. Then there are curves C_4, C_5, C_6, C_7 such that

$$C_1 = C_4 + C_5, \quad C_2 = C_5 + C_4, \quad C_2 = C_6 + C_7, \quad C_3 = C_7 + C_6.$$
$$\tag{6}$$

Let $C_2 = \mathscr{C}(g, a, c)$. Then, by (6) and Exercise 9.3(i), there are numbers b, b' such that $a < b < c$, $a < b' < c$, and

$$C_5 = \mathscr{C}(g, a, b), \qquad C_4 = \mathscr{C}(g, b, c), \qquad C_6 = \mathscr{C}(g, a, b'),$$
$$C_7 = \mathscr{C}(g, b', c).$$

Hence, if $b = b'$, then $C_5 = C_6$, $C_4 = C_7$, and so, by (6), $C_1 = C_3$, which implies that $C_1 \sim C_3$. If $b < b'$, let $C_8 = \mathscr{C}(g, b, b')$. Then $C_4 = C_8 + C_7$, $C_6 = C_5 + C_8$, and so, by (6), $C_1 = C_8 + (C_7 + C_5)$ and $C_3 = (C_7 + C_5) + C_8$, which again implies that $C_1 \sim C_3$. Similarly $C_1 \sim C_3$ if $b > b'$, and thus in all cases, which was to be proved. The equivalence is therefore transitive.

9.10. With every dissection into arcs $C_1, C_2, \ldots, C_k$ of a curve C, there is associated a number s, defined as follows: Let z_0 be the first point of C, and let z_m be the last point of C_m ($m = 1, 2, \ldots, k$). Then

$$s = \sum_{m=1}^{k} |z_m - z_{m-1}|.$$

Consider the set α of all numbers s associated in this way with dissections of C into arcs. If (and only if) α is bounded above, C is said to be *rectifiable*, and the *length* of C is defined as the upper bound of α.

EXERCISES

9.7. Prove that, if $C = C_1 + C_2 + \ldots + C_k$, where $C_1, C_2, \ldots, C_k$ are rectifiable curves of lengths $l_1, l_2, \ldots, l_k$ respectively, then C is a rectifiable curve of length $l_1 + l_2 + \ldots + l_k$.

9.8. Prove that the length of the line segment $\{z_1, z_2\}$ is $|z_2 - z_1|$.

9.11. THEOREM 9.4. *Let C be the curve represented by $z = g(t)$, $a \leqslant t \leqslant b$, and let g' be continuous in $[a, b]$. Then C is rectifiable, and its length is*

$$\int_a^b |g'(t)| dt.$$

Proof. Denote the integral by J, and let s be any member of the aggregate α of §9.10. Then, by Exercise 9.3(ii), there are numbers $t_0, t_1, \ldots, t_k$ such that $a = t_0 < t_1 < \ldots < t_k = b$ and

$$s = \sum_{m=1}^{k} |g(t_m) - g(t_{m-1})|.$$

Now, by Theorem 4.9 and Exercise 4.2,

$$|g(t_m) - g(t_{m-1})| = \left| \int_{t_{m-1}}^{t_m} g'(t)dt \right| \leqslant \int_{t_{m-1}}^{t_m} |g'(t)|dt.$$

Hence

$$s \leqslant \sum_{m=1}^{k} \int_{t_{m-1}}^{t_m} |g'(t)|dt = \int_{t_0}^{t_k} |g'(t)|dt = J.$$

It follows that α is bounded above, and that its upper bound is less than or equal to J. This means that C is rectifiable, and that, denoting its length by l, we have $l \leqslant J$.

It remains to prove that $l \geqslant J$. Let δ be any positive number. Choose numbers $t_0, t_1, \ldots, t_k$ so that $a = t_0 < t_1 < \ldots < t_k = b$, and that, in each of the intervals $[t_0, t_1], [t_1, t_2], \ldots, [t_{k-1}, t_k]$, the oscillation of g' is less than δ. This is possible by Theorem 4.10. Then

$$|g'(t)| - |g'(t_m)| \leqslant |g'(t) - g'(t_m)| < \delta \quad (t_{m-1} \leqslant t \leqslant t_m, \\ m = 1, 2, \ldots, k),$$

and hence

$$\int_{t_{m-1}}^{t_m} |g'(t)|dt - (t_m - t_{m-1})|g'(t_m)|$$
$$= \int_{t_{m-1}}^{t_m} \{|g'(t)| - |g'(t_m)|\}dt \leqslant (t_m - t_{m-1})\delta$$

and

$$(t_m - t_{m-1})|g'(t_m)| - |g(t_m) - g(t_{m-1})|$$
$$= \left| \int_{t_{m-1}}^{t_m} g'(t_m)dt \right| - \left| \int_{t_{m-1}}^{t_m} g'(t)dt \right|$$
$$\leqslant \left| \int_{t_{m-1}}^{t_m} g'(t_m)dt - \int_{t_{m-1}}^{t_m} g'(t)dt \right| = \left| \int_{t_{m-1}}^{t_m} \{g'(t_m) - g'(t)\}dt \right|$$
$$\leqslant \int_{t_{m-1}}^{t_m} |g'(t) - g'(t_m)|dt \leqslant (t_m - t_{m-1})\delta.$$

It follows that

$$\int_{t_{m-1}}^{t_m} |g'(t)|\,dt - |g(t_m) - g(t_{m-1})| \;\leqslant\; 2(t_m - t_{m-1})\delta$$

$$(m = 1, 2, \ldots, k). \quad (7)$$

Now let

$$s = \sum_{m=1}^{k} |g(t_m) - g(t_{m-1})|.$$

Then s is a member of α, and hence $s \leqslant l$. Also, by (7),

$$J - s = \sum_{m=1}^{k} \left\{ \int_{t_{m-1}}^{t_m} |g'(t)|\,dt - |g(t_m) - g(t_{m-1})| \right\}$$

$$\leqslant 2\delta \sum_{m=1}^{k} (t_m - t_{m-1}) = 2\delta(b - a).$$

Thus $J - l \leqslant 2\delta(b - a)$ for every positive number δ, which implies that $l \geqslant J$. This completes the proof.

*9.12. THEOREM 9.5. *Let* $\mathscr{C}(g, a, b)$ *be a rectifiable curve. If* $a < u \leqslant b$, *let* $h(u)$ *be the length of* $\mathscr{C}(g, a, u)$, *and let* $h(a) = 0$. *Then* h *is continuous in* $[a, b]$.

Proof. Let S_1 be the set of those points u for which $a < u \leqslant b$, S_2 the set of those for which $a \leqslant u < b$. Then it is sufficient to prove that h is (i) continuous to the left at every point of S_1, and (ii) continuous to the right at every point of S_2.

Let $a < u \leqslant b$. It is trivial that h is non-decreasing in $[a, b]$. Hence $\lim\limits_{t \to u-} h(t)$ exists and, putting

$$\lim_{t \to u-} h(t) = L, \quad (8)$$

we have

$$L \leqslant h(u). \quad (9)$$

Now let $\epsilon > 0$. Then, by §9.10 and Exercise 9.3(ii), there are numbers $t_0, t_1, \ldots, t_k$ such that $a = t_0 < t_1 < \ldots < t_k = u$ and

$$\sum_{m=1}^{k} |g(t_m) - g(t_{m-1})| > h(u) - \epsilon. \quad (10)$$

Let $t_{k-1} < u' < u$, and let the set α' be related to the curve

$\mathscr{C}(g, a, u')$ in the same way as the set α of §9.10 to C. Then the number

$$s' = \sum_{m=1}^{k-1} |g(t_m) - g(t_{m-1})| + |g(u') - g(t_{k-1})|$$

is a member of α', and hence $s' \leqslant h(u')$. From this and (10) it follows that

$$h(u') > h(u) - \epsilon - |g(u) - g(t_{k-1})| + |g(u') - g(t_{k-1})|$$
$$\geqslant h(u) - \epsilon - |g(u') - g(u)|.$$

Since g is continuous to the left at u, the right-hand side of the last inequality tends to $h(u) - \epsilon$ as $u' \to u-$, while, by (8), the left-hand side tends to L. Hence $L \geqslant h(u) - \epsilon$. Since this holds for every $\epsilon > 0$, we have $L \geqslant h(u)$, which, together with (9) and (8), proves (i).

Now let $j(u)$ be the length of $\mathscr{C}(g, u, b)$ if $a \leqslant u < b$. Then j is continuous to the right at every point of S_2. This can be proved in the same way as (i). Now, by Exercise 9.7, $h(u) = h(b) - j(u)$ $(a \leqslant u < b)$, and (ii) follows.

9.13. THEOREM 9.6. *Let f be a function, continuous in the interval $[a, b]$, which does not assume the value 0 in $[a, b]$. Then there is a real function h, continuous in $[a, b]$, such that $e^{ih(t)}$ $= f(t)/|f(t)|$ for every point t in $[a, b]$.*

Proof. By Theorem 4.3, there is a point t_1 in $[a, b]$, such that $|f(t_1)| \leqslant |f(t)|$ for every point t of $[a, b]$. By hypothesis, $f(t_1) \neq 0$, i.e. $|f(t_1)| > 0$. Now, by Theorem 4.11, f is uniformly continuous in $[a, b]$. Hence there is a positive number δ, such that, for every pair of points t, t' of $[a, b]$ for which $|t' - t| < \delta$, we have $|f(t') - f(t)| < 2|f(t_1)| \leqslant |f(t')| + |f(t)|$, which implies that $f(t')/f(t)$ cannot be real and negative. Choose δ accordingly, take $n = [(b-a)/\delta] + 1$, and let $1 \leqslant m \leqslant n$,

$$g_m(t) = f\left\{a + \frac{m}{n}(t-a)\right\} \bigg/ f\left\{a + \frac{m-1}{n}(t-a)\right\},$$

and $h_m(t) = \operatorname{am} g_m(t)$. Then g_m is continuous in $[a, b]$, and $g_m(t)$ is not 0 or real and negative for any point t in $[a, b]$. Hence, by Exercises 7.3 and 4.1, h_m is continuous in $[a, b]$. Now let

$$h(t) = \operatorname{am} f(a) + \sum_{m=1}^{n} h_m(t).$$

Then h is continuous in $[a, b]$, and

$$e^{ih(t)} = e^{i \text{ am } f(a)} \prod_{m=1}^{n} e^{ih_m(t)} = \frac{f(a)}{|f(a)|} \prod_{m=1}^{n} \frac{g_m(t)}{|g_m(t)|} = \frac{f(t)}{|f(t)|}$$

for every point t in $[a, b]$.

9.14. The function h of Theorem 9.6 is not uniquely determined by a, b and f; for if h is a function with the required properties, and k is any integer, then the function h^* defined by $h^*(t) = h(t) + 2k\pi$ also has the required properties. I shall show, however, that the number $h(b) - h(a)$ is uniquely determined by a, b and f.

THEOREM 9.7. *Let the function g be continuous in $[a, b]$, and suppose that, for every point t in $[a, b]$, $g(t)$ is an integer. Then $g(a) = g(b)$.*

This follows immediately from Hardy, §101; for, between any two different real numbers, there are numbers which are not integers.

THEOREM 9.8. *Let C be a curve, leading from z_0 to z_1. Let the function f be continuous on C, and suppose that, for every point z of C, $f(z)$ is an integer. Then $f(z_0) = f(z_1)$.*

This follows easily from Theorem 9.7.

Now suppose the functions h and h^* have the properties mentioned in Theorem 9.6, and let $g(t) = \{h^*(t) - h(t)\}/(2\pi)$. Then g is continuous in $[a, b]$ and, for every point t in $[a, b]$, $e^{2\pi i g(t)} = e^{ih^*(t)}/e^{ih(t)} = 1$, which implies that $g(t)$ is an integer. Hence, by Theorem 9.7, $g(a) = g(b)$, i.e. $h^*(a) - h(a) = h^*(b) - h(b)$, i.e. $h(b) - h(a) = h^*(b) - h^*(a)$. Thus the number $h(b) - h(a)$ is the same for all functions h with the said properties. This number is called the *variation of the amplitude* of $f(t)$ in $[a, b]$.

9.15. THEOREM 9.9. *Let (g_1, a_1, b_1) and (g_2, a_2, b_2) be representations of the curve C, and suppose the function f is continuous on C, and does not assume the value 0 there. Then the variation of the amplitude of $f\{g_1(t)\}$ in $[a_1, b_1]$ is equal to that of $f\{g_2(t)\}$ in $[a_2, b_2]$.*

Proof. By §9.2, there is a function ϕ, continuous and strictly increasing in $[a_1, b_1]$, such that $\phi(a_1) = a_2$, $\phi(b_1) = b_2$, and $g_2\{\phi(t)\} = g_1(t)$ for every point t in $[a_1, b_1]$. Let the variation of the amplitude of $f\{g_m(t)\}$ in $[a_m, b_m]$ be v_m $(m = 1, 2)$. Then, by §§9.13–9.14, there is a function h_2, continuous in $[a_2, b_2]$, such that

$$e^{ih_2(t)} = \frac{f\{g_2(t)\}}{|f\{g_2(t)\}|} \quad (a_2 \leqslant t \leqslant b_2) \tag{11}$$

and $h_2(b_2) - h_2(a_2) = v_2$. Let

$$h_1(t) = h_2\{\phi(t)\} \quad (a_1 \leqslant t \leqslant b_1). \tag{12}$$

Then, since $\phi([a_1, b_1]) = [a_2, b_2]$, it follows from Exercise 7.3 that h_1 is continuous in $[a_1, b_1]$, and from (11) that

$$e^{ih_1(t)} = e^{ih_2\{\phi(t)\}} = \frac{f[g_2\{\phi(t)\}]}{|f[g_2\{\phi(t)\}]|} = \frac{f\{g_1(t)\}}{|f\{g_1(t)\}|} \quad (a_1 \leqslant t \leqslant b_1).$$

Hence, by §§9.13–9.14, $h_1(b_1) - h_1(a_1) = v_1$. Now, by (12), $h_1(a_1) = h_2\{\phi(a_1)\} = h_2(a_2)$ and $h_1(b_1) = h_2\{\phi(b_1)\} = h_2(b_2)$. Hence $v_1 = v_2$, which was to be proved.

Thus, if C is any curve, and f any function, continuous on C, which does not assume the value 0 on C, then the variation of the amplitude of $f\{g(t)\}$ in $[a, b]$ is the same number for all representations (g, a, b) of C. I call this number the *variation of the amplitude of $f(z)$ as z describes C*, and denote it by var am (f, C). If the point w is not on C, I define $\chi(w, C)$ as the variation of the amplitude of $z - w$ as z describes C. If $w \in |C|$, I say that $\chi(w, C)$ does not exist.

EXERCISES

9.9. If the point w is not on the curve C, and C^* is 'C described backward' (see §9.3), show that $\chi(w, C^*) = -\chi(w, C)$.

9.10. If the point w is not on the curve C, and $C = C_1 + C_2$ (see §§9.4–9.5), show that $\chi(w, C) = \chi(w, C_1) + \chi(w, C_2)$.

9.11. If C is the broken line $\{z_0, z_1, \ldots, z_k\}$, and the point w is not on C, show that

$$\chi(w, C) = \sum_{m=1}^{k} \text{am} \frac{z_m - w}{z_{m-1} - w}.$$

9.12. If C is a curve leading from z_1 to z_2, and the line segment $\{w_1, w_2\}$ does not meet C, show that

$$\chi(w_2, C) - \chi(w_1, C) = \text{am} \frac{z_2 - w_2}{z_2 - w_1} - \text{am} \frac{z_1 - w_2}{z_1 - w_1}.$$

9.13. If C is a curve, and the function f is defined by $f(w) = \chi(w, C)$, show that f is fully continuous at all points other than those of C.

9.14. (i) If C is a curve, leading from z_1 to z_2, and the point w is not on C, show that

$$e^{i\chi(w,\,C)} = \frac{z_2 - w}{|z_2 - w|} \times \frac{|z_1 - w|}{z_1 - w}.$$

(ii) If C is a closed curve, and the point w is not on C, show that $\chi(w, C)/(2\pi)$ is an integer.

9.15. If C is a closed curve, and the line segment $\{w_1, w_2\}$ does not meet C, show that $\chi(w_1, C) = \chi(w_2, C)$.

9.16. State and prove generalisations of the results of Exercises 9.9, 9.10 and 9.14, dealing with var am (f, C) instead of $\chi(w, C)$.

9.17. If the functions f and g are continuous on the curve C, and $h(z) = f(z)g(z) \neq 0$ $(z \in |C|)$, show that

var am (h, C) = var am (f, C) + var am (g, C).

9.18. C is a curve leading from z_1 to z_2. The function f is continuous on C, and $f(z)$ is neither 0 nor real and negative for any point z of C. Prove that var am $(f, C) =$ am $f(z_2) -$ am $f(z_1)$.

9.19. On the hypotheses obtained from those of Exercise 9.18 by substituting 'positive' for 'negative', prove that

var am (f, C) = am $\{-f(z_2)\} -$ am $\{-f(z_1)\}$.

9.16. If C is a closed curve, and w a point which is not on C, then the number $\chi(w, C)/(2\pi)$ (which, by Exercise 9.14(ii), is an integer) is called the *winding number* of C with respect to w.

For any closed curve C, I define $E(C)$ as the set of those points w for which $\chi(w, C) = 0$, and $I(C)$ as the set of those points w for which $\chi(w, C) \neq 0$. (This inequality is taken to imply the existence of $\chi(w, C)$. Thus $I(C)$, like $E(C)$, consists entirely of points which are not on C.) I further define $E'(C)$ and $I'(C)$ by the equations $E'(C) = E(C) \cup |C|$ and $I'(C) = I(C) \cup |C|$.

EXERCISE

9.20. Prove that, if C is any closed curve, then $E(C)$ and $I(C)$ are open sets, and $E'(C)$ and $I'(C)$ are closed sets.

If C is a *simple* closed curve (see §9.7), then $E(C)$ and $I(C)$ are called the *exterior* and the *interior* of C respectively, and the phrase *within C* means 'in $I(C)$'.

9.17. A *domain* is a non-empty open set D with the property that every pair of points of D can be joined by a broken line contained in D.

A domain D is said to be *simply connected* if and only if, for every simple polygon Π, for which $|\Pi| \subset D$, we have $I(\Pi) \subset D$.

I define a *Jordan curve* as a simple closed curve whose exterior and interior are domains. In fact, the so-called *Jordan curve theorem* states that *every* simple closed curve is a Jordan curve. The distinction between these two notions is therefore unnecessary. It is, however, usually quite easy to prove that a *particular* simple closed curve is a Jordan curve; and it is very difficult to prove the Jordan curve theorem in all its generality. Those proofs of it that I have seen are either very complicated, or assume a fair amount of topology, or contain mistakes or hidden appeals to geometrical intuition, or leave many details to the reader. Some have several of these defects. Jordan's own supposed proof is perhaps an intelligent attempt, but very inadequate and marred by serious misconception. To make it part of the *definition* of a Jordan curve that its exterior and interior are domains is one way out of the difficulty. For those readers who do not like this procedure, I shall give my own proof of the theorem, for what it is worth, later on.

A *Jordan polygon* is defined as a polygon which is a Jordan curve. It is comparatively easy to prove that every simple polygon is a Jordan polygon.

9.18. A set of points S is called a *half-line* if and only if there are two distinct points z_0, z_1, such that S consists of those points z for which $(z - z_0)/(z_1 - z_0) \geqslant 0$. The meaning of the phrases 'a half-line from z_0' and 'the half-line from z_0 through z_1' is now obvious.

EXERCISES

9.21. Prove that, if C is a closed curve, and there is a half-line from z_0 which does not meet C, then $z_0 \in E(C)$.

9.22. Prove that any disc is a simply connected domain.

9.23. It is assumed that z_1, z_2, z_3 are distinct points. Prove that $\{z_1, z_2, z_3, z_1\}$ is a simple polygon if and only if im $\{(z_3 - z_1)/(z_2 - z_1)\} \neq 0$. Prove also that, if im $\{(z_3 - z_1)/(z_2 - z_1)\} = 0$, then either $\{z_1, z_3\} = \{z_1, z_2, z_3\}$, or $\{z_2, z_1\} = \{z_2, z_3, z_1\}$ or $\{z_3, z_2\} = \{z_3, z_1, z_2\}$.

9.24. If $k \geqslant 4$, $z_k = z_0$, and the polygon $\{z_0, z_1, \ldots, z_k\}$ is not a simple polygon, prove that there are integers m, n such that $0 \leqslant m < n < k$, $2 \leqslant n - m \leqslant k - 2$, and the line segments $\{z_m, z_{m+1}\}$, $\{z_n, z_{n+1}\}$ have at least one point in common.

9.19. The *diameter* of a set S is defined as the upper bound of $|w - z|$ for all pairs of points w, z of S. The diameter of a curve

C is defined as the diameter of $|C|$. It follows from §4.11 and §9.3 that, if $C = \mathscr{C}(g, a, b)$, then the diameter of C is the oscillation of g in $[a, b]$. We can, therefore, re-state Theorem 4.10 in the following form:

THEOREM 9.10. *Let C be any curve, δ any positive number. Then there is a dissection of C into arcs whose diameters are less than δ.*

EXERCISES

9.25. Prove that, if S is an open set, and the points z_1, z_2 can be joined by a curve contained in S, then they can also be joined by a broken line contained in S. Deduce that, if a non-empty open set S has the property that every pair of points of S can be joined by a curve contained in S, then S is a domain.

9.26. S is a closed set with diameter d. Show that there are points z, w in S such that $|z - w| = d$.

9.27. Show that the diameter of any rectifiable curve is less than or equal to the length of the curve.

9.28. Show that, if C is any closed curve, then the diameter of $I'(C)$ (see §9.16) is equal to that of C.

9.29. Show that, if $z_1 \neq z_2$, and $\Pi = \{z_1, z_2, z_1\}$, then $I(\Pi)$ is empty.

9.30. If z_1, z_2, z_3 are distinct points, im $\{(z_3 - z_1)/(z_2 - z_1)\} = 0$, and $\Pi = \{z_1, z_2, z_3, z_1\}$, show that $I(\Pi)$ is empty.

9.31. (i) If a closed curve C and a domain D have no point in common, show that $\chi(w, C)$ has the same value for all points w of D.

(ii) If a closed curve C and a curve C' have no point in common, show that $\chi(w, C)$ has the same value for all points w of C'.

9.32. S is a set of points whose complement is an unbounded domain. C is a closed curve, and $|C| \subset S$. Show that $I(C) \subset S$.

*9.20. Let z_1, z_2, z_3 be distinct points, and suppose

$$\text{im } \{(z_3 - z_1)/(z_2 - z_1)\} \neq 0. \tag{13}$$

Then, corresponding to every point z, there are real numbers t_1, t_2, t_3, uniquely determined, such that

$$t_1 + t_2 + t_3 = 1 \tag{14}$$

and

$$z = t_1 z_1 + t_2 z_2 + t_3 z_3. \tag{15}$$

To see this, put $z = x + iy$ and $z_m = x_m + iy_m$ $(m = 1, 2, 3)$. Then the above statement is equivalent to the following:

The three simultaneous equations

$$t_1 + t_2 + t_3 = 1,$$
$$x_1 t_1 + x_2 t_2 + x_3 t_3 = x,$$
$$y_1 t_1 + y_2 t_2 + y_3 t_3 = y,$$

with the unknowns t_1, t_2, t_3, have exactly one solution.   This is true if

$$\begin{vmatrix} 1 & 1 & 1 \\ x_1 & x_2 & x_3 \\ y_1 & y_2 & y_3 \end{vmatrix} \neq 0, \tag{16}$$

and it is easily seen that (16) is equivalent to (13).

EXERCISE

9.33. Prove that

$$t_1 = \frac{\operatorname{im}\{(z - z_2)/(z_3 - z_2)\}}{\operatorname{im}\{(z_1 - z_2)/(z_3 - z_2)\}}.$$

Now let $\Delta = \{z_1, z_2, z_3, z_1\}$, and denote the numbers t_1, t_2, t_3 by $g_1(z)$, $g_2(z)$, $g_3(z)$ respectively, to indicate their dependence on z.

EXERCISE

9.34. Prove that $z \in |\Delta|$ if and only if (i) at least one of the three numbers $g_1(z)$, $g_2(z)$, $g_3(z)$ is 0, and (ii) none of them is negative.

Now suppose $g_1(w) < 0$, and let S be the half-line from w through $2w - z_1$ (i.e. in the direction away from z_1).   Let z be any point of S, and $t = (z - w)/(w - z_1)$.   Then, by §9.18, $t \geqslant 0$.   Also

$$z = w + t(w - z_1) = (1 + t)\{g_1(w)z_1 + g_2(w)z_2 + g_3(w)z_3\} - tz_1$$
$$= \{(1 + t)g_1(w) - t\}z_1 + (1 + t)g_2(w)z_2 + (1 + t)g_3(w)z_3.$$

Here the coefficients of z_1, z_2 and z_3 are real, and their sum is 1.   Hence $g_1(z) = (1 + t)g_1(w) - t < 0$.   From this and Exercise 9.34 it follows that z is not on Δ.   Thus the half-line S does not meet Δ.   Hence, by Exercise 9.21, $w \in E(\Delta)$.   This has been proved on the assumption that $g_1(w) < 0$.   It holds, similarly, if $g_2(w) < 0$ or $g_3(w) < 0$.   Thus $w \in E(\Delta)$ if at least one of the three numbers $g_1(w)$, $g_2(w)$, $g_3(w)$ is negative.   If none of them is negative, but at least one is 0, then, by Exercise 9.34, $w \in |\Delta|$.   There remains only the case in which all three are positive.

Suppose, then,

$$g_1(w) > 0, \qquad g_2(w) > 0, \qquad g_3(w) > 0, \tag{17}$$

and consider first the case in which

$$\text{im } \{(z_1 - z_2)/(z_3 - z_2)\} > 0. \tag{18}$$

By Exercise 9.34, w is not on Δ. Hence, by Exercise 9.11,

$$\chi(w, \Delta) = \text{am } \frac{z_2 - w}{z_1 - w} + \text{am } \frac{z_3 - w}{z_2 - w} + \text{am } \frac{z_1 - w}{z_3 - w}. \tag{19}$$

Now, by (17), (18) and Exercise 9.33,

$$\text{im } \{(w - z_2)/(z_3 - z_2)\} > 0. \tag{20}$$

Also

$$\frac{z_3 - w}{z_2 - w} = 1 - \left(\frac{w - z_2}{z_3 - z_2}\right)^{-1}.$$

Hence, by (20), im $\{(z_3 - w)/(z_2 - w)\} > 0$, which implies that

$$\text{am } \{(z_3 - w)/(z_2 - w)\} > 0. \tag{21}$$

Now

$$\frac{z_2 - z_3}{z_1 - z_3} = \left(1 - \frac{z_1 - z_2}{z_3 - z_2}\right)^{-1}, \qquad \frac{z_3 - z_1}{z_2 - z_1} = 1 - \left(\frac{z_1 - z_2}{z_3 - z_2}\right)^{-1}.$$

Hence, by (18),

$$\text{im } \{(z_2 - z_3)/(z_1 - z_3)\} > 0, \qquad \text{im } \{(z_3 - z_1)/(z_2 - z_1)\} > 0.$$

From this it follows in the same way as (21) from (18) that

$$\text{am } \{(z_1 - w)/(z_3 - w)\} > 0, \qquad \text{am } \{(z_2 - w)/(z_1 - w)\} > 0. \tag{22}$$

Since a principal amplitude is never greater than π, it follows from (19), (21) and (22) that $0 < \chi(w, \Delta) \leqslant 3\pi$, and from this and Exercise 9.14(ii) that $\chi(w, \Delta) = 2\pi$.

Similarly if, instead of (18), we assume

$$\text{im } \{(z_1 - z_2)/(z_3 - z_2)\} < 0, \tag{23}$$

we obtain $\chi(w, \Delta) = -2\pi$.

The results of this section can be summed up as follows:

$I(\Delta)$ is the set of those points w for which (17) holds, and $I'(\Delta)$ the set of those for which $g_1(w) \geqslant 0$, $g_2(w) \geqslant 0$ and $g_3(w) \geqslant 0$.

For any point w of $I(\Delta)$, we have $\chi(w, \Delta) = 2\pi$ or -2π according as (18) or (23) holds.

EXERCISES

9.35. It is assumed that z_1, z_2, z_3 are distinct points, that

$$\Delta_1 = \{z_1, z_2, z_3, z_1\},$$

that w_1, w_2, w_3 are distinct points of $I'(\Delta_1)$, and that $\Delta_2 = \{w_1, w_2, w_3, w_1\}$. Prove that $I'(\Delta_2) \subset I'(\Delta_1)$. If, moreover, (13) holds, and none of the three points w_1, w_2, w_3 coincides with z_3, prove that z_3 is not in $I'(\Delta_2)$.

9.36. It is assumed that $a < b$, $\alpha < \beta$, $z_1 = a + i\alpha$, $z_2 = b + i\alpha$, $z_3 = b + i\beta$, $z_4 = a + i\beta$ and $\Pi = \{z_1, z_2, z_3, z_4, z_1\}$. Prove that $I(\Pi)$ is the set of those points w for which $a < \operatorname{re} w < b$ and $\alpha < \operatorname{im} w < \beta$, that $I'(\Pi)$ is the set of those for which $a \leqslant \operatorname{re} w \leqslant b$ and $\alpha \leqslant \operatorname{im} w \leqslant \beta$, and that $\chi(w, \Pi) = 2\pi$ for every point w of $I(\Pi)$. Prove also that Π is a Jordan polygon.

9.37. If $r > 0$ and $C = \{ir, 0, r\} + \mathscr{C}(t; re^{it}, 0, \tfrac{1}{2}\pi)$, prove that $I(C)$ is the set of those points z for which $\operatorname{re} z > 0$, $\operatorname{im} z > 0$ and $|z| < r$, and that $\chi(z, C) = 2\pi$ for every point z of $I(C)$.

9.38. C is a curve, leading from z_1 to z_2. Prove that, if the half-line from w through $w - 1$ does not meet C, then $\chi(w, C) = \operatorname{am}(z_2 - w) - \operatorname{am}(z_1 - w)$, and if the half-line from w through $w + 1$ does not meet C, then $\chi(w, C) = \operatorname{am}(w - z_2) - \operatorname{am}(w - z_1)$.

9.39. Prove that, if C is a simple closed curve, then the points of C cannot all have the same imaginary part.

*9.21. Let C be a simple closed curve. Choose points z_1, z_2 of C such that

$$\operatorname{im} z_1 \leqslant \operatorname{im} z \leqslant \operatorname{im} z_2 \tag{24}$$

for every point z of C. This is possible, for instance by Theorems 4.3 and 9.2 and Exercise 9.2(i). Then, by Exercise 9.39, $\operatorname{im} z_1 < \operatorname{im} z_2$.

It easily follows from §9.8 that there are two simple curves C_1, C_2, such that C_1 leads from z_1 to z_2, C_2 from z_2 to z_1, and

$$C \sim C_1 + C_2. \tag{25}$$

Let

$$\phi_m(w) = \chi(w, C_m) - (-1)^m \operatorname{am}(iz_1 - iw)$$
$$+ (-1)^m \operatorname{am}(iw - iz_2) \quad (m = 1, 2). \tag{26}$$

Let H_1, H_2 be the half-lines from z_1 through $z_1 - i$ and from z_2 through $z_2 + i$ respectively. Then, by Exercises 4.1 and 9.13,

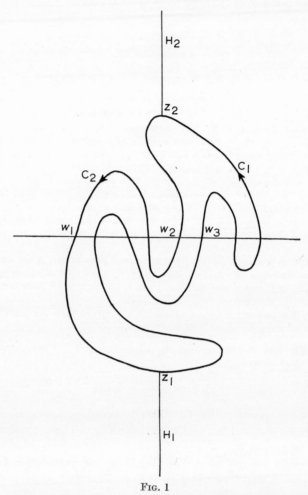

FIG. 1

ϕ_m is fully continuous at all points other than those of $|C_m| \cup H_1 \cup H_2$ ($m = 1, 2$). Also, by Exercise 9.14,

$$e^{i\chi(w,\,C_1)} = \frac{z_2 - w}{|z_2 - w|} \times \frac{|z_1 - w|}{z_1 - w},$$

and hence, by (26), $\exp\{i\phi_1(w)\} = -1$, if w is not on C_1. This means that $\phi_1(w)/\pi$ is an odd integer whenever it exists. Similarly, so is $\phi_2(w)/\pi$.

*9.22. LEMMA 1. $\phi_1(w)$ *has the same value for all points w of C_2 other than $w = z_1$ and $w = z_2$.*

Proof. Let w_1 and w_2 be any two points of C_2, distinct from z_1 and z_2 and from each other. Then there is an arc C' of C_2 with end points w_1 and w_2. Now C' has no point in common with $|C_1| \cup H_1 \cup H_2$. Hence, by §9.21, ϕ_1 is continuous on C', and $\phi_1(w)/\pi$ is an integer for every point w of C'. From this and Theorem 9.8 it follows that $\phi_1(w_1) = \phi_1(w_2)$. This proves the lemma.

LEMMA 2. *Let*

$$\operatorname{im} z_1 < \operatorname{im} w < \operatorname{im} z_2, \qquad (27)$$

and suppose the half-line from w through $w - 1$ does not meet C_1. Then $\phi_1(w) = \pi$.

Proof. By (26) and Exercise 9.38,

$\phi_1(w) = \operatorname{am}(z_2 - w) - \operatorname{am}(z_1 - w) + \operatorname{am}(iz_1 - iw) - \operatorname{am}(iw - iz_2)$.

Now, by (27), $\operatorname{im}(z_1 - w) < 0$ and $\operatorname{im}(z_2 - w) > 0$. Hence, by Exercise 1.1(ii),

$\operatorname{am}(iz_1 - iw) = \operatorname{am}(z_1 - w) + \operatorname{am} i = \operatorname{am}(z_1 - w) + \tfrac{1}{2}\pi$

and

$\operatorname{am}(iw - iz_2) = \operatorname{am}(z_2 - w) + \operatorname{am}(-i) = \operatorname{am}(z_2 - w) - \tfrac{1}{2}\pi$,

and the results follows.

LEMMA 3. *Suppose that (27) holds. If the half-line from w through $w - 1$ does not meet C_2, then $\phi_2(w) = -\pi$. If the half-line from w through $w + 1$ does not meet C_1, then $\phi_1(w) = -\pi$, and if it does not meet C_2, then $\phi_2(w) = \pi$.*

This can be proved in the same way as Lemma 2.

Now let b be any number such that

$$\operatorname{im} z_1 < b < \operatorname{im} z_2, \qquad (28)$$

and let S_m (for $m = 1$ and $m = 2$) be the set of those real numbers x for which $x + ib \in |C_m|$. Then it is easily seen that S_m is closed and bounded. Moreover, S_1 is not empty. For if it were, then neither of the half-lines from ib through $ib - 1$ and $ib + 1$ would meet C_1, and it would follow from Lemma 2 that $\phi_1(ib) = \pi$, and from Lemma 3 that $\phi_1(ib) = -\pi$. Thus the set of real numbers $S_1 \cup S_2$ is closed, bounded, and not empty. It therefore has a least member x_1, say. Now either $x_1 \in S_1$ or $x_1 \in S_2$. Suppose, first, $x_1 \in S_2$, let x_2 be the greatest member of S_2, and let $w_m = x_m + ib$ $(m = 1, 2)$. Then, by Lemma 2, $\phi_1(w_1) = \pi$, and, by Lemma 1, $\phi_1(w_1) = \phi_1(w_2)$. Hence

$$\phi_1(w_2) = \pi. \tag{29}$$

From this and Lemma 3 it follows that the half-line from w_2 through $w_2 + 1$ must meet C_1. This means that the set S_3, of those points x of S_1 for which $x \geqslant x_2$, is not empty. Now S_3 is bounded below and closed, and therefore has a least member x_3, say. It is trivial that $x_3 > x_2$. Let $w_3 = x_3 + ib$. Then $w_2 \in |C_2|$ and $w_3 \in |C_1|$. Hence, by (25), both end points of the line segment $\{w_2, w_3\}$ are on C. Now let w' be any other point of this line segment, and let re $w' = x'$. Then $w' = x' + ib$ and

$$x_2 < x' < x_3. \tag{30}$$

From this and the definition of x_3 it follows that no number between x_2 and x' (inclusive) is in S_1. This means that the line segment $\{w_2, w'\}$ does not meet C_1, and it follows from (28) that it does not meet either H_1 or H_2. Arguing as in the proof of Lemma 1, but with $\{w_2, w'\}$ instead of C', we obtain $\phi_1(w') = \phi_1(w_2)$. From this and (29) it follows that

$$\phi_1(w') = \pi. \tag{31}$$

Now, by (30) and the definition of x_2, no number $x \geqslant x'$ is in S_2. This means that the half-line from w' through $w' + 1$ does not meet C_2. Hence, by Lemma 3,

$$\phi_2(w') = \pi. \tag{32}$$

Now, by (25), §9.8 and Exercise 9.10, $\chi(w', C) = \chi(w', C_1) + \chi(w', C_2)$. Hence, by (26), (31) and (32), $\chi(w', C) = 2\pi$.

So far we have assumed that $x_1 \in S_2$. The assumption that $x_1 \in S_1$ would similarly have led to $\chi(w', C) = -2\pi$. In either case, $w' \in I(C)$.

9.23. The results of the last two sections can be summed up as follows:

THEOREM 9.11. *Let C be a simple closed curve. Let z_1 and z_2 respectively be points of least and greatest imaginary part on C, and let* im $z_1 < b <$ im z_2. *Then the straight line* im $z = b$ *contains a line segment whose end points are on C, and whose* *other points are in* $I(C)$. *Also, if* w *is any one of these other points, then* $\chi(w, C) = \pm 2\pi$; *and there are two simple curves* C_1, C_2, *such that* C_1 *leads from* z_1 *to* z_2, C_2 *from* z_2 *to* z_1, $C \sim C_1 + C_2$, *and one of the end points of the said line segment is on* C_1, *the other on* C_2.

A Jordan curve C is said to be *described in the positive sense* if and only if, for every point w of $I(C)$, we have $\chi(w, C) = 2\pi$. It is said to be *described in the negative sense* if and only if, for every such point w, we have $\chi(w, C) = -2\pi$. It follows from Theorem 9.11 and Exercises 9.39 and 9.31(i) that any Jordan curve is described in either the positive or the negative sense.

EXERCISES

9.40. C is a closed curve, equivalent to $C_1 + C_2$ (see §9.8 and §9.5). The function f is continuous on C, and $f(z) \neq 0$ ($z \in |C|$). Prove that var am $(f, C) =$ var am $(f, C_1) +$ var am (f, C_2).

9.41. Prove that the end points of the line segment mentioned in Theorem 9.11 are also the end points of two simple curves C', C'', such that $z_1 \in |C'|$, $z_2 \in |C''|$, and $C \sim C' + C''$.

9.42. Prove that, if $z_1 \neq z_2$, then $\{z_2, z_1\}$ is '$\{z_1, z_2\}$ described backward'.

9.43. The function g_1 is defined as in §9.20, and $z \in |\{w, w'\}|$. Prove that, (i) if $g_1(w) \leqslant g_1(w')$, then $g_1(w) \leqslant g_1(z) \leqslant g_1(w')$, and (ii) if $g_1(w) < g_1(w')$, $z \neq w$ and $z \neq w'$, then $g_1(w) < g_1(z) < g_1(w')$.

CHAPTER 10

THE ROOTS OF
AN ALGEBRAIC EQUATION

10.1. *A polynomial of degree n* is an expression of the form

$$\sum_{m=0}^{n} a_m z^m,$$

where $a_n \neq 0$. It can be deduced from the fundamental theorem of algebra (see §4.8) by the methods of elementary algebra that any polynomial of degree $n \geqslant 1$ can be expressed in the form

$$c \prod_{m=1}^{n} (z - z_m).$$

This means that, for every polynomial $p(z)$ of degree $n \geqslant 1$, there are constants $c, z_1, z_2, \ldots, z_n$, such that

$$p(z) = c \prod_{m=1}^{n} (z - z_m) \tag{1}$$

for every number z. It can also be shown by the methods of elementary algebra that this factorisation of $p(z)$ is unique apart from the order of the factors. The numbers $z_1, z_2, \ldots,$ z_n are called the *roots* of the algebraic equation $p(z) = 0$ or the *zeros* of the polynomial $p(z)$. By the number of roots of the equation $p(z) = 0$ (or of zeros of $p(z)$) in the set of points S we do not mean the number of points z of S for which $p(z) = 0$, but the number of integers m for which $1 \leqslant m \leqslant n$ and $z_m \in S$. In other words, multiple roots are counted according to their multiplicities. Thus the equation $z^5 = 0$ has 5 roots in the unit disc.

10.2. Suppose that C is a Jordan curve, described in the positive sense (see §9.23), that (1) holds, and that $p(z) \neq 0$ for any point z of C (i.e. that none of the points $z_1, z_2, \ldots, z_n$ is on C). Then, by §9.16 and §9.23, for any integer m from

1 to n, $\chi(z_m, C) = 2\pi$ or 0 according as z_m is or is not in $I(C)$. Hence, denoting the number of zeros of $p(z)$ in $I(C)$ by k, we have

$$\sum_{m=1}^{n} \chi(z_m, C) = 2\pi k.$$

Now, by (1), Exercise 9.17 and the definition of $\chi(w, C)$ (§9.15),

$$\text{var am } (p, C) = \sum_{m=1}^{n} \chi(z_m, C).$$

Hence $k = (2\pi)^{-1}$ var am (p, C).

10.3. *Example.* Find the number of zeros of the polynomial $f(z) = z^5 + z^2 + 1$ in the set S of those points z for which $-1 < \text{re } z < 0$ and $0 < \text{im } z < 1$.

Solution. Let the number in question be k.

By Exercise 9.36 and §9.23, $S = I(C)$, where $C = \{-1, 0, i, -1+i, -1\}$, and C is described in the positive sense. Hence, if f has no zeros on C, it follows from §10.2 that

$$2\pi k = \text{var am } (f, C). \tag{2}$$

The evaluation of the right-hand side of (2) can be based on Exercises 9.40, 9.18 and 9.19.

Let us consider each of the four sides of C. The points of $\{i, -1+i\}$ are of the form $x+i$, where $-1 \leqslant x \leqslant 0$. Now

$$\text{re } f(x+i) = x^5 - 10x^3 + x^2 + 5x,$$
$$\text{im } f(x+i) = 5x^4 - 10x^2 + 2x + 1. \tag{3}$$

Hence, if $f(x+i)$ is real, then $x \neq 0$ and

$$f(x+i) = \text{re } f(x+i) - x \text{ im } f(x+i)$$
$$= -4x^5 - x^2 + 4x = 4x(1-x^4) - x^2,$$

which is negative if $-1 \leqslant x < 0$. Thus $f(z)$ is neither 0 nor real and positive for any point z of $\{i, -1+i\}$. The points of $\{-1+i, -1\}$ are of the form $-1+iy$, where $0 \leqslant y \leqslant 1$. Now $\text{re } f(-1+iy) = 1 + 9y^2 - 5y^4$, which is positive if $0 \leqslant y \leqslant 1$. On $\{-1, 0\}$, $f(z)$ is obviously positive. The points of $\{0, i\}$ are of the form iy, and $\text{re } f(iy) = 1 - y^2$, which is positive if $0 \leqslant y < 1$, while $f(i)$ is not real. Thus, taking $C_1 = \{i, -1+i\}$

and $C_2 = \{-1+i, \ -1, \ 0, \ i\}$, we see that $f(z)$ is not 0 for any point z of either C_1 or C_2, not positive for any point z of C_1, and not negative for any point z of C_2. Also $C \sim C_1 + C_2$. Hence f has no zeros on C, so that (2) holds, and it follows from Exercise 9.40 that

$$\text{var am } (f, C) = \text{var am } (f, C_1) + \text{var am } (f, C_2).$$

Also, by Exercise 9.19,

$$\text{var am } (f, C_1) = \text{am } \{-f(-1+i)\} - \text{am } \{-f(i)\},$$

and, by Exercise 9.18,

$$\text{var am } (f, C_2) = \text{am } f(i) - \text{am } f(-1+i).$$

From (2) and the last three formulae we obtain

$$2\pi k = \text{am } w_1 - \text{am } (-w_1) + \text{am } w_2 - \text{am } (-w_2),$$

where $w_1 = -f(-1+i)$ and $w_2 = f(i)$. Now, by (3), im $w_1 > 0$ and im $w_2 > 0$. Hence, by formula (15) of §1.17,

$$\text{am } w_1 - \text{am } (-w_1) = \text{am } w_2 - \text{am } (-w_2) = \pi.$$

It follows that $k = 1$.

10.4. *Example.* Find the number of zeros of the polynomial $f(z) = z^5 + z^3 + 3z^2 + 1$ in the first quadrant of the plane.

Solution. Let

$$g(z) = 1 + z^{-2} + 3z^{-3} + z^{-5}, \tag{4}$$

so that

$$f(z) = z^5 g(z) \quad (z \neq 0). \tag{5}$$

Then, by (4),

$$|g(z)-1| \leqslant |z|^{-2} + 3|z|^{-3} + |z|^{-5} \leqslant \tfrac{1}{4} + \tfrac{3}{8} + \tfrac{1}{32} < 1 \quad (|z| \geqslant 2), \tag{6}$$

which implies that $g(z)$ is neither 0 nor real and negative if $|z| \geqslant 2$. From this and (5) it follows that all the zeros of f are in the disc $|z| < 2$. Thus what we have to find is the number of zeros of f in the first quadrant of this disc. Let this number be k.

Let $\Gamma = \mathscr{C}(t; 2e^{it}, 0, \tfrac{1}{2}\pi)$ and

$$C = \{2i, 0, 2\} + \Gamma. \tag{7}$$

Then, by Exercise 9.37, C is described in the positive sense, and $I(C)$ is the first quadrant of the disc $|z| < 2$. Hence, by §10.2,

$$2\pi k = \text{var am} \ (f, C), \tag{8}$$

provided that f has no zeros on C. We know already that f has no zeros on Γ, since $|z| = 2$ for every point z of Γ. It is trivial that $f(z) > 0$, $(0 \leqslant z \leqslant 2)$. Also

$$\text{re} \, f(iy) = 1 - 3y^2, \qquad \text{im} \, f(iy) = y^3(y^2 - 1). \tag{9}$$

Hence the only points on $\{2i, 0\}$ at which $f(z)$ is real are 0 and i, and we have $f(0) > 0$ and $f(i) < 0$. Thus f has no zeros on C, and (8) is proved. Moreover, $f(z)$ is not real and positive for any point z of $\{2i, \frac{1}{2}i\}$, and not real and negative for any point z of $\{\frac{1}{2}i, 0, 2\}$. Hence, by Exercises 9.19 and 9.18,

$$\text{var am} \ (f, \{2i, \tfrac{1}{2}i\}) = \text{am} \ \{-f(\tfrac{1}{2}i)\} - \text{am} \ \{-f(2i)\} \tag{10}$$

and

$$\text{var am} \ (f, \{\tfrac{1}{2}i, 0, 2\}) = \text{am} \, f(2) - \text{am} \, f(\tfrac{1}{2}i). \tag{11}$$

Now, by (5) and Exercise 9.17,

$$\text{var am} \ (f, \Gamma) = 5 \, \text{var am} \ (h, \Gamma) + \text{var am} \ (g, \Gamma),$$

where the function h is defined by $h(z) = z$, and it is trivial that var am $(h, \Gamma) = \frac{1}{2}\pi$. Hence

$$\text{var am} \ (f, \Gamma) = \tfrac{5}{2}\pi + \text{var am} \ (g, \Gamma). \tag{12}$$

We have noted that $g(z)$ is neither 0 nor real and negative if $|z| \geqslant 2$, and this condition is satisfied if z is on Γ. Hence, by Exercise 9.18, var am $(g, \Gamma) = \text{am} \, g(2i) - \text{am} \, g(2)$, and am $g(2) = 0$. It therefore follows from (12) that

$$\text{var am} \ (f, \Gamma) = \tfrac{5}{2}\pi + \text{am} \, g(2i). \tag{13}$$

Also, since am $f(2) = 0$, it follows from (10), (11) and Exercise 9.40 that

$$\text{var am} \ (f, \{2i, 0, 2\}) = \text{am} \ \{-f(\tfrac{1}{2}i)\} - \text{am} \, f(\tfrac{1}{2}i) - \text{am} \ \{-f(2i)\}.$$

Hence, by (8), (7), Exercise 9.40 and (13),

$$2\pi k = \tfrac{5}{2}\pi + \text{am} \ \{-f(\tfrac{1}{2}i)\} - \text{am} \, f(\tfrac{1}{2}i) + \text{am} \, g(2i) - \text{am} \ \{-f(2i)\}. \tag{14}$$

Now, by (9), im $f(\frac{1}{2}i) < 0$.   Hence, by formula (15) of §1.17,

$$\text{am}\,\{-f(\tfrac{1}{2}i)\} - \text{am}\, f(\tfrac{1}{2}i) = \pi. \tag{15}$$

Also, by (5) and (6), $-f(2i) = -32ig(2i)$ and re $g(2i) > 0$. Hence, by Exercise 1.1(i), am $\{-f(2i)\} = $ am $(-32i) + $ am $g(2i)$ $= -\frac{1}{2}\pi + $ am $g(2i)$. From this and (14) and (15) we obtain $k = 2$.

CHAPTER 11

CONTOUR INTEGRALS

11.1. The integral of a function f along a curve C is usually defined only on the assumption that f is continuous on C, and that C has a conveniently chosen property. A curve with that property is usually called a *contour*, and the integral is accordingly called a *contour integral*. The choice of the property is not always the same, and therefore different mathematicians use the term 'contour' with different meanings. In this book it will simply mean 'rectifiable curve' (see §9.10). Some mathematicians, however, use it in the more restricted sense of 'smooth curve', which I now explain.

11.2. A curve is said to be *smooth* if and only if it has a representation (g, a, b) in which the derivative (relative to the real axis; see §4.5) g' is continuous in $[a, b]$. A curve which can be dissected into smooth arcs (see §9.4) may be said to be *piecewise smooth*. This term is, however, superfluous, since every piecewise smooth curve is smooth, as the reader will probably learn from the next two exercises.

EXERCISES

11.1. If $g(t) = it^2$ or t^2 according as $t < 0$ or $t \geqslant 0$, show that $\{i, 0, 1\} = \mathscr{C}(g, -1, 1)$. Deduce that the broken line $\{i, 0, 1\}$ is a smooth curve.

11.2. If C_1 and C_2 are smooth curves, and the last point of C_1 is the first point of C_2, show that $C_1 + C_2$ is a smooth curve.

11.3. Let C be a contour (i.e. a rectifiable curve), starting at z_0, and let the function f be continuous on C. Then I associate with every dissection Δ of C into arcs a number $s(\Delta)$, defined as follows: If Δ is the dissection $C_1, C_2, \ldots, C_k$, and z_n is the last point of C_n $(n = 1, 2, \ldots, k)$, then

$$s(\Delta) = \sum_{n=1}^{k} (z_n - z_{n-1}) f(z_n). \tag{1}$$

Now let Δ' be the dissection $C_1', C_2', \ldots, C_{k'}'$. I say that Δ' contains Δ if and only if there are integers $m_0, m_1, m_2 \ldots, m_k$, such that $0 = m_0 < m_1 < m_2 < \ldots < m_k = k'$, and that, for every integer n from 1 to k, we have

$$C_n = C'_{m_{n-1}+1} + C'_{m_{n-1}+2} + \ldots + C'_{m_n}. \tag{2}$$

Let l be the length of C.

LEMMA 1. *Let* $\epsilon > 0$, $\delta > 0$, *and suppose that, for every pair of points* z, z' *of* C, *for which* $|z - z'| < \delta$, *we have* $|f(z) - f(z')| < \epsilon$. *Suppose also that* Δ *is a dissection of* C *into arcs whose diameters are less than* δ, *and that* Δ' *is a dissection which contains* Δ. *Then* $|s(\Delta') - s(\Delta)| \leqslant \epsilon l$.

Proof. Let the notation be as above. Also, for $m = 1, 2, \ldots, k'$, let z'_m be the last point of C'_m; and let $z'_0 = z_0$. Then

$$s(\Delta') = \sum_{m=1}^{k'} (z'_m - z'_{m-1}) f(z'_m) = \sum_{n=1}^{k} \sum_{m=m_{n-1}+1}^{m_n} (z'_m - z'_{m-1}) f(z'_m). \tag{3}$$

Now, by (2) and the definitions of z_n and z'_m, $z_n = z'_{m_n}$ $(n = 0, 1, 2, \ldots, k)$. Hence

$$z_n - z_{n-1} = \sum_{m=m_{n-1}+1}^{m_n} (z'_m - z'_{m-1}) \quad (n = 1, 2, \ldots, k),$$

and hence, by (1) and (3),

$$s(\Delta') - s(\Delta) = \sum_{n=1}^{k} \sum_{m=m_{n-1}+1}^{m_n} (z'_m - z'_{m-1})\{f(z'_m) - f(z_n)\}. \tag{4}$$

Now, if $m_{n-1} < m \leqslant m_n$, then z_m and z_n are points of the arc C_n, whose diameter is less than δ. Hence $|z'_m - z_n| < \delta$, and hence, by hypothesis, $|f(z'_m) - f(z_n)| < \epsilon$ $(m_{n-1} < m \leqslant m_n)$. From this and (4) it follows that

$$|s(\Delta') - s(\Delta)| \leqslant \epsilon \sum_{n=1}^{k} \sum_{m=m_{n-1}+1}^{m_n} |z'_m - z'_{m-1}| = \epsilon \sum_{m=1}^{k'} |z'_m - z'_{m-1}|.$$

Now, by §9.10 and the definition of l,

$$\sum_{m=1}^{k'} |z'_m - z'_{m-1}| \leqslant l,$$

and the result follows.

LEMMA 2. *For every positive number* ϵ, *there is a positive number* δ, *such that, if* Δ_1 *and* Δ_2 *are any dissections of* C *into arcs of diameters less than* δ, *then* $|s(\Delta_1) - s(\Delta_2)| < \epsilon$.

Proof. The case $l=0$ is trivial. Suppose, therefore, that $l>0$. Let ϵ be any positive number. Choose the positive number δ so that, for every pair of points z, z' of C, for which $|z-z'|<\delta$, we have $|f(z)-f(z')|<\epsilon/(3l)$. This is possible by Theorems 4.11 and 9.2 and Exercise 9.2(i). Now let Δ_1 and Δ_2 be any dissections of C into arcs of diameters less than δ. It is trivial that there is a dissection Δ' which contains both Δ_1 and Δ_2, and it follows from Lemma 1 (with $\epsilon/(3l)$ instead of ϵ) that $|s(\Delta')-s(\Delta_1)|\leqslant\frac{1}{3}\epsilon$ and $|s(\Delta')-s(\Delta_2)|\leqslant\frac{1}{3}\epsilon$. Hence $|s(\Delta_1)-s(\Delta_2)|\leqslant\frac{2}{3}\epsilon<\epsilon$, which proves the lemma.

11.4. LEMMA 3. *There is one and only one number J with the following property: For every positive number ϵ, there is a positive number δ, such that, for every dissection Δ of C into arcs of diameters less than δ, we have $|s(\Delta)-J|<\epsilon$.*

Proof. By Exercise 9.2(ii), there is a number M such that

$$|f(z)| \leqslant M \quad (z\in|C|). \tag{5}$$

From this it easily follows that

$$|s(\Delta)| \leqslant Ml \tag{6}$$

for any dissection Δ of C into arcs.

For every natural number n, choose a dissection Δ_n of C into arcs of diameters less than $1/n$. This is possible by Theorem 9.10. Then, by (6), the sequence $s(\Delta_1)$, $s(\Delta_2)$, $s(\Delta_3)$, ... is bounded. It is, in fact, convergent, but it is not worth while to prove this here. As the sequence is bounded, it has, by Theorem 2.7, a convergent sub-sequence. This means that there are integers n_1, n_2, n_3, ..., such that $0<n_1<n_2<...$, and that $\lim_{m\to\infty} s(\Delta_{n_m})$ exists. Put

$$\lim_{m\to\infty} s(\Delta_{n_m}) = J. \tag{7}$$

To show that J has the required property, let ϵ be any positive number. Choose the positive number δ so that, if Δ and Δ' are any dissections of C into arcs of diameters less than δ, then

$$|s(\Delta)-s(\Delta')| < \tfrac{1}{2}\epsilon. \tag{8}$$

This is possible by Lemma 2. Now choose the natural number m so that $m\delta>1$ and

$$|s(\Delta_{n_m})-J| < \tfrac{1}{2}\epsilon. \tag{9}$$

This is possible by (7). Then $1/n_m \leqslant 1/m < \delta$, and Δ_{n_m} is, therefore, a dissection of C into arcs of diameters less than δ. Thus, if Δ is also such a dissection, we have (8) with $\Delta' = \Delta_{n_m}$, i.e. $|s(\Delta) - s(\Delta_{n_m})| < \frac{1}{2}\epsilon$. From this and (9) we obtain $|s(\Delta) - J| < \epsilon$, which shows that J has the required property. That at most one number J can have it follows at once from Theorem 9.10.

The number J of Lemma 3 (which, of course, depends on C and f) is denoted by

$$\int_C f(z)dz.$$

11.5. The next five theorems are trivial.

THEOREM 11.1.   *Let C be a contour, leading from z_1 to z_2. Then*

$$\int_C 1dz = z_2 - z_1.$$

Note.   It is customary to write $\int dz$ for $\int 1dz$.

THEOREM 11.2.   *Let C be a contour, f a function continuous on C, and c a constant (i.e. a number independent of z).   Then*

$$\int_C cf(z)dz = c\int_C f(z)dz.$$

THEOREM 11.3.   *Let C be a contour, and let the functions f and g be continuous on C.   Then*

$$\int_C \{f(z) + g(z)\}dz = \int_C f(z)dz + \int_C g(z)dz.$$

THEOREM 11.4.   *Let C be a contour, $C = C_1 + C_2$, and let the function f be continuous on C.   Then*

$$\int_C f(z)dz = \int_{C_1} f(z)dz + \int_{C_2} f(z)dz.$$

THEOREM 11.5.   *Let C be a contour of length l, M a constant, let the function f be continuous on C, and let $|f(z)| \leqslant M$ for every point z of C.   Then*

$$\left|\int_C f(z)dz\right| \leqslant Ml.$$

The next theorem is not quite trivial. Its proof may, nevertheless, be left to the reader.

THEOREM 11.6. *Let C be a contour, let C^* be 'C described backward', and let the function f be continuous on C.   Then*

$$\int_{C^*} f(z)dz = -\int_C f(z)dz.$$

11.6. THEOREM 11.7.   *Let $C = \mathscr{C}(g, a, b)$, and suppose that the derivative g' is continuous in $[a, b]$, and that the function f is continuous on C.   Then*

$$\int_C f(z)dz = \int_a^b f\{g(t)\}g'(t)dt. \tag{10}$$

Proof.   Denote the left-hand side of (10) by J, the right-hand side by I, and let $\epsilon > 0$.

It follows from Exercise 7.3 that $f\{g(t)\}$, considered as a function of t, is continuous in $[a, b]$.   Hence, by Theorem 4.10, there are numbers $t_0, t_1, \ldots, t_k$, such that $a = t_0 < t_1 < \ldots < t_k = b$, and that the oscillation of $f\{g(t)\}$ in each of the intervals $[t_{n-1}, t_n]$, $(n = 1, 2, \ldots, k)$, is less than ϵ.   This implies that

$$|f\{g(t)\} - f\{g(t_n)\}| < \epsilon \quad (t_{n-1} \leqslant t \leqslant t_n; n = 1, 2, \ldots, k). \tag{11}$$

Let

$$z_n = g(t_n), \qquad C_n = \mathscr{C}(g, t_{n-1}, t_n), \qquad J_n = \int_{C_n} f(z)dz,$$

$$I_n = \int_{t_{n-1}}^{t_n} f\{g(t)\}g'(t)dt. \tag{12}$$

Then

$$J = \sum_{n=1}^k J_n, \qquad I = \sum_{n=1}^k I_n. \tag{13}$$

Let

$$l = \int_a^b |g'(t)|dt, \qquad l_n = \int_{t_{n-1}}^{t_n} |g'(t)|dt. \tag{14}$$

Then, by Theorem 9.4, l and l_n are the lengths of C and C_n respectively.

Now, by Theorems 11.1, 11.2 and 11.3,

$$J_n - (z_n - z_{n-1})f(z_n) = \int_{C_n} \{f(z) - f(z_n)\}dz,$$

and, by (11) and (12), $|f(z) - f(z_n)| < \epsilon$ $(z\epsilon|C_n|)$. Hence, by Theorem 11.5,

$$|J_n - (z_n - z_{n-1})f(z_n)| \leqslant \epsilon l_n. \tag{15}$$

Also, by (12) and Theorem 4.9,

$$I_n - (z_n - z_{n-1})f(z_n) = \int_{t_{n-1}}^{t_n} [f\{g(t)\} - f\{g(t_n)\}]g'(t)dt.$$

Hence, by Exercise 4.2, (11) and (14),

$$|I_n - (z_n - z_{n-1})f(z_n)| \leqslant \epsilon \int_{t_{n-1}}^{t_n} |g'(t)|dt = \epsilon l_n.$$

From this and (15) it follows that $|J_n - I_n| \leqslant 2\epsilon l_n$ $(n = 1, 2, \ldots, k)$, and from this and (13) that

$$|J - I| \leqslant 2\epsilon \sum_{n=1}^{k} l_n = 2\epsilon l.$$

Thus $|J - I| \leqslant 2\epsilon l$ for every positive number ϵ. This means that $J = I$, which was to be proved.

EXERCISES

11.3. If C is the circle with centre z_0 and radius r, described counter-clockwise (i.e. $C \sim \mathscr{C}(t; z_0 + re^{it}, 0, 2\pi)$), prove that

$$\int_C \frac{dz}{z - z_0} = 2\pi i.$$

11.4. If C is the upper half of the ellipse $x^2 + 4y^2 = 4$ (where $z = x + iy$), described from 2 to -2, evaluate

$$\int_C |z|dz.$$

11.5. If C is the circle $|z| = 2$, described counter-clockwise, evaluate

$$\text{(i) } \int_C \frac{dz}{z - 1}, \qquad \text{(ii) } \int_C \frac{dz}{z - 3}.$$

11.6. C is a contour, $C = \mathscr{C}(g, a, b)$, and f is continuous on C. $H(a) = 0$, and if $a < u \leqslant b$, then

$$H(u) = \int_{C(u)} f(z)dz,$$

where $C(u) = \mathscr{C}(g, a, u)$.   Prove that H is continuous in $[a, b]$.   (Hint: use Theorems 9.5, 11.4 and 11.5.)

11.7. THEOREM 11.8. *Let C be a contour, leading from z_1 to z_2, and suppose that the function f is fully differentiable at all points of C, and that f' is continuous on C. Then*

$$\int_C f'(z)dz = f(z_2) - f(z_1). \tag{16}$$

Note. If C is a smooth curve, the result is easily obtained thus: By §11.2, there are numbers a, b and a function g, such that $C = \mathscr{C}(g, a, b)$, and the derivative g' is continuous in $[a, b]$. From this and Theorem 11.7 it follows that

$$\int_C f'(z)dz = \int_a^b f'\{g(t)\}g'(t)dt. \tag{17}$$

Let the function h be defined by the equation $h(t) = f\{g(t)\}$. Then, by Theorem 4.2, $h'(t) = f'\{g(t)\}g'(t)$ $(a \leqslant t \leqslant b)$, and it is easily seen that h' is continuous in $[a, b]$. Hence, by (17) and Theorem 4.9,

$$\int_C f'(z)dz = \int_a^b h'(t)dt = h(b) - h(a) = f\{g(b)\} - f\{g(a)\}.$$

Now $g(a) = z_1$ and $g(b) = z_2$, and (16) follows.

EXERCISE

11.7. Prove that, if the function f is fully differentiable at all points of the domain D, and $f'(z) = 0$ for every point z of D, then f is constant (i.e. assumes only one value) in D. Prove also that the domains are the only non-empty open sets with this property.

*11.8. *Proof* of Theorem 11.8. Let $C = \mathscr{C}(g, a, b)$,

$$H(a) = 0, \qquad H(u) = \int_{\mathscr{C}(g, a, u)} f'(z)dz \quad (a < u \leqslant b), \tag{18}$$

and

$$G(u) = H(u) - f\{g(u)\} + f(z_1) \quad (a \leqslant u \leqslant b). \tag{19}$$

Then $H(b)$ is equal to the left-hand side of (16), and $g(b) = z_2$, and so (16) is equivalent to

$$G(b) = 0. \qquad (20)$$

So this is what we have to prove.

Let $h(u)$ be the length of $\mathscr{C}(g, a, u)$ if $a < u \leqslant b$, and $h(a) = 0$. Then, by Theorem 9.5, h is continuous in $[a, b]$, and, by (18), (19) and Exercises 11.6 and 7.3, so is G. Let

$$F(u) = 2|G(u)|h(b) - |G(b)|h(u) \quad (a \leqslant u \leqslant b). \qquad (21)$$

Then, since h and G are continuous in $[a, b]$, so is F. Hence the set α of those numbers u of $[a, b]$ for which $F(u) = 0$ is closed. Also $F(a) = 0$, which means that $a \in \alpha$, and so α is not empty, and α is obviously bounded. Hence α has a greatest member u_0, say. This means that

$$a \leqslant u_0 \leqslant b, \qquad (22)$$

$$F(u_0) = 0, \qquad (23)$$

and if $u_0 < u \leqslant b$, then $F(u) \neq 0$.

Now $h(b) \geqslant 0$, and the case $h(b) = 0$ (in which C has only one point) is trivial. Suppose, therefore, that $h(b) > 0$, and that (20) does not hold. Then, by (21), $F(b) > 0$, and hence, by (22) and (23),

$$a \leqslant u_0 < b. \qquad (24)$$

Also, as we have seen, $F(u) \neq 0$ $(u_0 < u \leqslant b)$. From this and the inequality $F(b) > 0$ and Hardy, §101, it follows that

$$F(u) > 0 \quad (u_0 < u \leqslant b). \qquad (25)$$

Let u be any number such that $u_0 < u \leqslant b$. Then, by (23), (24) and (21),

$$F(u) = F(u) - F(u_0)$$
$$= 2\{|G(u)| - |G(u_0)|\}h(b) - |G(b)|\{h(u) - h(u_0)\}. \qquad (26)$$

Also, by (19), (18), and Theorems 11.4, 11.2 and 11.1,

$$G(u) - G(u_0) = \int_{\mathscr{C}(g, u_0, u)} f'(z)dz - f\{g(u)\} + f\{g(u_0)\}$$
$$= \int_{\mathscr{C}(g, u_0, u)} [f'(z) - f'\{g(u_0)\}]dz - f\{g(u)\} + f\{g(u_0)\}$$
$$+ \{g(u) - g(u_0)\}f'\{g(u_0)\}. \qquad (27)$$

Now $f'\{g(t)\}$, considered as a function of t, is continuous in $[a, b]$. Hence there is a positive number δ_1, such that, for every number t in $[a, b]$ for which $|t - u_0| \leqslant \delta_1$, we have $|f'\{g(t)\} - f'\{g(u_0)\}| < |G(b)|/\{4h(b)\}$. It follows that, if $u_0 < u \leqslant \min(b, u_0 + \delta_1)$, then $|f'(z) - f'\{g(u_0)\}| < |G(b)|/\{4h(b)\}$ for every point z of $\mathscr{C}(g, u_0, u)$. Also, by the definition of h and Exercise 9.7, the length of $\mathscr{C}(g, u_0, u)$ is $h(u) - h(u_0)$. Hence, by Theorem 11.5,

$$\left| \int_{\mathscr{C}(g, u_0, u)} [f'(z) - f'\{g(u_0)\}] dz \right|$$
$$\leqslant \{h(u) - h(u_0)\}|G(b)|/\{4h(b)\} \quad \{u_0 < u \leqslant \min(b, u_0 + \delta_1)\}.$$
$$(28)$$

Since f is fully differentiable at $g(u_0)$, there is a positive number δ_2, such that, for every number z for which $0 < |z - g(u_0)| < \delta_2$, we have

$$\left| \frac{f(z) - f\{g(u_0)\}}{z - g(u_0)} - f'\{g(u_0)\} \right| < \frac{|G(b)|}{4h(b)}.$$

Hence, for every number z for which $|z - g(u_0)| < \delta_2$, we have

$$|f(z) - f\{g(u_0)\} - \{z - g(u_0)\}f'\{g(u_0)\}|$$
$$\leqslant |z - g(u_0)|\,|G(b)|/\{4h(b)\}. \quad (29)$$

Thus, if

$$|g(u) - g(u_0)| < \delta_2, \qquad (30)$$

then (29) holds with $z = g(u)$. If, moreover, $u_0 < u \leqslant b$, then, by Exercise 9.27, $|g(u) - g(u_0)| \leqslant h(u) - h(u_0)$, and hence

$$|f\{g(u)\} - f\{g(u_0)\} - \{g(u) - g(u_0)\}f'\{g(u_0)\}|$$
$$\leqslant \{h(u) - h(u_0)\}|G(b)|/\{4h(b)\}. \quad (31)$$

Choose u so that the inequalities $u_0 < u \leqslant \min(b, u_0 + \delta_1)$ and (30) hold. This is possible since g is continuous in $[a, b]$. Then, by (27), (28) and (31),

$|G(u)| - |G(u_0)| \leqslant \{h(u) - h(u_0)\}|G(b)|/\{2h(b)\}$, and hence, by (26), $F(u) \leqslant 0$, which contradicts (25). This proves (20), and so completes the proof of the theorem.

EXERCISE

11.8. C is a contour, leading from z_1 to z_2. The function f is fully differentiable at all points of C, its derivative f' is continuous on C, and $f(z) \neq 0$ $(z \in |C|)$. (i) Prove that, if $f(z)$ is not negative for any point z of C, then

$$\int_C \frac{f'(z)}{f(z)}\, dz = \log f(z_2) - \log f(z_1),$$

and if $f(z)$ is not positive for any point z of C, then

$$\int_C \frac{f'(z)}{f(z)}\, dz = \log\{-f(z_2)\} - \log\{-f(z_1)\}.$$

(ii) Deduce that, in both these cases,

$$\int_C \frac{f'(z)}{f(z)}\, dz = \log|f(z_2)| - \log|f(z_1)| + i \text{ var am } (f, C).$$

(Hint: use §6.2(ii), Theorems 4.1 and 11.8, and Exercises 9.18 and 9.19.)

11.9. The function g is called a *primitive* or an *indefinite integral* of the function f in the set of points S if and only if, at every point z of S, g is fully differentiable, and $g'(z) = f(z)$.

THEOREM 11.9. *Let C be a closed contour, and let the function f be continuous on C and have an indefinite integral on C. Then*

$$\int_C f(z)dz = 0.$$

This follows immediately from Theorem 11.8. As explained in §9.3, the phrase 'on C' means 'in $|C|$'.

EXERCISE

11.9.\ Find the flaw in the following argument: If $C = \mathscr{C}(t; e^{it}, 0, 2\pi)$, then $\log z$ (or should it be $\operatorname{Log} z$?) is an indefinite integral of $1/z$ on C. Hence, by Theorem 11.9,

$$\int_C \frac{dz}{z} = 0,$$

which contradicts Exercise 11.3.

THEOREM 11.10. *Let C be a contour, leading from z_0 to w. Suppose that the function f is fully differentiable at all points of*

*C, that its derivative f' is continuous on C, and that $f(z) \neq 0$
($z \in |C|$). Then*

$$\int_C \frac{f'(z)}{f(z)} \, dz = \log |f(w)| - \log |f(z_0)| + i \text{ var am } (f, C).$$

Proof. By Theorem 9.2 and Exercise 9.2, $|C|$ is closed and
bounded. Hence, by Theorem 4.3, there is a point z' on C
such that

$$|f(z)| \geqslant |f(z')| \tag{32}$$

for every point z of C. Also, by Theorem 4.11, f is uniformly
continuous on C, and, by hypothesis, $f(z') \neq 0$. Hence there
is a positive number δ, such that, for any points z_1, z_2 of C for
which $|z_1 - z_2| < \delta$, we have $|f(z_1) - f(z_2)| < 2|f(z')|$. From this
and (32) it follows that f cannot assume both positive and
negative values on any arc of C whose diameter is less than δ.
Thus, if C' is any such arc, leading from w_1 to w_2, say, then,
by Exercise 11.8(ii),

$$\int_{C'} \frac{f'(z)}{f(z)} \, dz = \log |f(w_2)| - \log |f(w_1)| + i \text{ var am } (f, C').$$

Now let C_1, C_2, ..., C_k be a dissection of C into arcs of
diameters less than δ (which exists by Theorem 9.10), and let
z_m be the last point of C_m. Then, by what has just been said,

$$\int_{C_m} \frac{f'(z)}{f(z)} \, dz = \log |f(z_m)| - \log |f(z_{m-1})|$$
$$+ i \text{ var am } (f, C_m) \quad (m = 1, 2, \ldots, k). \tag{33}$$

Now, by Theorem 11.4,

$$\int_C \frac{f'(z)}{f(z)} \, dz = \sum_{m=1}^{k} \int_{C_m} \frac{f'(z)}{f(z)} \, dz,$$

and, by Exercise 9.16,

$$\text{var am } (f, C) = \sum_{m=1}^{k} \text{var am } (f, C_m).$$

Hence, by (33),

$$\int_C \frac{f'(z)}{f(z)} \, dz = \log |f(z_k)| - \log |f(z_0)| + i \text{ var am } (f, C),$$

which proves the result stated, since $z_k = w$.

THEOREM 11.11.   *On the hypotheses of Theorem 11.10,*

$$\exp \int_C \frac{f'(z)}{f(z)} \, dz = \frac{f(w)}{f(z_0)}.$$

Proof.   By Exercise 9.16,

$$\exp \{i \text{ var am } (f, C)\} = \{f(w)/|f(w)|\}\{|f(z_0)|/f(z_0)\}.$$

The result therefore follows from Theorem 11.10.

THEOREM 11.12.   *Let C be a contour, leading from z_0 to z_1, and suppose the point w is not on C.   Then*

$$\int_C \frac{dz}{z-w} = \log|z_1 - w| - \log|z_0 - w| + i\chi(w, C).$$

This follows from the definition of $\chi(w, C)$ (§9.15) and Theorem 11.10 with $f(z) = z - w$.

THEOREM 11.13.   *Let C be a Jordan contour, described in the positive sense, and let $w \in I(C)$.   Then*

$$\int_C \frac{dz}{z-w} = 2\pi i.$$

This follows from Theorem 11.12 and §9.23.

11.10. THEOREM 11.14.   *Let the function f be continuous in the disc $|z - z_0| < r$, and let*

$$g(z) - g(z_0) = \int_{\{z_0, z\}} f(w) \, dw$$

for every point z for which $0 < |z - z_0| < r$.   Then g is fully differentiable at z_0, and $g'(z_0) = f(z_0)$.

Proof.   By §11.5,

$$\frac{g(z) - g(z_0)}{z - z_0} - f(z_0)$$

$$= \frac{1}{z - z_0} \int_{\{z_0, z\}} \{f(w) - f(z_0)\} \, dw \quad (0 < |z - z_0| < r). \quad (34)$$

Now let ϵ be any positive number.   Then, since f is continuous at z_0, there is a positive number δ_0, such that, for every number w for which $|w - z_0| < \delta_0$, we have $|f(w) - f(z_0)| < \epsilon$.   Let

$\delta = \min (r, \delta_0)$, and suppose that $0 < |z - z_0| < \delta$. Then, for every point w of $\{z_0, z\}$, we have $|w - z_0| < \delta_0$ and hence $|f(w) - f(z_0)| < \epsilon$. From this and (34), Theorem 11.5 and Exercise 9.8 it follows that

$$\left| \frac{g(z) - g(z_0)}{z - z_0} - f(z_0) \right| \leqslant \epsilon. \tag{35}$$

Thus, for every positive number ϵ, there is a positive number δ, such that, for every number z for which $0 < |z - z_0| < \delta$, we have (35). This means that

$$\lim_{z \to z_0} \frac{g(z) - g(z_0)}{z - z_0} = f(z_0),$$

and the result follows.

THEOREM 11.15. *Let the function f be continuous in the open set S, and let*

$$g(z') - g(z) = \int_{\{z, z'\}} f(w) dw$$

for every pair of distinct points z, z' for which $|\{z, z'\}| \subset S$. Then g is an indefinite integral of f in S.

This follows immediately from Theorem 11.14.

11.11. This and the next two sections deal with what may be called contour integration by parts and by substitution.

THEOREM 11.16. *Let C be a contour, leading from z_1 to z_2, and suppose that the functions g and h are fully differentiable at all points of C, and that g' and h' are continuous on C. Then*

$$\int_C g(z) h'(z) dz = g(z_2) h(z_2) - g(z_1) h(z_1) - \int_C g'(z) h(z) dz.$$

This follows from Theorem 11.8 with $f(z) = g(z) h(z)$.

THEOREM 11.17. *Let C be a closed contour, and suppose that the functions g and h are fully differentiable at all points of C, and that g' and h' are continuous on C. Then*

$$\int_C g(z) h'(z) dz = - \int_C g'(z) h(z) dz.$$

This follows at once from Theorem 11.16.

11.12. In §7.1, I defined the expression $f(S)$ under certain conditions. I shall now do the same with $f(C)$, where C is a curve.

Let (g_1, a_1, b_1) and (g_2, a_2, b_2) be any two representations of the same curve C (see §§9.1–9.2). Let f be continuous on C, and let the functions h_1, h_2 be defined by $h_m(t) = f\{g_m(t)\}$, $(m = 1, 2)$. Then, by Exercise 7.3, h_m is continuous in $[a_m, b_m]$. Hence the expressions (h_1, a_1, b_1) and (h_2, a_2, b_2) are curve representations, and it is trivial that they are equivalent. Thus the curve $\mathscr{C}[t; f\{g(t)\}, a, b]$ is the same for all representations (g, a, b) of C. I define $f(C)$ as this curve.

EXERCISES

11.10. Prove that, if the function f is continuous on the curve C, then $|f(C)| = f(|C|)$.

11.11. The function f is fully differentiable at all points of the curve C, and f' is continuous on C. Prove that, (i) if C is smooth (see §11.2), then so is $f(C)$, and (ii) if C is rectifiable (see §9.10), then so is $f(C)$.

11.13. THEOREM 11.18. *Let C be a smooth curve, and suppose that the function f is fully differentiable at all points of C, that f' is continuous on C, and that the function h is continuous on $f(C)$. Then*

$$\int_{f(C)} h(w)dw = \int_C h\{f(z)\}f'(z)dz.$$

Proof. Let (g, a, b) be a representation of C such that g' is continuous in $[a, b]$. Such a representation exists by §11.2. Then, by Theorem 11.7,

$$\int_C h\{f(z)\}f'(z)dz = \int_a^b h[f\{g(t)\}]f'\{g(t)\}g'(t)dt. \qquad (36)$$

Now, by §11.12, $f(C) = \mathscr{C}[t; f\{g(t)\}, a, b]$. Let the function F be defined by $F(t) = f\{g(t)\}$. Then $f(C) = \mathscr{C}(F, a, b)$. Also, by Theorem 4.2, F is differentiable relative to the real axis at all points of $[a, b]$, and $F'(t) = f'\{g(t)\}g'(t)$, $(a \leqslant t \leqslant b)$. From this and Exercises 7.3 and 4.6 it follows that F' is continuous in $[a, b]$. Hence, by Theorem 11.7,

$$\int_{f(C)} h(w)dw = \int_a^b h\{F(t)\}F'(t)dt = \int_a^b h[f\{g(t)\}]f'\{g(t)\}g'(t)dt,$$

which, together with (36), proves the result stated.

The theorem obtained by substituting 'contour' for 'smooth curve' in Theorem 11.18 is also true, but not so easily proved.

11.14. It is one of the remarkable results of the theory of functions of a complex variable that, if a function is fully differentiable at all points of an open set S, then its derivative is continuous in S. This cannot, at present, be proved directly; all the existing proofs depend on contour integration. The following theorem is useful in this connection.

THEOREM 11.19. *Let C be a contour, S an open set, and suppose that C and S have no point in common. Let the function f be continuous on C, and let*

$$g(z) = \int_C \frac{f(w)}{w-z}\, dw \qquad (37)$$

for every point z of S. Then (i) *g is fully differentiable, and*

$$g'(z) = \int_C \frac{f(w)}{(w-z)^2}\, dw,$$

at all points z of S, and (ii) *g' is continuous in S.*

Proof. By Exercise 9.2(ii), there is a number M such that

$$|f(w)| \leqslant M \quad (w \in |C|). \qquad (38)$$

Now let z_0 be any point of S. Then, since S is open, there is a disc D about z_0 such that $D \subset S$. Let the radius of D be r, and let

$$0 < |z - z_0| < \tfrac{1}{2}r. \qquad (39)$$

Then, for any point w of C,

$$|w - z_0| \geqslant r, \qquad |w - z| > \tfrac{1}{2}r. \qquad (40)$$

Also, by (37),

$$\frac{g(z) - g(z_0)}{z - z_0} - \int_C \frac{f(w)}{(w - z_0)^2}\, dw$$

$$= \int_C f(w) \left\{ \frac{1}{z - z_0} \left(\frac{1}{w - z} - \frac{1}{w - z_0} \right) - \frac{1}{(w - z_0)^2} \right\} dw$$

$$= (z - z_0) \int_C \frac{f(w)}{(w - z)(w - z_0)^2}\, dw. \qquad (41)$$

Now, by (38) and (40), $|f(w)(w-z)^{-1}(w-z_0)^{-2}| \leqslant 2Mr^{-3}$ $(w \in |C|)$. From this and (41) and Theorem 11.5 it follows that

$$\left| \frac{g(z)-g(z_0)}{z-z_0} - \int_C \frac{f(w)}{(w-z_0)^2}\, dw \right| \leqslant 2Mr^{-3}l|z-z_0|,$$

where l is the length of C. This inequality holds for every number z satisfying (39), and its right-hand side tends to 0 as $z \to z_0$. Hence so does its left-hand side, which means that g is fully differentiable at z_0, and

$$g'(z_0) = \int_C \frac{f(w)}{(w-z_0)^2}\, dw.$$

This proves (i).

To prove (ii), let z_0 again be any point of S, choose r as before, and suppose again that (39) holds. Then, by (i),

$$g'(z)-g'(z_0) = \int_C f(w)\left(\frac{1}{(w-z)^2} - \frac{1}{(w-z_0)^2} \right) dw. \qquad (42)$$

Now, by (38) and (40),

$$\left| f(w)\left(\frac{1}{(w-z)^2} - \frac{1}{(w-z_0)^2} \right) \right| = \left| f(w)\left(\frac{1}{w-z} + \frac{1}{w-z_0} \right) \frac{z-z_0}{(w-z)(w-z_0)} \right|$$
$$\leqslant 6Mr^{-3}|z-z_0| \quad (w \in |C|).$$

From this and (42) and Theorem 11.5 it follows that

$$|g'(z)-g'(z_0)| \leqslant 6Mr^{-3}l|z-z_0|.$$

Here, by the same argument as before, the left-hand side tends to 0 as $z \to z_0$. This means that g' is fully continuous at z_0, and so completes the proof.

EXERCISES

11.12. Prove that any circle described counter-clockwise, as defined in Exercise 11.3, is described in the positive sense, as defined in §9.23.

11.13. Prove that, if $a > 0$, then

$$\left| \int_{\{a,\, a+ia\}} e^{-z^2}\, dz \right| < \frac{1}{a}.$$

CHAPTER 12

CAUCHY'S THEOREM

12.1. Cauchy's theorem, in its usual form, states that, if a function f is regular within and on a Jordan contour C (see §§9.17 and 11.1), then

$$\int_C f(z)dz = 0.$$

I shall deal first with the case in which C is a *triangle*, i.e. a polygon of the form $\{z_1, z_2, z_3, z_1\}$. A necessary and sufficient condition for this to be a simple polygon was given in Exercise 9.23. I call it a *proper triangle* or a *line-triangle* according as it is or is not a simple polygon.

EXERCISE

12.1. Prove that every proper triangle is a Jordan polygon.

In what follows, it will be convenient to have a general notation for the length of a contour C. I shall denote it by le C.

12.2. THEOREM 12.1. *Let the function f be fully differentiable at the point z_0, and let $\epsilon > 0$. Then there is a disc D about z_0, such that, for every closed contour C for which (i) $z_0 \in I'(C)$, (ii) $|C| \subset D$, and (iii) f is continuous on C, we have*

$$\left| \int_C f(z)dz \right| \leqslant \epsilon(\text{le } C)^2.$$

Proof. By hypothesis and §4.5 and §4.3, there is a positive number δ, such that, for every number z for which $0 < |z - z_0| < \delta$, we have $|\{f(z) - f(z_0)\}/(z - z_0) - f'(z_0)| < \epsilon$. Choose δ accordingly, and let D be the disc with centre z_0 and radius δ. Then

$$|f(z) - f(z_0) - f'(z_0)(z - z_0)| \leqslant \epsilon|z - z_0| \quad (z \in D). \qquad (1)$$

Let

$$g(z) = f(z_0) + f'(z_0)(z - z_0), \qquad (2)$$

and let C be any contour satisfying (ii). Then, by (1),

$$|f(z) - g(z)| \leqslant \epsilon |z - z_0| \quad (z \in |C|). \tag{3}$$

If, moreover, C is a closed contour, and satisfies (i), then, by Exercises 9.28 and 9.27, $|z - z_0| \leqslant \text{le } C$, $(z \in |C|)$, and hence, by (3),

$$|f(z) - g(z)| \leqslant \epsilon \text{ le } C \quad (z \in |C|). \tag{4}$$

If, moreover, C satisfies (iii), it follows from (4) and Theorem 11.5 that

$$\left| \int_C \{f(z) - g(z)\} dz \right| \leqslant \epsilon(\text{le } C)^2. \tag{5}$$

Now, by (2), $g(z)$ has the indefinite integral

$$f(z_0)z + \tfrac{1}{2}f'(z_0)(z - z_0)^2$$

everywhere. Hence, by Theorem 11.9,

$$\int_C g(z) dz = 0$$

for every closed contour C. From this and Theorem 11.3 it follows that

$$\int_C f(z) dz = \int_C \{f(z) - g(z)\} dz$$

for every closed contour C satisfying (iii), and from this and (5) we obtain the result stated.

12.3. THEOREM 12.2. *Let C be a triangle, and let the function f be continuous in $I'(C)$. Then there is a triangle C' with the following properties:*

$$(i) \ I'(C') \subset I'(C), \qquad (ii) \ \text{le } C' = \tfrac{1}{2} \text{ le } C, \quad \text{and}$$

$$(iii) \ \left| \int_C f(z) dz \right| \leqslant 4 \left| \int_{C'} f(z) dz \right|.$$

Proof. Let $C = \{z_1, z_2, z_3, z_1\}$, $z_4 = \tfrac{1}{2}(z_2 + z_3)$, $z_5 = \tfrac{1}{2}(z_3 + z_1)$, $z_6 = \tfrac{1}{2}(z_1 + z_2)$, $C_1 = \{z_1, z_6, z_5, z_1\}$, $C_2 = \{z_6, z_2, z_4, z_6\}$, $C_3 = \{z_5, z_4, z_3, z_5\}$ and $C_4 = \{z_4, z_5, z_6, z_4\}$. Then it is trivial that each of the four triangles C_1, C_2, C_3, C_4 has property (ii), and it follows from Exercise 9.35 that it has property (i). It is therefore sufficient to prove that at least one of them has property (iii). Now, by Theorems 11.4 and 11.6 and Exercise 9.42,

$$\int_C f(z)dz = \sum_{m=1}^{4} \int_{C_m} f(z)dz,$$

which implies that

$$\left|\int_C f(z)dz\right| \leqslant \sum_{m=1}^{4} \left|\int_{C_m} f(z)dz\right| \leqslant 4\left|\int_{C_n} f(z)dz\right|,$$

where n is one of the numbers $m = 1, 2, 3, 4$—the one (or one of those) for which

$$\left|\int_{C_m} f(z)dz\right|$$

is greatest—and the result follows.

12.4. THEOREM 12.3. *Let C_0 be a triangle, and let the function f be fully differentiable at all points of $I'(C_0)$. Then*

$$\int_{C_0} f(z)dz = 0.$$

Proof. By Theorem 12.2, there is a triangle C_1, such that $I'(C_1) \subset I'(C_0)$, le $C_1 = \frac{1}{2}$ le C_0, and

$$\left|\int_{C_0} f(z)dz\right| \leqslant 4\left|\int_{C_1} f(z)dz\right|.$$

Similarly there is a triangle C_2, such that $I'(C_2) \subset I'(C_1)$, le $C_2 = \frac{1}{2}$ le C_1, and

$$\left|\int_{C_1} f(z)dz\right| \leqslant 4\left|\int_{C_2} f(z)dz\right|;$$

and so on. We thus obtain a sequence of triangles $C_0, C_1, C_2, \ldots$, such that

$$I'(C_{n+1}) \subset I'(C_n) \quad (n = 0, 1, 2, \ldots), \tag{6}$$

le $C_{n+1} = \frac{1}{2}$ le C_n, and

$$\left|\int_{C_n} f(z)dz\right| \leqslant 4\left|\int_{C_{n+1}} f(z)dz\right| \quad (n = 0, 1, 2, \ldots),$$

from which it follows by induction that

$$\text{le } C_n = 2^{-n} \text{ le } C_0 \quad (n = 0, 1, 2, \ldots) \tag{7}$$

and

$$\left| \int_{C_0} f(z)dz \right| \leqslant 4^n \left| \int_{C_n} f(z)dz \right| \quad (n = 0, 1, 2, \ldots). \tag{8}$$

Now it is obvious that $I'(C_n)$ is not empty, and it follows from Exercises 9.20 and 9.28 (since an unbounded set has no diameter) that it is closed and bounded. Hence, by (6) and Theorem 3.5, there is a point z_0 such that

$$z_0 \in I'(C_n) \quad (n = 0, 1, 2, \ldots). \tag{9}$$

In particular, $z_0 \in I'(C_0)$, which implies that f is fully differentiable at z_0.

Let ϵ be any positive number, and choose the disc D in accordance with Theorem 12.1. Choose the natural number n so that $2^{-n} \text{ le } C_0$ is less than the radius of D. Then, by (7), (9) and Exercises 9.28 and 9.27, $|C_n| \subset D$. Hence, by (9) and Theorem 12.1,

$$\left| \int_{C_n} f(z)dz \right| \leqslant \epsilon(\text{le } C_n)^2.$$

From this and (8) and (7) it follows that

$$\left| \int_{C_0} f(z)dz \right| \leqslant \epsilon(\text{le } C_0)^2.$$

Since this holds for every positive number ϵ, the theorem is proved.

EXERCISE

12.2. It is assumed that $a < b$ and $\alpha < \beta$, that Π is defined as in Exercise 9.36, and that the function f is fully differentiable at every point $x + iy$ for which $a \leqslant x \leqslant b$ and $\alpha \leqslant y \leqslant \beta$. Prove that

$$\int_\Pi f(z)dz = 0.$$

12.5. THEOREM 12.4. *Let* $0 < r_1 < r_2$,

$$C_m = \mathscr{C}(t; w_0 + r_m e^{it}, 0, 2\pi) \quad (m = 1, 2), \tag{10}$$

and let the function h be fully differentiable at every point w for which $r_1 \leqslant |w - w_0| \leqslant r_2$. *Then*

$$\int_{C_1} h(w)dw = \int_{C_2} h(w)dw. \tag{11}$$

Proof. Let C_1^* be 'C_1 described backward', and

$$C = \{w_0 + r_1,\, w_0 + r_2\} + C_2 + \{w_0 + r_2,\, w_0 + r_1\} + C_1^*.$$

Then, by Theorems 11.4 and 11.6,

$$\int_C h(w)dw = \int_{C_2} h(w)dw - \int_{C_1} h(w)dw.$$

It is, therefore, sufficient to prove that

$$\int_C h(w)dw = 0. \tag{12}$$

Let

$$f(z) = w_0 + e^z, \tag{13}$$

$$H(z) = h\{f(z)\}f'(z) \tag{14}$$

and $\Pi = \{\log r_1,\, \log r_2,\, \log r_2 + 2\pi i,\, \log r_1 + 2\pi i,\, \log r_1\}$. Then, by §§4.6 and 6.2, H is fully differentiable at every point z for which $\log r_1 \leqslant \operatorname{re} z \leqslant \log r_2$. Hence, by Exercise 12.2,

$$\int_\Pi H(z)dz = 0. \tag{15}$$

Also, by (13) and §11.12, $f(\Pi) = C$. Hence, by Theorem 11.18 and (14),

$$\int_C h(w)dw = \int_\Pi H(z)dz.$$

From this and (15) we obtain (12).

EXERCISE

12.3. If C is any of the curves called 'the circle with centre z_0 and radius r' (see Exercise 11.3), and the function f is fully differentiable at every point z for which $|z - z_0| \leqslant r$, prove that

$$\int_C f(z)dz = 0.$$

12.6. A set of points S is said to be *convex* if and only if, for every pair of distinct points z_0, z_1 of S, the line segment $\{z_0, z_1\}$ is contained in S.

A *star set* is defined as a set of points S with the following property: there is a point z_0 of S, such that, for every point z_1 of S, other than z_0, the line segment $\{z_0, z_1\}$ is contained in S. Such a point z_0 is called a *centre* of the star set S.

It is obvious that every non-empty convex set is a star set, and that every point of it is a centre of it. It is also obvious that every open star set is a domain. Such a set is therefore usually called a *star domain*. Similarly a non-empty open convex set is usually called a *convex domain*.

EXERCISE

12.4. S is a star set with centre z_1, and Δ is the triangle $\{z_1, z_2, z_3, z_1\}$. Prove that, if $|\{z_2, z_3\}| \subset S$, then $I'(\Delta) \subset S$.

12.7. THEOREM 12.5. *Let the function f be regular in the star domain S. Then f has an indefinite integral in S.*

Proof. Let z_0 be a centre of S. Let

$$g(z_0) = 0, \tag{16}$$

and

$$g(z) = \int_{\{z_0, z\}} f(w)dw \tag{17}$$

for every point z of S, other than z_0. Then, in virtue of Theorem 11.15, it is sufficient to show that

$$g(z') - g(z) = \int_{\{z, z'\}} f(w)dw \tag{18}$$

for every pair of distinct points z, z' for which $|\{z, z'\}| \subset S$.

Suppose, then, that z, z' is such a pair of points. Suppose, first, that $z \neq z_0$ and $z' \neq z_0$. Then (17) holds, and

$$g(z') = \int_{\{z_0, z'\}} f(w)dw. \tag{19}$$

From this and Theorem 11.6 and Exercise 9.42 it follows that

$$-g(z') = \int_{\{z', z_0\}} f(w)dw. \tag{20}$$

Now, by Theorem 12.3 and Exercise 12.4,

$$\int_{\{z_0, z, z', z_0\}} f(w)dw = 0.$$

Hence, by (17), (20) and Theorem 11.4,

$$g(z) + \int_{\{z, z'\}} f(w)dw - g(z') = 0.$$

This proves (18), except in the cases $z = z_0$ and $z' = z_0$. In the former of these, (18) follows from (16) and (19), in the latter from (16), (17), Theorem 11.6 and Exercise 9.42.

THEOREM 12.6. *Let the function f be regular in the star domain D, and let C be a closed contour, contained in D. Then*

$$\int_C f(z)dz = 0.$$

This follows from Theorems 12.5 and 11.9.

*12.8. In §11.12, I defined the expression $f(C)$ for any curve C and any function f, continuous on C. The definition can be applied to the function f defined by $f(z) = \operatorname{im} z$. I denote the curve $f(C)$ so obtained by $\operatorname{im} C$. Thus, if $C = \mathscr{C}(g, a, b)$, then $\operatorname{im} C = \mathscr{C}\{t; \operatorname{im} g(t), a, b\}$. The Concise Oxford Dictionary (2nd edn. Oxford, 1929) defines a curve as a line of which no part is straight. The curve $\operatorname{im} C$ is not a curve in this sense, but is, on the contrary, entirely straight, being contained in the real axis; and $|\operatorname{im} C|$ is either a closed interval, or consists of only one point. Geometrically, $\operatorname{im} C$ can be described as the projection of C on the imaginary axis, turned clockwise about the origin through a right angle.

I define the *height* of any curve C as the diameter of $\operatorname{im} C$, and denote it by $\operatorname{he} C$. The reader will easily see that $\operatorname{he} C$ is the difference between the greatest and the least of the imaginary parts of the points of C.

EXERCISE

12.5. (i) Prove that, if C is a contour, then so is $\operatorname{im} C$, and $\operatorname{he} C \leqslant \operatorname{le} \operatorname{im} C \leqslant \operatorname{le} C$. (ii) Prove that, if C is a *closed* contour, then $\operatorname{le} \operatorname{im} C \geqslant 2 \operatorname{he} C$.

*12.9. THEOREM 12.7.   *Let C be a curve, S a set of points, T the complement of S, and suppose that the height of C is less than the distance d between $|C|$ and T.   Then there is a convex domain D such that $|C| \subset D \subset S$.*

Proof.   Let $C = \mathscr{C}(g, a, b)$.   Then, by Hardy, §103, Theorem 2, there are numbers t_1, t_2, t_3, t_4 in $[a, b]$, such that

$$\operatorname{re} g(t_1) \leqslant \operatorname{re} g(t) \leqslant \operatorname{re} g(t_2), \qquad \operatorname{im} g(t_3) \leqslant \operatorname{im} g(t) \leqslant \operatorname{im} g(t_4)$$
(21)

for every number t in $[a, b]$.   By §12.8,

$$\operatorname{he} C = \operatorname{im} g(t_4) - \operatorname{im} g(t_3). \tag{22}$$

Now, by hypothesis, $\operatorname{he} C < d$.   Hence, putting

$$\delta = \tfrac{1}{2}(d - \operatorname{he} C), \tag{23}$$

we have

$$\delta > 0. \tag{24}$$

Let D be the set of those points z for which

$$\operatorname{re} g(t_1) - \delta < \operatorname{re} z < \operatorname{re} g(t_2) + \delta, \qquad \operatorname{im} g(t_3) - \delta < \operatorname{im} z$$
$$< \operatorname{im} g(t_4) + \delta. \tag{25}$$

Then it follows from (21) and (24) that $|C| \subset D$, and it is trivial that D is a convex domain.   Thus it only remains to prove that $D \subset S$, i.e. that no point of D can be a point of T.   Now, by §3.4, if $z \in T$ and $z' \in |C|$, then $|z - z'| \geqslant d$.   Hence it is sufficient to prove that, for every point z of D, there is a point z' of C, such that $|z - z'| < d$.

Let z, then, be any point of D.   Then (25) holds.   Hence, by (21), (22) and (23),

$$|\operatorname{im} z - \operatorname{im} z'| < \operatorname{he} C + \delta = d - \delta \tag{26}$$

for every point z' of C.   If $\operatorname{re} z \leqslant \operatorname{re} g(t_1)$ or $\operatorname{re} z \geqslant \operatorname{re} g(t_2)$, take $z' = g(t_1)$ or $g(t_2)$ respectively.   Then, by (25),

$$|\operatorname{re} z - \operatorname{re} z'| < \delta. \tag{27}$$

If, however, $\operatorname{re} g(t_1) < \operatorname{re} z < \operatorname{re} g(t_2)$, there is, by Hardy, §101, a number t' in $[a, b]$ such that $\operatorname{re} g(t') = \operatorname{re} z$.   Choose t' accordingly, and take $z' = g(t')$.   Then $\operatorname{re} z = \operatorname{re} z'$, and so (27) holds in all cases.   From (27) and (26) we obtain $|z-z'| < d$, which completes the proof.

   *$\textbf{12.10.}$ THEOREM 12.8.   *Let S_0 be a bounded set, whose complement is a domain, and let the function f be regular in S_0. Then, for every simple closed contour C, contained in S_0, we have*

$$\int_C f(z)dz = 0. \tag{28}$$

Proof.   Let S be the set of those points at which f is regular. Then, by Exercise 6.1, S is open, and, by hypothesis,

$$S_0 \subset S. \tag{29}$$

If S is the whole plane, the result follows from Theorem 12.6. Suppose, therefore, that S is not the whole plane, let T be the complement of S, and let d_0 be the distance between S_0 and T. Then, by (29) and Theorems 3.2 and 3.4,

$$d_0 > 0. \tag{30}$$

I shall prove the theorem by induction.   To this end, I define the aggregate α—an aggregate of natural numbers—as follows: $k \in \alpha$ if and only if, for every simple closed contour C, contained in S_0, for which

$$\text{le im } C < kd_0, \tag{31}$$

we have (28).   Since every contour C satisfies (31) for some natural number k, it is sufficient to prove that every natural number is a member of α. Thus, in virtue of the axiom of induction, it is sufficient to prove the following two lemmas:

   LEMMA 1. $1 \in \alpha$.
   LEMMA 2.   *Let $k \in \alpha$.   Then $k+1 \in \alpha$.*
   Proof of Lemma 1.   Let C be a closed contour, $|C| \subset S_0$, le im $C < d_0$, and let d be the distance between $|C|$ and T. Then, by Exercise 12.5(i), he $C < d_0$, and it is trivial that $d \geqslant d_0$. Hence, he $C < d$.   From this and Theorem 12.7 it follows that there is a convex domain D such that $|C| \subset D \subset S$.   Hence, by the definition of S, f is regular in D.   We now obtain (28) from Theorem 12.6.   Thus (28) holds for every simple closed contour C, contained in S_0, for which (31) holds with $k = 1$. This means that $1 \in \alpha$.

Proof of Lemma 2.   Let C be a simple closed contour,

$$|C| \subset S_0, \tag{32}$$

and

$$\text{le im } C \ < \ (k+1)d_0. \tag{33}$$

If he $C < d_0$, we obtain (28) as in the proof of Lemma 1. Suppose, therefore, that

$$\text{he } C \ \geqslant \ d_0. \tag{34}$$

By hypothesis, the complement of S_0 is an unbounded domain.   Hence, by (32), Exercise 9.32 and §9.16,

$$I'(C) \subset S_0. \tag{35}$$

Let z_1 and z_2 respectively be points of least and greatest imaginary part on C.   Then

$$\text{he } C \ = \ \text{im } z_2 \ - \text{im } z_1. \tag{36}$$

Also, by Theorem 9.11—with $b = \frac{1}{2}(\text{im } z_2 + \text{im } z_1)$—and Exercise 9.41, there are points z_3, z_4 and simple curves C', C'' with the following properties:

$$\text{im } z_3 \ = \ \text{im } z_4 \ = \ \tfrac{1}{2}(\text{im } z_2 + \text{im } z_1), \tag{37}$$

$$|\{z_3, z_4\}| \subset I'(C), \tag{38}$$

$$z_1 \in |C'|, \qquad z_2 \in |C''|, \tag{39}$$

$$C \ \sim \ C' + C'', \tag{40}$$

$$C' \text{ leads from } z_3 \text{ to } z_4, \tag{41}$$

and $\{z_3, z_4\}$ and C have no point other than z_3 and z_4 in common. From this and (40) it follows that $\{z_3, z_4\}$ and C' have no point other than z_3 and z_4 in common.   Hence, by (41), $C' + \{z_4, z_3\}$ is a simple closed curve.   Similarly $C'' + \{z_3, z_4\}$ is a simple closed curve; for it follows from (40) and (41) that C'' leads from z_4 to z_3.

Let

$$C_1 \ = \ C' + \{z_4, z_3\}, \qquad C_2 \ = \ C'' + \{z_3, z_4\}. \tag{42}$$

Then C_1 and C_2 are simple closed curves, and it is easily seen that they are contours.   Also, by (42), (40), (38) and (35),

$$|C_1| \subset S_0, \qquad |C_2| \subset S_0. \tag{43}$$

Hence f is continuous on C_1 and C_2, and hence, by (40), (42), Theorems 11.4 and 11.6, and Exercise 9.42,

$$\int_C f(z)dz = \int_{C_1} f(z)dz + \int_{C_2} f(z)dz. \qquad (44)$$

Now, by (40) and §9.8 and §12.8, im $C \sim$ im $C' +$ im C''. Hence, by Exercise 9.7,

$$\text{le im } C = \text{le im } C' + \text{le im } C''. \qquad (45)$$

Similarly, by (42), le im $C_1 =$ le im $C' +$ le im$\{z_4, z_3\}$. Now, by (37), im$\{z_4, z_3\}$ has only one point. Thus le im$\{z_4, z_3\} = 0$, and le im $C_1 =$ le im C'. Similarly le im $C_2 =$ le im C''. It therefore follows from (45) that

$$\text{le im } C = \text{le im } C_1 + \text{le im } C_2. \qquad (46)$$

By (39) and (42), z_1 and z_3 are points of C_1. Hence, by §12.8, he $C_1 \geqslant$ im $z_3 -$ im z_1. From this and Exercise 12.5(ii), (37), (36) and (34) it follows that

le im $C_1 \geqslant 2$ he $C_1 \geqslant 2$ im $z_3 - 2$ im z_1
$$= \text{im } z_2 - \text{im } z_1 = \text{he } C \geqslant d_0.$$

Hence, by (33) and (46), le im $C_2 < kd_0$. Since C_2 is a simple closed contour, and (43) holds, and $k \in \alpha$, it follows that

$$\int_{C_2} f(z)dz = 0.$$

Similarly

$$\int_{C_1} f(z)dz = 0.$$

From these two equations and (44) we obtain (28).

Thus (28) holds for every simple closed contour C, contained in S_0, for which (33) holds. This means that $k+1 \in \alpha$, which proves Lemma 2, and thereby completes the proof of the theorem.

12.11. THEOREM 12.9. *Let C be a simple closed contour, whose exterior is a domain, and let the function f be regular within and on C. Then*

$$\int_C f(z)dz = 0.$$

This follows from Theorem 12.8 with $S_0 = I'(C)$, and obviously implies Cauchy's theorem as stated in §12.1.

*12.12. Theorem 12.6 can be re-stated in the following form:
Every star domain D has the property that, for every function f, regular in D, and every closed contour C, contained in D, we have

$$\int_C f(z)dz = 0.$$

The star domains are not the only sets of points with this property, and the problem of finding *all* these sets is outside the scope of this book, but I shall give its solution as far as it refers to domains. It will be found that all simply connected domains (see §9.17) have this property, and that no other domains have it. The second of these two statements is the easier, and I shall prove it first.

*12.13. THEOREM 12.10. *Let D be a domain, but not simply connected. Then there are a function f, regular in D, and a closed contour C, contained in D, such that*

$$\int_C f(z)dz \neq 0.$$

Proof. By §9.17, there is a simple polygon C, such that $|C| \subset D$, and that $I(C)$ is *not* contained in D. This means that there is a point w, such that w is in $I(C)$, but not in D. Let the function f be defined by $f(z) = 1/(z-w)$. Then f is regular in D, and, by Theorem 11.12,

$$\int_C f(z)dz = i\chi(w, C).$$

From this and §9.16 we obtain the result stated.

*12.14. In §9.6, the *broken line* $\{z_0, z_1, \ldots, z_k\}$ was defined as a certain curve. For some purposes, it is better to define it as the ordered collection of the line segments $\{z_0, z_1\}, \{z_1, z_2\}, \ldots, \{z_{k-1}, z_k\}$—the *sides* of the broken line. From this point of view, $\{i, 0, 2\}$ and $\{i, 0, 1, 2\}$ are distinct. From that of §9.6, they are identical, and it has no meaning to speak of the number of sides of a broken line. It is, however, not worth while to distinguish pedantically between the said curve and the said collection of line segments.

The points $z_0, z_1, \ldots, z_k$ are called the *corners* or *vertices* of the broken line $\{z_0, z_1, \ldots, z_k\}$. In the particular case $z_k = z_0$, when the broken line is a polygon Π, say, a *diagonal* of Π is defined as a line segment $\{z_m, z_n\}$, where m and n are integers between 0 and k (inclusive), and $2 \leqslant |m - n| \leqslant k - 2$. The diagonal is said to be *interior* if and only if all its points except its end points are in $I(\Pi)$.

EXERCISES

12.6. Prove that any two sides of a simple polygon cannot have more than one point in common; and that, if they have a point in common, it is the last point of one of them and the first point of the other.

12.7. Prove that, if $\{z_0, z_1, \ldots, z_k\}$ is a simple polygon, then the points $z_1, z_2, \ldots, z_k$ are distinct.

The next theorem is not absolutely necessary for the purposes of this book, but I think it is of considerable interest in itself. Several proofs of it, which I have seen in the literature, contain definite mistakes, quite apart from appeals to geometrical intuition.

*12.15. THEOREM 12.11. *Let Π be a simple polygon of four or more sides. Then Π has an interior diagonal.*

Proof. Let $\Pi = \{w_0, w_1, \ldots, w_k\}$. Then $k \geqslant 4$ and $w_k = w_0$. Let n be the integer with the following three properties:

(i) $1 \leqslant n \leqslant k$.

(ii) re $w_n \leqslant$ re w_m for every integer m for which $1 \leqslant m \leqslant k$.

(iii) im $w_n <$ im w_m for every integer m (see the remark on modern mathematical logic in §3.2) for which $1 \leqslant m \leqslant k$, $m \neq n$ and re $w_m =$ re w_n. In other words: among those of the numbers $w_1, w_2, \ldots, w_k$ with least real part, let w_n be the one with least imaginary part. (ii) and (iii) together are equivalent to

$$-\tfrac{1}{2}\pi < \text{am} \, (w_m - w_n) \leqslant \tfrac{1}{2}\pi \quad (1 \leqslant m \leqslant k, m \neq n). \quad (47)$$

Let $z_1 = w_n$, $z_3 = w_{n-1}$, and $z_2 = w_{n+1}$ or w_1 according as $n < k$ or $n = k$. Then, by (47),

$$-\tfrac{1}{2}\pi < \text{am} \, (z_2 - z_1) \leqslant \tfrac{1}{2}\pi \quad \text{and} \quad -\tfrac{1}{2}\pi < \text{am} \, (z_3 - z_1) \leqslant \tfrac{1}{2}\pi.$$

Also, by Exercise 12.6, am $(z_2 - z_1) \neq$ am $(z_3 - z_1)$, for otherwise $\{z_3, z_1\}$ and $\{z_1, z_2\}$ would have more than one point in common. Hence $0 < |$am $(z_3 - z_1) -$ am $(z_2 - z_1)| < \pi$, and so

$$\text{im } \{(z_3 - z_1)/(z_2 - z_1)\} \neq 0. \tag{48}$$

Let

$$\Delta = \{z_1, z_2, z_3, z_1\}. \tag{49}$$

Then, by (48) and §12.1, Δ is a proper triangle. Let S_0 be the set of the points of the line segment $\{z_2, z_3\}$, other than its end points; let

$$S = I(\Delta) \cup S_0, \tag{50}$$

and let g_1, g_2, g_3 be defined as in §9.20. Then S is the set of those points z for which $g_1(z) \geqslant 0$, $g_2(z) > 0$ and $g_3(z) > 0$.

LEMMA 1. *For every point z of $S \cap |\Pi|$, there is a corner w' of Π, such that*

$$w' \in S \tag{51}$$

and

$$g_1(w') \geqslant g_1(z). \tag{52}$$

Proof. Let $z \in S \cap |\Pi|$. Then there is an integer m such that $1 \leqslant m \leqslant k$ and $z \in |\{w_{m-1}, w_m\}|$. If $g_1(w_{m-1}) \leqslant g_1(w_m)$, let $w = w_{m-1}$, $w' = w_m$, and if $g_1(w_m) < g_1(w_{m-1})$, let $w = w_m$, $w' = w_{m-1}$. Then w' is a corner of Π, and (52) follows from Exercise 9.43(i).

Suppose, first, $g_1(z) > 0$, and disregard the trivial case $w' = z$. Then, by (52) and Exercise 9.43(i), $g_1(z') > 0$ for every point z' of $\{z, w'\}$. Hence $\{z, w'\}$ cannot meet $\{z_2, z_3\}$. Nor, by Exercise 12.6, can it meet the remainder of Δ. Hence, by Exercise 9.15, $\chi(w', \Delta) = \chi(z, \Delta)$. Since $z \in S$, it follows that $\chi(w', \Delta) \neq 0$, which proves (51) in this case.

Next suppose that $g_1(z) = 0 < g_1(w')$. Then, by Exercise 9.43(ii), $0 < g_1(z') < g_1(w')$ for every point z' of $\{z, w'\}$ except its end points. If, moreover, z' is near enough to z, it follows from the continuity of g_2 and g_3 that also $g_2(z') > 0$ and $g_3(z') > 0$, i.e. $z' \in I(\Delta)$, and we obtain (51) by the same argument as before, but with z' instead of z.

Finally suppose that $g_1(z) = 0 = g_1(w')$, and again disregard the trivial case $w' = z$. Then, by Exercise 9.43(ii), we cannot have $g_1(w) < 0$. It therefore follows that $w = w_{m-1}$, $w' = w_m$, and $g_1(w_{m-1}) = g_1(w_m) = 0$. Hence, by §9.20, $w_m = g_2(w_m)z_2 + g_3(w_m)z_3$, and $g_2(w_m) + g_3(w_m) = 1$, so that $w_m - z_3 = g_2(w_m)$ $(z_2 - z_3)$. Similarly $z - z_3 = g_2(z)(z_2 - z_3)$, and hence (since we disregard the case $w' = z$)

$$z_3 = z + t(w_m - z) \qquad (53)$$

with $t = g_2(z)/\{g_2(z) - g_2(w_m)\}$.

We cannot have $g_2(w_m) < 0$; for this would imply (53) with $0 < t < 1$, which would imply that z_3 is a point, other than an end point, of $\{z, w_m\}$, and hence of $\{w_{m-1}, w_m\}$; which is inconsistent with Exercise 12.6. Hence

$$g_2(w_m) \geqslant 0. \qquad (54)$$

Similarly

$$g_3(w_m) \geqslant 0, \qquad g_2(w_{m-1}) \geqslant 0, \qquad g_3(w_{m-1}) \geqslant 0. \qquad (55)$$

If $g_2(w_m) > 0$ and $g_3(w_m) > 0$, then $w_m \in S_0$, i.e. $w' \in S_0$, which implies (51). If $g_3(w_m) = 0$, then $w_m = z_2$. It therefore follows from Exercise 12.7 and the definition of z_1 and z_2 that $w_{m-1} = z_1$, which is impossible, if only because $g_1(w_{m-1}) = 0$ and $g_1(z_1) = 1$. There remains only the case in which $g_2(w_m) = 0$. In this case $w_m = z_3$, which implies that

$$m - (n - 1) = 0 \text{ or } k. \qquad (56)$$

Then we cannot have $g_2(w_{m-1}) = 0$, for this would imply $w_{m-1} = z_3 = w_m$. Nor can we have $g_3(w_{m-1}) = 0$, for this would imply $w_{m-1} = z_2$, so that $m - 1 - (n + 1) = 0$ or $-k$. From this and (56) it would follow that $k = 3$, whereas $k \geqslant 4$. Thus $g_1(w_{m-1}) = 0 = g_1(z)$, $g_2(w_{m-1}) > 0$ and $g_3(w_{m-1}) > 0$, which (since $w = w_{m-1}$) implies that

$$w \in S \qquad (57)$$

and

$$g_1(w) \geqslant g_1(z). \qquad (58)$$

I have not proved (51) in this case (nor is it true); but the statement 'there is a corner w of Π for which (57) and (58) hold', which I have proved, is equivalent to the statement 'there is a corner w' of Π for which (51) and (52) hold'; and this is what I had to prove. The lemma is therefore established.

Continuing the proof of the theorem, let $w'_h = w_{h+n}$, $(0 < h \leqslant k - n)$, $w'_h = w_{h+n-k}$, $(k - n < h \leqslant k)$, $C' = \{w'_1, w'_2, \ldots, w'_{k-1}\}$ and $C = C' + \{z_3, z_2\}$. Then C is a polygon, and, by §9.8 and (49),

$$\Pi \sim C' + \{z_3, z_1, z_2\} \tag{59}$$

and

$$\Delta \sim \{z_3, z_1, z_2\} + \{z_2, z_3\}. \tag{60}$$

Hence, by Exercises 9.9, 9.10 and 9.42,

$$\chi(w, \Pi) = \chi(w, C) + \chi(w, \Delta) \tag{61}$$

for any point w which is neither on Π nor on $\{z_2, z_3\}$.

LEMMA 2.   *Let $w \in I(\Delta)$, and suppose z_1 is the only point common to Π and $\{w, z_1\}$. Then $w \in I(\Pi)$.*

Proof. Let H be the half-line from w through z_1. It is easily seen that $\mathrm{re}\, z \geqslant \mathrm{re}\, z_1$ for any point z of C, and that $\mathrm{re}\, w > \mathrm{re}\, z_1$, from which it follows that $\mathrm{re}\, z < \mathrm{re}\, z_1$ for any point z of H that is not on $\{w, z_1\}$. Hence any such point cannot be on C. Also z_1 is not on C, and the other points of $\{w, z_1\}$ are, by hypothesis, not on Π, and therefore not on C'. It is easily seen that they are in $I(\Delta)$. Hence they are not on $\{z_3, z_2\}$ either, and therefore not on C. Thus H does not meet C, and hence, by Exercise 9.21, $w \in E(C)$, i.e. $\chi(w, C) = 0$. On the other hand, since $w \in I(\Delta)$, we have $\chi(w, \Delta) \neq 0$. It therefore follows from (61) that $\chi(w, \Pi) \neq 0$, which means that $w \in I(\Pi)$. This proves Lemma 2.

Now suppose that there is at least one corner of Π in S. If there is only one, call it w'. If there are several, let w' be the one (or one of those) for which $g_1(w')$ is greatest. Then, by Lemma 1, there is no point w in $S \cap |\Pi|$ for which $g_1(w) > g_1(w')$. On the other hand, every point w of $\{w', z_1\}$, other than its end points, satisfies this inequality (by Exercise 9.43(ii)), and is in S. Hence no such point w is on Π. In other words, Π and $\{w', z_1\}$ have only the two points w' and z_1 in common. Thus, if w is any other point of $\{w', z_1\}$, then Π and $\{w, z_1\}$ have only the point z_1 in common, and since it is trivial that $w \in I(\Delta)$, it follows from Lemma 2 that $w \in I(\Pi)$. This shows that $\{w', z_1\}$ is an interior diagonal of Π.

Finally suppose that there is no corner of Π in S. Then, by Lemma 1, there is no point of Π in S. Hence, if w' is any point of S_0 (see the definition preceding (50)), then Π and $\{w', z_1\}$ have only the point z_1 in common. We cannot, however, use Lemma 2 with w' instead of w; for w' is not in $I(\Delta)$. So take $w = \frac{1}{2}(w' + z_1)$. Then $w \in I(\Delta)$, and it follows from Lemma 2 that $w \in I(\Pi)$, i.e. $\chi(w, \Pi) \neq 0$. Also $\{w', w\}$ does not meet Π. Hence, by Exercise 9.15, $\chi(w', \Pi) \neq 0$, i.e. $w' \in I(\Pi)$. It follows that $S_0 \subset I(\Pi)$, which means that $\{z_2, z_3\}$ is an interior diagonal of Π. This completes the proof of the theorem.

A somewhat easier result, namely that Π has a diagonal contained in $I'(\Pi)$, would have been good enough for my purposes.

EXERCISE

12.8. Find the mistake in the following proof of the last theorem: Knopp, vol. 1, §4, proof of Lemma 2.

*12.16. THEOREM 12.12. *Let the function f be regular in the simply connected domain D. Then*

$$\int_C f(z)dz = 0 \tag{62}$$

for every polygon C contained in D.

Proof. In order to use induction, I define the aggregate α—an aggregate of natural numbers—as follows: $k \in \alpha$ if and only if (62) holds for every polygon C of less than k sides, contained in D.

LEMMA. *Let $k \geqslant 4$ and $k \in \alpha$. Then $k+1 \in \alpha$.*

Proof. Let C be a polygon of k sides, contained in D; say $C = \{z_0, z_1, \ldots, z_k\}$.

Suppose, first, that C is not a simple polygon. Then, by Exercise 9.24, there are integers m, n and a point w such that $0 \leqslant m < n < k$, $2 \leqslant n - m \leqslant k - 2$, $w \in |\{z_m, z_{m+1}\}|$ and $w \in |\{z_n, z_{n+1}\}|$. Let $C_1 = \{w, z_{m+1}, z_{m+2}, \ldots, z_n, w\}$ (omitting z_{m+1} if $z_{m+1} = w$, and z_n if $z_n = w$) and $C_2 = \{w, z_{n+1}, z_{n+2}, \ldots, z_k, z_1, \ldots, z_m, w\}$ (with similar omissions if appropriate). Then, by §9.8, $C \sim C_1 + C_2$, and hence, by Theorem 11.4,

$$\int_C f(z)dz = \int_{C_1} f(z)dz + \int_{C_2} f(z)dz. \tag{63}$$

Now C_1 and C_2 are polygons, contained in D, and C_1 has at most $n - m + 1$ sides, while C_2 has at most $k - n + m + 1$, so that either has less than k. Since $k \in \alpha$, it follows that

$$\int_{C_1} f(z)dz = \int_{C_2} f(z)dz = 0, \qquad (64)$$

which, together with (63), proves (62).

Now suppose that C is a simple polygon. Then, by Theorem 12.11, C has an interior diagonal $\{z_m, z_n\}$, say, where again $0 \leqslant m < n < k$ and $2 \leqslant n - m \leqslant k - 2$. Let $C_1 = \{z_m, z_{m+1}, \ldots, z_n\}$ and $C_2 = \{z_n, z_{n+1}, \ldots, z_k, z_1, z_2, \ldots, z_m\}$ (with the right interpretation if $m = 0$). Then (63) holds as before, but C_1 and C_2, though contained in D, are not polygons. So let

$$C_1' = C_1 + \{z_n, z_m\}, \qquad C_2' = C_2 + \{z_m, z_n\}. \qquad (65)$$

Then C_1' and C_2' are polygons, the former having exactly $n - m + 1$ sides, the latter $k - n + m + 1$. Also, by the definitions of a simply connected domain (§9.17) and an interior diagonal (§12.14), C_1' and C_2' are contained in D. So, by the argument which led to (64) in the other case, we now obtain

$$\int_{C_1'} f(z)dz = \int_{C_2'} f(z)dz = 0. \qquad (66)$$

Also, by (63), (65), Theorems 11.4 and 11.6, and Exercise 9.42,

$$\int_C f(z)dz = \int_C f(z)dz + \int_{C'} f(z)dz,$$

which, together with (66), again proves (62).

Thus (62) holds for every polygon C, contained in D, of k sides. It also holds, by hypothesis, for every such polygon of less than k sides. Hence $k + 1 \in \alpha$, which proves the lemma.

Now there is no polygon of less than two sides, and it follows from Theorems 11.4, 11.6 and 12.3 and the definition of a simply connected domain that (62) holds for every polygon C, contained in D, of two or three sides. This means that $4 \in \alpha$. It therefore follows from the lemma and the axiom of induction that every integer $k \geqslant 4$ is in α. This proves the theorem.

*12.17. THEOREM 12.13. *Let the function f be regular in the simply connected domain D, and let C_1 and C_2 be broken lines, contained in D, with the same first point and the same last point. Then*

$$\int_{C_1} f(z)dz = \int_{C_2} f(z)dz.$$

Proof. Let C_2^* be 'C_2 described backward'. Then $C_1 + C_2^*$ is a polygon, and the result follows from Theorems 12.12, 11.4 and 11.6.

THEOREM 12.14. *Let the function f be regular in the simply connected domain D. Then f has an indefinite integral in D.*

Proof. Choose a point z_0 in D. Then, by the definition of a domain (§9.17), for any point z of D, there is a broken line C, contained in D, leading from z_0 to z; and it follows from Theorem 12.13 that

$$\int_C f(w)dw$$

has the same value for all such broken lines C. Denote this value by $g(z)$.

Now let z and z' be any distinct points of D, such that $|\{z, z'\}| \subset D$. Let C be a broken line, contained in D, leading from z_0 to z, and let $C' = C + \{z, z'\}$. Then C' is a broken line, contained in D, leading from z_0 to z'. Hence

$$g(z) = \int_C f(w)dw, \qquad g(z') = \int_{C'} f(w)dw,$$

and hence, by Theorem 11.4,

$$g(z') - g(z) = \int_{\{z, z'\}} f(w)dw.$$

From this and Theorem 11.15 we obtain the result stated.

THEOREM 12.15. *Let the function f be regular in the simply connected domain D. Then*

$$\int_C f(z)dz = 0$$

for every closed contour C, contained in D.

This follows from Theorems 12.14 and 11.9.

EXERCISES

12.9. The function f is continuous in the domain D, and (62) holds for every simple polygon C contained in D.   Prove that (62) holds for every closed contour C contained in D.

12.10. The function f is continuous in the star domain D, and (62) holds for every proper triangle C contained in D.   Prove that f has an indefinite integral in D.

CHAPTER 13

CAUCHY'S INTEGRAL FORMULAE

13.1 A remark made at the beginning of §11.14, so far without proof, is equivalent to the statement that the derivative of any function is fully continuous at any point at which this function is regular. As already mentioned, this can be proved, at present, only by means of contour integration. In particular, the proof depends on a formula, valid for any function regular within and on a Jordan contour C, which expresses the value of the function at any point within C in terms of its values on C. This and a similar formula for the derivatives (of all orders) of the function are called *Cauchy's integral formulae.* Before dealing with them, I shall obtain some slight generalizations of Theorem 12.3.

13.2. THEOREM 13.1. *Let $C = \{z_1, z_2, z_3, z_1\}$ be a proper triangle, and suppose the function f is continuous in $I'(C)$, and fully differentiable at all points of $I'(C)$ other than z_3.* Then

$$\int_C f(z)dz = 0.$$

Proof. Let $0 < t < 1$, $z_4 = z_3 + t(z_1 - z_3)$, $z_5 = z_3 + t(z_2 - z_3)$, $C_1 = \{z_4, z_5, z_3, z_4\}$, $C_2 = \{z_1, z_2, z_4, z_1\}$ and $C_3 = \{z_2, z_5, z_4, z_2\}$. Then, by Exercise 9.35, $I'(C_m) \subset I'(C)$, $(m = 1, 2, 3)$, and z_3 is not in either $I'(C_2)$ or $I'(C_3)$. Hence f is continuous on C_1, and fully differentiable at all points within and on C_2 and C_3. Hence, by Theorems 11.4 and 11.6 and Exercise 9.42,

$$\int_C f(z)dz = \sum_{m=1}^{3} \int_{C_m} f(z)dz, \tag{1}$$

and, by Theorem 12.3,

$$\int_{C_m} f(z)dz = 0 \quad (m = 2, 3).$$

Thus

$$\int_C f(z)dz = \int_{C_1} f(z)dz. \tag{2}$$

Now, by the corollary to Theorem 4.3, there is a number M such that, for every point z of $I'(C)$, $|f(z)| \leqslant M$. Hence, by Theorem 11.5,

$$\left| \int_{C_1} f(z)dz \right| \leqslant M \text{ le } C_1. \qquad (3)$$

Also le $C_1 = t$ le C. Thus, by (2) and (3),

$$\left| \int_C f(z)dz \right| \leqslant tM \text{ le } C.$$

Since this holds for every number t in $(0, 1)$, the result follows.

THEOREM 13.2. *Let C be a proper triangle, w a point within C, and suppose the function f is fully continuous at w and fully differentiable at all other points within and on C. Then*

$$\int_C f(z)dz = 0.$$

Proof. Let $C = \{z_1, z_2, z_3, z_1\}$, $C_1 = \{z_1, z_2, w, z_1\}$, $C_2 = \{z_2, z_3, w, z_2\}$ and $C_3 = \{z_3, z_1, w, z_3\}$. Then (1) holds as before, and it follows from Theorem 13.1 that

$$\int_{C_m} f(z)dz = 0 \quad (m = 1, 2, 3).$$

Hence the result.

13.3. THEOREM 13.3. *Let C be a proper triangle, described in the positive sense, w a point within C, and suppose the function f is fully differentiable at all points within and on C. Then*

$$f(w) = \frac{1}{2\pi i} \int_C \frac{f(z)}{z - w} dz.$$

Proof. Let $g(z) = \{f(z) - f(w)\}/(z - w)$ where this exists, and $g(w) = f'(w)$. Then, by §§4.4–4.6, g is fully continuous at w and fully differentiable at all other points within and on C. Hence, by Theorem 13.2,

$$\int_C g(z)dz = 0. \qquad (4)$$

Now, for every point z of C, $f(z)/(z-w) = g(z) + f(w)/(z-w)$. Hence, by (4) and Theorems 11.3 and 11.2,

$$\int_C \frac{f(z)}{z-w}\,dz = f(w) \int_C \frac{dz}{z-w},$$

and the result follows from Theorem 11.13.

13.4. THEOREM 13.4. *Let C be a proper triangle, described in the positive sense, and suppose the function f is fully differentiable at all points within and on C. Then*

$$f'(z) = \frac{1}{2\pi i} \int_C \frac{f(w)}{(w-z)^2}\,dw$$

for every point z of $I(C)$, and f' is continuous in $I(C)$.

Proof. Let

$$g(z) = 2\pi i f(z). \tag{5}$$

Then, by Theorem 13.3,

$$g(z) = \int_C \frac{f(w)}{w-z}\,dw$$

for every point z of $I(C)$. Hence, by Theorem 11.19,

$$g'(z) = \int_C \frac{f(w)}{(w-z)^2}\,dw$$

for every point z of $I(C)$, and g' is continuous in $I(C)$. The result therefore follows from (5).

THEOREM 13.5. *Let the function f be regular at z_0. Then f' is fully continuous at z_0.*

Proof. By §6.3, there is a positive number r, such that f is fully differentiable at all points z for which $|z - z_0| < r$. Let $z_1 = z_0 + \frac{1}{2}r$, $z_2 = z_0 + \frac{1}{2}r(-1+i)$, $z_3 = z_0 + \frac{1}{2}r(-1-i)$ and $C = \{z_1, z_2, z_3, z_1\}$. Then, by §12.1, §9.23 and §9.20, C is a proper triangle, described in the positive sense, and $z_0 \in I(C)$. Also, for all points z within and on C, $|z - z_0| < r$, so that f is fully differentiable at all these points. Hence, by Theorem 13.4. f' is continuous in $I(C)$, and the result follows.

EXERCISE

13.1. Show that, if the function f is fully differentiable at all points z of the open set S, then the four partial derivatives occurring in the

Cauchy-Riemann equations are continuous at the corresponding points (x, y).

13.5. THEOREM 13.6. *Let the function f be regular at z_0. Then so is f'.*

Proof. Choose r and C as in the proof of Theorem 13.5, and note that f is not only fully differentiable, but regular, at every point of the disc with centre z_0 and radius r. Hence, by Theorem 13.5, f' is continuous on C. From this and Theorem 11.17 it follows that

$$\int_C f(w)(w-z)^{-2}dw = \int_C f'(w)(w-z)^{-1}dw$$

for every point z that is not on C. Hence, by Theorem 13.4,

$$f'(z) = \frac{1}{2\pi i} \int_C \frac{f'(w)}{w-z}\,dw$$

for every point z of $I(C)$. Thus, putting $g(z) = 2\pi i f'(z)$, we obtain

$$g(z) = \int_C \frac{f'(w)}{w-z}\,dw \quad \{z \in I(C)\},$$

and it follows from Theorem 11.19 that g is fully differentiable at all points of $I(C)$. So, therefore, is f'; which implies the result stated.

EXERCISE

13.2. Show that, in the notation of Chapter 6, $\partial^2 u/\partial x^2 + \partial^2 u/\partial y^2 = \partial^2 v/\partial x^2 + \partial^2 v/\partial y^2 = 0$ at every point at which f is regular. Show that these differential equations need not hold at a point at which f is merely fully differentiable.

13.6. THEOREM 13.7. *Let the function f be regular at z_0. Let $r > 0, g(z_0) = f'(z_0)$, and $g(z) = \{f(z) - f(z_0)\}/(z - z_0), (0 < |z - z_0| < r)$. Then g is regular at z_0.*

Proof. By Theorem 13.6, f' is fully differentiable at z_0, This means that there is a number a such that

$$\{f'(z) - f'(z_0)\}/(z - z_0) \to a \quad \text{as} \quad z \to z_0. \tag{6}$$

Let ϵ be any positive number, and choose the positive number δ so that, for every number z for which $0 < |z - z_0| < \delta$, we have $|\{f'(z)-f'(z_0)\}/(z-z_0)-a| < \epsilon$. This is possible by (6). Then

$$|f'(z)-f'(z_0)-a(z-z_0)| \leqslant \epsilon|z-z_0| \quad (|z-z_0| < \delta). \tag{7}$$

By Exercise 6.1, there is a positive number r' such that $f(z)$ is regular for $|z-z_0| < r'$. Let $\delta' = \min(\delta, r, r')$, $h(z) = f(z) - f'(z_0)(z-z_0) - \frac{1}{2}a(z-z_0)^2$, and suppose that $0 < |w-z_0| < \delta'$. Then an easy calculation shows that

$$\{g(w)-g(z_0)\}/(w-z_0) - \tfrac{1}{2}a = \{h(w)-h(z_0)\}/(w-z_0)^2. \tag{8}$$

Also, by (7), $|h'(z)| \leqslant \epsilon|z-z_0|$ ($|z-z_0| < \delta$), and, by Theorem 13.5, h' is continuous in the disc $|z-z_0| < r'$. Hence $|h'(z)| \leqslant \epsilon|w-z_0|$ ($z \in |\{z_0, w\}|$), and, by Theorems 11.8 and 11.5,

$$|h(w)-h(z_0)| = \left|\int_{\{z_0,\,w\}} h'(z)dz\right| \leqslant \epsilon|w-z_0|^2.$$

From this and (8) it follows that

$$|\{g(w)-g(z_0)\}/(w-z_0) - \tfrac{1}{2}a| \leqslant \epsilon. \tag{9}$$

I have shown that, for every positive number ϵ, there is a positive number δ', such that, for every complex number w, for which $0 < |w-z_0| < \delta'$, we have (9). This means that $\{g(w)-g(z_0)\}/(w-z_0) \to \frac{1}{2}a$ as $w \to z_0$, and so implies that g is fully differentiable at z_0. Now, by §4.6, g is also fully differentiable at every point z for which $0 < |z-z_0| < \min(r, r')$. Hence g is regular at z_0.

13.7. THEOREM 13.8. *Let D be a disc with centre z_0, and suppose the function g is fully continuous at z_0 and regular at all other points of D. Then g is regular also at z_0.*

Proof. Let $f(z) = (z-z_0)g(z)$, ($z \in D$). Then

$$\lim_{z \to z_0} \frac{f(z)-f(z_0)}{z-z_0} = \lim_{z \to z_0} g(z) = g(z_0).$$

Hence f is fully differentiable at z_0, and $f'(z_0) = g(z_0)$. It is trivial (see §4.6) that f is fully differentiable at all other points of D. Hence f is regular at z_0. The hypotheses of Theorem 13.7 are therefore satisfied with r equal to the radius of D, and the result follows from that theorem.

THEOREM 13.9. *Let D be a disc with centre z_0, and suppose the function f is regular at all points of D other than z_0, and $\lim\limits_{z\to z_0}\{(z-z_0)f(z)\}=0$. Then $\lim\limits_{z\to z_0}f(z)$ exists.*

Proof. Let $g(z_0)=0$ and $g(z)=(z-z_0)f(z)$, $(z\in D,\ z\neq z_0)$. Then, by hypothesis, $\lim\limits_{z\to z_0}g(z)=g(z_0)$, i.e. g is fully continuous at z_0; and it follows from Theorem 6.3 that g is regular at all other points of D. Hence, by Theorem 13.8, g is fully differentiable at z_0. This means that $\lim\limits_{z\to z_0}[\{g(z)-g(z_0)\}/(z-z_0)]$ exists, which is equivalent to the result stated.

13.8. **THEOREM 13.10.** *Let C be a Jordan contour, described in the positive sense, w a point within C, and f a function regular within and on C. Then*

$$f(w) = \frac{1}{2\pi i}\int_C \frac{f(z)}{z-w}\,dz.$$

Proof. Let $g(z)=\{f(z)-f(w)\}/(z-w)$ where this exists, and $g(w)=f'(w)$. Then, by Theorem 13.7, g is regular at w, and it follows from Theorem 6.3 that g is regular at all other points at which f is regular. Hence g is regular within and on C, and hence, by Theorem 12.9,

$$\int_C g(z)dz = 0. \tag{10}$$

Now $f(z)/(z-w)=g(z)+f(w)/(z-w)$ $(z\in|C|)$. Hence, by Theorems 11.3 and 11.2,

$$\int_C \frac{f(z)}{z-w}\,dz = \int_C g(z)dz + f(w)\int_C \frac{dz}{z-w}.$$

From this and (10) and Theorem 11.13 we obtain the result stated.

13.9. For any natural number n, $f^{(n)}$ denotes the nth derivative of f, and it follows from Theorem 13.6 (applied n times) that $f^{(n)}$ is regular at any point at which f is regular.

THEOREM 13.11. *Suppose the hypotheses of Theorem 13.10 hold, and let n be any natural number. Then*

$$f^{(n)}(w) = \frac{n!}{2\pi i}\int_C f(z)(z-w)^{-n-1}dz.$$

Proof. By what has just been said, $f^{(n)}$ is regular within and on C. Hence, by Theorem 13.10,

$$f^{(n)}(w) = \frac{1}{2\pi i} \int_C f^{(n)}(z)(z-w)^{-1}dz.$$

Now, by Theorem 11.17 (applied n times),

$$\int_C f^{(n)}(z)(z-w)^{-1}dz = n! \int_C f(z)(z-w)^{-n-1}dz,$$

and the result follows.

Theorem 13.11 is usually proved by differentiation under the integral sign. The justification of this process is somewhat tedious. I have not avoided it altogether, as it occurs in the proof of Theorem 11.19.

13.10. THEOREM 13.12. *Let S be an open set, f a function continuous in S, and suppose that*

$$\int_C f(z)dz = 0 \qquad (11)$$

for every proper triangle C for which $I'(C) \subset S$.   Then f is regular in S.

Proof. Let z_0 be any point of S. Then, since S is open, there is a disc D about z_0, such that $D \subset S$. By Exercise 12.10, f has an indefinite integral in D. This means that there is a function g, fully differentiable at all points of D (and therefore regular at z_0), such that

$$g'(z) = f(z) \quad (z \in D). \qquad (12)$$

It now follows from Theorem 13.6 that g' is regular at z_0. Hence, by (12), so is f. Thus f is regular at every point z_0 of S, which was to be proved.

The following weakened version of Theorem 13.12 is called 'Morera's theorem':

Let the function f be continuous in the simply connected domain D, and suppose that (11) holds for every simple closed contour C contained in D.   Then f is regular in D.

EXERCISE

13.3. Find the value of

$$\int_C \frac{(z-1)dz}{(z+1)^2(z-2)},$$

where C is the circle $|z+i| = 2$.   [London, 1949.]
   [Hint: use Theorem 13.11 with $f(z) = (z-1)/(z-2)$ and $w = -1$.]

CHAPTER 14

FUNCTIONS REPRESENTED BY INFINITE SERIES

14.1. I assume that the reader knows the elements of the theory of uniform convergence of sequences and series of functions of a real variable, and that he has no difficulty in obtaining straight-forward extensions of results of this theory to functions of a complex variable. It may, therefore, be left to him to prove the next theorem.

THEOREM 14.1. *Let the functions f_1, f_2, f_3, ... be continuous on the contour C, and suppose that the series $\sum f_n(z)$ converges uniformly on C. Then*

$$\int_C \sum_{n=1}^{\infty} f_n(z)dz = \sum_{n=1}^{\infty} \int_C f_n(z)dz.$$

In what follows, '$f^{(0)}$' means 'f'.

THEOREM 14.2. *Let $f(z)$ be regular for $|z - z_0| < r$. Then*

$$f(z) = \sum_{n=0}^{\infty} \frac{f^{(n)}(z_0)}{n!}(z - z_0)^n \quad (|z - z_0| < r). \tag{1}$$

Proof. Let z_1 be any number such that $|z_1 - z_0| < r$. Choose the number r_1 so that $|z_1 - z_0| < r_1 < r$, and let C be the circle $|z - z_0| = r_1$, described in the positive sense {i.e. $C \sim \mathscr{C}(t; z_0 + r_1 e^{it}, 0, 2\pi)$}. Then, by Theorem 13.10,

$$f(z_1) = \frac{1}{2\pi i}\int_C \frac{f(z)}{z - z_1}dz = \frac{1}{2\pi i}\int_C \sum_{n=0}^{\infty} \frac{f(z)}{(z - z_0)^{n+1}}(z_1 - z_0)^n dz, \tag{2}$$

and it easily follows from Exercise 9.2(ii) that the series on the right-hand side of (2) converges uniformly on C. Hence, by Theorems 14.1, 11.2, 13.10 and 13.11,

$$f(z_1) = \sum_{n=0}^{\infty} \frac{f^{(n)}(z_0)}{n!}(z_1 - z_0)^n,$$

which proves the theorem.

A series of the form of that in (1) is called a *Taylor series*. The series in (1) itself is called the *Taylor expansion* of $f(z)$ about z_0.

It follows from Theorem 14.2 that, if f is an integral function (see §6.5), then (1) holds for every pair of numbers z_0, z.

14.2. The phrase *locally uniformly at z_0* means 'uniformly in some disc about z_0'. The phrase *locally uniformly in S*, where S is a set of points, means 'locally uniformly at all points of S'.

The fundamental properties of *power series* are given in Hardy, §§198–201. It may be left to the reader to prove that any power series which has a circle of convergence converges locally uniformly (though not necessarily uniformly) in the interior of that circle, and that any power series which converges in the whole plane converges locally uniformly in the whole plane.

THEOREM 14.3. *Let the functions $f_0, f_1, f_2, \ldots$ be regular in the open set S, and suppose that $\sum f_n(z)$ converges for every point z of S, and that $\sum f'_n(z)$ converges locally uniformly in S. Then*

$$\frac{d}{dz} \sum_{n=0}^{\infty} f_n(z) = \sum_{n=0}^{\infty} f'_n(z) \quad (z \in S).$$

Proof. Let

$$f(z) = \sum_{n=0}^{\infty} f_n(z), \qquad g(z) = \sum_{n=0}^{\infty} f'_n(z),$$

and let z_0 be any point of S. Then we have to prove that

$$f'(z_0) = g(z_0). \tag{3}$$

Now z_0 is interior to S, and $\sum f'_n(z)$ converges locally uniformly at z_0. Hence there is a disc D about z_0, such that $D \subset S$, and that $\sum f'_n(z)$ converges uniformly in D. Let z be any point of D other than z_0. Then, by Theorems 14.1 and 11.8,

$$\int_{\{z_0, z\}} g(w)dw = \sum_{n=0}^{\infty} \int_{\{z_0, z\}} f'_n(w)dw$$

$$= \sum_{n=0}^{\infty} \{f_n(z) - f_n(z_0)\} = f(z) - f(z_0).$$

From this and Theorem 11.14 (with f and g interchanged) we obtain (3).

It is easily seen that, if $\sum a_n(z-z_0)^n$ converges for every point z of a disc D about z_0, then $\sum na_n(z-z_0)^{n-1}$ converges locally uniformly in D. It therefore follows from Theorem 14.3 that any power series which has a circle of convergence may be differentiated term by term within that circle, and that any power series which converges everywhere may be differentiated term by term everywhere. Thus the sum of a power series which has a circle of convergence is regular within that circle, and the sum of a power series which converges everywhere is an integral function.

EXERCISE

14.1. Justify the term by term differentiation of power series by a method which does not depend on integration.

14.3. The next theorem also deals with term by term differentiation, but, unlike the last, has no analogue in the theory of functions of a real variable.

THEOREM 14.4. *Let the functions $f_0, f_1, f_2, \ldots$ be regular in the open set S, and suppose that*

$$\sum_{n=0}^{\infty} f_n(z) = f(z) \quad (z \in S),$$

the convergence being locally uniform in S. Then f is regular in S, and

$$f^{(m)}(z) = \sum_{n=0}^{\infty} f_n^{(m)}(z) \quad (m = 1, 2, 3, \ldots; z \in S).$$

Proof. Let z_0 be any point of S. Then there is a disc D about z_0, such that $D \subset S$, and $\sum f_n(z)$ converges uniformly in D. Let $\triangle$ be any triangle contained in D. Then, by Theorems 14.1 and 12.3,

$$\int_{\triangle} f(z)dz = \sum_{n=0}^{\infty} \int_{\triangle} f_n(z)dz = 0.$$

From this and Theorem 13.12 (with D instead of S) it follows that f is regular at z_0. Since this holds for every point z_0 of S, f is regular in S.

9—C.N.F.

Now let C be a circle about z_0, described in the positive sense, with a radius smaller than that of D. Then, by Theorems 14.1 and 13.11,

$$f^{(m)}(z_0) = \frac{m!}{2\pi i} \int_C \frac{f(z)}{(z-z_0)^{m+1}} \, dz$$

$$= \sum_{n=0}^{\infty} \frac{m!}{2\pi i} \int_C \frac{f_n(z)}{(z-z_0)^{m+1}} \, dz = \sum_{n=0}^{\infty} f_n^{(m)}(z_0) \quad (m = 1, 2, 3, \ldots).$$

This completes the proof.

14.4. THEOREM 14.5. *Let* $r > 0$, *and suppose that, for every number z for which* $|z - z_0| < r$, *we have*

$$f(z) = \sum_{n=0}^{\infty} a_n(z-z_0)^n. \tag{4}$$

Then

$$a_m = \frac{f^{(m)}(z_0)}{m!} \quad (m = 0, 1, 2, \ldots). \tag{5}$$

Also, if C is any circle about z_0 whose radius is less than r (described in the positive sense), then

$$a_m = \frac{1}{2\pi i} \int_C \frac{f(z)}{(z-z_0)^{m+1}} \, dz. \tag{6}$$

Proof. Formula (5) is obtained by applying term by term differentiation m times to (4) (see the end of §14.2) and substituting z_0 for z. Formula (6) then follows from Theorems 13.10 and 13.11.

The next theorem is called 'Cauchy's inequality for the coefficients of a power series'.

THEOREM 14.6. *Let* $0 < r < r'$, *and suppose that, for every number z for which* $|z - z_0| < r'$, *we have*

$$f(z) = \sum_{n=0}^{\infty} a_n(z-z_0)^n,$$

and that, for every number z for which $|z - z_0| = r$, *we have* $|f(z)| \leqslant M$. *Then* $|a_m| r^m \leqslant M \quad (m = 0, 1, 2, \ldots)$.

Proof.   Let C be the circle $|z-z_0| = r$, described in the positive sense.   Then, by Theorem 14.5 (with r' instead of r),

$$a_m = \frac{1}{2\pi i} \int_C \frac{f(z)}{(z-z_0)^{m+1}} \, dz.$$

The result now follows from Theorem 11.5.

The next theorem is due to Liouville.

THEOREM 14.7.   *Any bounded integral function is a constant.*

Proof.   Let f be an integral function, and suppose that $|f(z)| \leqslant M$ for every number z.   Then, by the remark at the end of §14.1,

$$f(z) = \sum_{n=0}^{\infty} a_n z^n$$

for every number z, where $a_n = f^{(n)}(0)/n!$.   From this and Theorem 14.6 it follows that $|a_m| \leqslant Mr^{-m}$ for every positive integer m and every positive number r.   Hence $a_m = 0$ for every positive integer m, and hence $f(z) = a_0$ for every number z.

EXERCISES

14.2.   Obtain a more direct proof of the last part of Theorem 14.5.

14.3.   Prove that, if c is a positive constant, and the integral function f satisfies the inequality $|f(z)| < |z|^c$ for every number z for which $|z| > c$, then $f(z)$ is a polynomial.

14.4.   Prove that the function f defined by

$$f(z) = \sum_{n=1}^{\infty} (-1)^{n-1} n^{-z}$$

(where n^{-z} has its principal value) is regular in the half-plane re $z > 0$.

14.5.   The function $f(z)$ is regular and such that $|f(z)| \geqslant 1$ for every finite value of z.   Show that $f(z)$ is a constant.

If $f(z) = u(x, y) + iv(x, y)$ is regular for every finite value of z and if $u(x, y)$ is never zero, show that $f(z)$ is a constant.   [London, 1950.]

CHAPTER 15

THE IDENTITY THEOREM FOR REGULAR FUNCTIONS

15.1. If a function f of a real variable is differentiable at all points of the interval $(0, 3)$, then the value of $f(2)$, for instance, is not determined (or in any way restricted) by the values of $f(x)$ for $0 < x < 1$. It is the object of this chapter to show that functions of a complex variable, considered in domains, differ in this respect from functions of a real variable, considered in intervals.

THEOREM 15.1. *Let D be a domain, and let z_0 and w be points of D. Then there are a finite number of discs D_0, D_1, D_2, . . ., D_k, contained in D, with the following properties:*

(i) *The centre of D_0 is z_0.*

(ii) *For $n = 1, 2, 3, . . ., k$, the centre of D_n is a point of D_{n-1}.*

(iii) *$w \in D_k$.*

Proof. The case in which D is the whole plane is trivial. Suppose, therefore, that D is not the whole plane, and let S be the complement of D. Then S is not empty. Also, by Theorem 3.2, S is closed. Now, by §9.17, there is a broken line Γ, contained in D, leading from z_0 to w. Let T be the set of the points of Γ. Then T is closed and bounded, and has no point in common with S. Let r be the distance between S and T. Then, by Theorem 3.4, $r > 0$. Now divide Γ into a finite number of line segments $\{z_0, z_1\}$, $\{z_1, z_2\}$, $\{z_2, z_3\}$, . . ., $\{z_{k-1}, z_k\}$, $\{z_k, w\}$, each of length less than r, and let D_n be the disc with centre z_n and radius r. Then the discs D_0, D_1, D_2, . . ., D_k have the properties stated.

15.2. A *zero* of f is a point z for which $f(z) = 0$.

THEOREM 15.2. *Let the function f be regular in the disc S, and let the centre of S be a limit point of the set of the zeros of f. Then $f(z) = 0$ for every point z of S.*

Proof.   Let z_0 be the centre of S.   Then, by Theorem 14.2,

$$f(z) = \sum_{n=0}^{\infty} a_n(z-z_0)^n \quad (z \in S), \tag{1}$$

where $a_n = f^{(n)}(z_0)/n!$.   Suppose, if possible, that the numbers a_n are not all 0, and let k be the least integer n for which $a_n \neq 0$.   Then

$$f(z) = \sum_{n=k}^{\infty} a_n(z-z_0)^n = (z-z_0)^k g(z) \quad (z \in S), \tag{2}$$

where

$$g(z) = \sum_{n=k}^{\infty} a_n(z-z_0)^{n-k} = \sum_{m=0}^{\infty} a_{m+k}(z-z_0)^m.$$

It is easily seen that g is fully continuous at z_0.   Also $g(z_0) = a_k \neq 0$.   Hence there is a positive number δ' such that $g(z) \neq 0$ $(|z-z_0| < \delta')$.   From this and (2) it follows that $f(z) \neq 0$ $(0 < |z-z_0| < \delta)$, where $\delta = \min(\delta', r)$, and r is the radius of S. This contradicts the hypothesis that z_0 is a limit point of the set of the zeros of f.   Hence $a_n = 0$ $(n = 0, 1, 2, \ldots)$, and the result follows from (1).

THEOREM 15.3.   *Let the function f be regular in the domain D, and suppose that the set of the zeros of f has a limit point in D.   Then $f(z) = 0$ for every point z of D.*

Proof.   Let T be the set of the zeros of f.   Then T has a limit point z_0, say, in D.   Let w be any point of D.   Then we have to prove that

$$f(w) = 0. \tag{3}$$

Choose discs $D_0, D_1, D_2, \ldots, D_k$ in accordance with Theorem 15.1.   By Theorem 15.2, any disc, which is contained in D, and whose centre is a limit point of T, is contained in T. Hence $D_0 \subset T$.   Now any point of D_0 is a limit point of D_0 and hence of T.   In particular, the centre of D_1 is a limit point of T.   Hence $D_1 \subset T$.   Repeating this argument, we obtain $D_2 \subset T, D_3 \subset T, \ldots$, and finally $D_k \subset T$, which implies (3).

The next theorem is the 'identity theorem'.

THEOREM 15.4. *Let the functions g and h be regular in the domain D, and suppose that $g(z) = h(z)$ for every point z of a set which has a limit point in D.   Then $g(z) = h(z)$ for every point z of D.*

This follows from Theorem 15.3 with $f(z) = g(z) - h(z)$.

COROLLARY. *Let the functions g and h be regular in the domain D, and suppose that $g(z) = h(z)$ for every point z of a non-empty open sub-set of D.   Then $g(z) = h(z)$ for every point z of D.*

CHAPTER 16

ANALYTIC CONTINUATION

16.1. The reader may find that my terminology is inconsistent with that of his favourite text-book. That cannot be helped. There is, as yet, no generally accepted terminology in connection with analytic continuation. I have already mentioned, in §4.2, two different meanings of the word 'function'. Many mathematicians use this word also—probably because Weierstrass did so a hundred years ago—for something which is, in fact, an aggregate of functions. Weierstrass should be forgiven, if only because he lived before the time of *Principia Mathematica*, but I see no reason to follow him in this matter. What Professor A calls a branch, Professor B calls a function element, and vice versa. Professor C may say that $(\sin z)/z$ is regular at $z = 0$, while Professor D says it has a removable singularity there—and I disagree with both. As to my own terminology, I make no claims for it, but only ask the reader to accept it for so long as he is reading this book.

16.2. I define an *analytic function* as a function with the following two properties: (i) Its region of existence is a domain. (ii) It is regular in its region of existence.

The term 'sub-function' was defined in §7.5. It is trivial that, if f is a function with region of existence S, and T is a non-empty sub-set of S, then there is one and only one sub-function of f with region of existence T. I call it the sub-function of f in T.

The function f defined by $f(z) = \log z$ is not analytic; for it is not regular at the point -1, and this point is in its region of existence. The sub-function of f in the plane cut along the negative real axis (see §7.4), however, is analytic.

I shall define the terms 'immediate continuation', 'analytic continuation', 'virtually regular' and 'singularity' only for analytic functions, except that the term 'isolated singularity' will be defined without this restriction.

16.3. Two analytic functions f, g, with regions of existence S, T respectively, are called *immediate continuations* of each other if and only if (i) $S \cap T$ is not empty, and (ii) $f(z) = g(z)$ for every point z of $S \cap T$.

It follows from this definition and the corollary to Theorem 15.4 that, corresponding to any analytic function f and any domain T, there is at most one immediate continuation of f with region of existence T. If there is one, I call it the immediate continuation of f into T. Otherwise I say that f has no immediate continuation into T. The sentence 'f has an immediate continuation to z_0' means that z_0 is a point of a domain into which f has an immediate continuation.

16.4. For any natural number k, I define the term *continuation in k steps*, by induction, as follows: (i) 'Continuation in one step' means 'immediate continuation'. (ii) A continuation of f in $k+1$ steps is an immediate continuation of a continuation of f in k steps.

I now define an *analytic continuation* as a continuation in any number of steps. By an analytic continuation of f into D I mean, as the reader may have guessed, an analytic continuation of f with region of existence D. The meaning of the sentence 'f has an analytic continuation to z_0' is now obvious.

16.5. Analytic continuation differs from immediate continuation in that a function f may have more than one analytic continuation into the same domain. According as this does or does not happen, f is said to be *multiform* or *uniform*.

EXERCISES

16.1. Prove that all integral functions are uniform.

16.2. Prove that the function f defined by

$$f(z) = \sum_{n=0}^{\infty} z^n$$

is uniform, and has no analytic continuation to the point 1.

16.6. To obtain an example of a multiform function, let D_1 be the plane cut along the negative real axis, D_2 the upper half-plane, D_3 the plane cut along the positive real axis, and D_4 the lower half-plane. Let f_1 be the analytic function mentioned in §16.2 {so that $f_1(z) = \log z$, $(z \in D_1)$}, f_2 the sub-function of f_1 in D_2, f_3 the function defined by $f_3(z) = f_1(-z) + \pi i$, f_4 the sub-function of f_3 in D_4, and f_5 the function defined by $f_5(z) = f_1(z) + 2\pi i$.

It is trivial that f_2 and f_4 are immediate continuations of f_1 and f_3 respectively. Now let $z \in D_2 \cap D_3$, i.e. im $z > 0$. Then, by the definitions and Exercise 5.13, $f_3(z) = \log(-z) + \pi i = \log z = f_2(z)$. Hence f_3 is an immediate continuation of f_2. Similarly, if z is in the intersection of the regions of existence of f_4 and f_5, then im $z < 0$ and $f_5(z) = \log z + 2\pi i = \log(-z) + \pi i = f_1(-z) + \pi i = f_3(z) = f_4(z)$. Hence f_5 is an immediate continuation of f_4. Thus f_{n+1} is an immediate continuation of f_n for $n = 1, 2, 3, 4$. It follows that f_5 is an analytic continuation of f_1. So is f_1 itself. Hence f_1 has more than one analytic continuation into D_1. This shows that f_1 is multiform.

16.7. A *boundary point* of an open set S is defined as a limit point of S which is not a point of S. (The general notion of a boundary point will not be needed here.) The *boundary* of S is the set of the boundary points of S.

An analytic function f is said to be *virtually regular* at a point w if and only if (i) w is a boundary point of the region of existence of f, and (ii) f has an immediate continuation to w.

E X E R C I S E S ·

16.3. Prove that the function f defined by $f(z) = (\sin z)/z$ is virtually regular at 0.

16.4. Find all the points at which the function f of Exercise 16.2 is virtually regular.

16.8. I define a *singularity* (other than ∞) of an analytic function f as a boundary point of the region of existence of f at which no analytic sub-function of f is virtually regular. Note that a sub-function of an analytic function is analytic if and only if its region of existence is a domain.

The point ∞ is called a singularity of f if and only if the point 0 is a singularity of the function g defined by $g(z) = f(1/z)$.

E X E R C I S E

16.5. Prove that the function f_1 of §16.6 is not virtually regular at any point, and that the point 0 is its only finite singularity.

16.9. Any analytic function f has infinitely many analytic continuations, namely its analytic sub-functions. I call these the *trivial analytic continuations* of f. By a *complete* analytic function I mean one whose only analytic continuations are the trivial ones. The reader should note, however, that some mathematicians use the term 'complete analytic function' in an entirely different sense.

EXERCISES

16.6. Prove that, if f is any analytic function, then the union of the regions of existence of all the analytic continuations of f is a domain.

16.7. Prove that an analytic function is uniform if and only if it is a sub-function of a complete analytic function.

16.10. For an analytic function f to be complete, it is a necessary condition that every boundary point of the region of existence of f should be a singularity of f. This follows at once from the relevant definitions. The condition is also sufficient, but this is, in my opinion, far from trivial, and I shall give a detailed proof of it.

16.11. THEOREM 16.1. *Let f_0 be an incomplete analytic function with region of existence S_0. Then f_0 has an analytic sub-function, which has an immediate continuation, whose region of existence is not contained in S_0.*

Proof. By hypothesis, f_0 has an analytic continuation which is not a sub-function of f_0. Let it be a continuation in k steps (see §16.4), and call it f_k. If $k = 1$, it is an immediate continuation of f_0, and f_0 is an analytic sub-function of itself. I shall come back to this case later. In the meantime, suppose $k > 1$. Then there are analytic functions $f_1, f_2, \ldots, f_{k-1}$, such that, for every integer n from 1 to k, f_n is an immediate continuation of f_{n-1}. Let α be the aggregate of those natural numbers $n \leqslant k$ for which f_n is not a sub-function of f_0. Then $k \in \alpha$, and so α is not empty. Let m be the least member of α. Then f_{m-1} is an analytic sub-function of f_0, and f_m is an immediate continuation of f_{m-1}, but not a sub-function of f_0. Thus, whether $k = 1$ or $k > 1$, f_0 has an analytic sub-function g, say, which has an immediate continuation h, say, which is not a sub-function of f_0.

Let the regions of existence of g and h be T and U respectively. Then $T \cap U$ is not empty. Also $f_0(z) = g(z)$ for every point z of T, and $g(z) = h(z)$ for every point z of $T \cap U$. Hence $f_0(z) = h(z)$ for every point z of the non-empty open sub-set $T \cap U$ of the domain U. Now h is regular in U. Thus, if f_0 were also regular in U, it would follow from the corollary to Theorem 15.4 that $f_0(z) = h(z)$ for every point z of U, i.e. that h is a sub-function of f_0; which is not so. Hence f_0 is not regular in U, i.e. U is not contained in S_0. This proves the theorem.

EXERCISES

16.8. S is an open set, $z_0 \in S$, and T is the set of those points which can be joined to z_0 by broken lines contained in S. Prove that T is a domain.

16.9. The point w is not in the open set S, but there is a point of S in every disc about w. Prove that w is a boundary point of S.

16.12. The next theorem is equivalent to the statement which I described in §16.10 as far from trivial.

THEOREM 16.2.   *Let f be an incomplete analytic function with region of existence S. Then S has at least one boundary point which is not a singularity of f.*

Proof. By Theorem 16.1, there are an analytic sub-function g of f, with region of existence T, say, and an immediate continuation h of g, with region of existence U, say, such that U is not contained in S. Now $T \cap U$ is not empty, i.e. there is a point z_0 in $T \cap U$; and there is a point w in U, which is not in S. Since U is a domain, there is a broken line C, contained in U, leading from z_0 to w. Let $C = \mathscr{C}(j, a, b)$, and let α be the set of those points t of $[a, b]$ for which $j(t)$ is not in S. Then α is obviously bounded, and it is easily seen that α is closed. Also, $b \in \alpha$, so that α is not empty. Hence α has a least member t_0, say, and obviously $a \leqslant t_0 \leqslant b$. Now $j(a) = z_0$, $z_0 \in T$, and $T \subset S$. Hence $j(a) \in S$, so that a is not in α, while t_0 is. Hence $a < t_0 \leqslant b$, and $j(t_0)$ is not in S.

It is easily shown—and will be shown later—that $j(t_0)$ is a boundary point of S. But this is not enough for our purpose; for, although g has an immediate continuation to $j(t_0)$, this does not imply that $j(t_0)$ is not a singularity of f. In fact, it can easily be shown by an example (see §16.19) that g may have an immediate continuation to a singularity of f. The trouble is that $j(t_0)$ is not necessarily a boundary point of T, and so g is not necessarily virtually regular at $j(t_0)$.

To overcome this difficulty, let V be the set of those points which can be joined to z_0 by broken lines contained in $S \cap U$. Note that $z_0 \in V$; for z_0 is joined to itself by the broken line $\{z_0, z_1, z_0\}$, which is contained in $S \cap U$ if z_1 is near enough to z_0. Also, if $a < t < t_0$, then $j(t) \in V$, for $j(t)$ is joined to z_0 by the broken line $\mathscr{C}(j, a, t)$. Thus, if D is any disc about $j(t_0)$, then there is a point of V in D; for $j(t)$ is such a point, if t is less than t_0 and near enough to t_0. Therefore, since $V \subset S$, and $j(t_0)$ is not in S, it follows from Exercise 16.9 that $j(t_0)$ is a boundary point of both S and V.

Now let ϕ be the sub-function of f in V, and note that, by Exercise 16.8, V is a domain. I shall show that h is an immediate continuation of ϕ.

Since $z_0 \in T \cap V$, this set is not empty; and, for any point z of it, we have $\phi(z) = f(z) = g(z) = h(z)$. Therefore, since $T \cap V$ is open, and both ϕ and h are regular in the domain V, it follows from the corollary to Theorem 15.4 that $\phi(z) = h(z)$ for every point z of V. Hence h is an immediate continuation of ϕ.

Now $j(t_0)$ is a boundary point of the region of existence of ϕ, and a point of that of h. Hence ϕ is virtually regular at $j(t_0)$, and so this point is not a singularity of f. This proves the theorem.

16.13. As an application of Theorem 16.2, consider an analytic function f whose region of existence is the unit disc, with the property that every point on the unit circle is a singularity of f. It follows from the said theorem that any such function is complete.

I shall show that, in order to prove that a point w on the unit circle is a singularity of f, it is sufficient to prove that f is not virtually regular at w. This is because w is what I call a simple boundary point of the unit disc. I define a *simple boundary point* of an open set S as a boundary point w of S with the following property: Every disc about w contains a domain D, such that (i) $w \in D$, and (ii) $D \cap S$ is a domain.

It is obvious that all boundary points of any disc are simple in this sense.

16.10. Prove that the point 0 is the only simple boundary point of the plane cut along the negative real axis.

16.14. THEOREM 16.3. *Let w be a simple boundary point of the region of existence S of the analytic function f, and suppose that w is not a singularity of f. Then f is virtually regular at w.*

Proof. By hypothesis, some analytic sub-function g of f, with region of existence T, say, is virtually regular at w. This means that w is a boundary point of T, and g has an immediate continuation h, say, to w. Let the region of existence of h be U. Then $w \in U$, $T \cap U$ is not empty, and

$$g(z) = h(z) \quad (z \in T \cap U). \tag{1}$$

Since U is open, it follows that w is interior to U. This means that there is a disc D about w such that $D \subset U$. Since w is a simple boundary point of S, there is a domain D_1, such that $w \in D_1$, $D_1 \subset D$, and $S \cap D_1$ is a domain.

Now $D_1 \subset U$. Hence, by (1), $g(z) = h(z)$, $(z \in T \cap D_1)$. Also $f(z) = g(z)$, $(z \in T)$. Hence

$$f(z) = h(z) \quad (z \in T \cap D_1). \tag{2}$$

The set $T \cap D_1$ is an open sub-set of the domain $S \cap D_1$. Also w, being a boundary point of T, is a limit point of T, and w is interior to D_1. Hence, by Exercise 3.5, w is a limit point of $T \cap D_1$, which implies that this set is not empty. It therefore follows from (2) and the corollary to Theorem 15.4 that $f(z) = h(z)$, $(z \in S \cap D_1)$. Thus the sub-function of h in D_1 is an immediate continuation of f, and the result follows.

16.11. Show that Theorem 16.3 becomes false if the word 'simple' is omitted.

16.12. Prove that the boundary of any open set is closed.

16.13. The analytic function f has region of existence S. T is the set of those boundary points of S at which f is not virtually regular. Prove that T is closed.

16.14. The function f is analytic, w is a boundary point of its region of existence, and $|f(rw)| \to \infty$ as $r \to 1-$. Prove that f is not virtually regular at w.

16.15. *Example.* Let the function f be defined by

$$f(z) = \sum_{n=1}^{\infty} z^{n!}.$$

Then f is analytic, and its region of existence is the unit disc. I shall prove that f is complete.

Let k be a natural number, $w^k = 1$, and $0 < r < 1$. Then

$$f(rw) = \sum_{n=1}^{k-1} r^{n!}w^{n!} + \sum_{n=k}^{\infty} r^{n!},$$

and hence

$$|f(rw)| > \sum_{n=k}^{\infty} r^{n!} - k.$$

It easily follows that $|f(rw)| \to \infty$ as $r \to 1-$. Hence, by Exercise 16.14, f is not virtually regular at w. This holds for any number w for which there is a natural number k such that $w^k = 1$. These numbers w are called the *roots of unity*. It is easily seen that any point on the unit circle is a limit point of the set of the roots of unity. Hence, by Exercise 16.13, f is not virtually regular at any point on the unit circle. It now follows from Theorem 16.3 that any such point is a singularity of f, and from this and Theorem 16.2 that f is complete.

EXERCISES

16.15. Prove that, if f is a complete analytic function, regular at z_0, but not an integral function, then the radius of convergence of the power series

$$\sum_{n=0}^{\infty} \frac{f^{(n)}(z_0)}{n!} (z-z_0)^n \qquad (3)$$

is equal to the distance of z_0 from the nearest singularity (or singularities) of f.

16.16. The function f_1 is defined as in §16.6, $z_0 = -2-i$, f is defined by either

(i) $f(z) = 1/\{f_1(z) - \log(-2+i)\}$

or

(ii) $f(z) = 1/\{f_1(z) - \log(-2+i) + 2\pi i\}$,

r is the radius of convergence of (3), and d is the distance of z_0 from the nearest singularity of f. In case (i), prove that $r = \sqrt{5}$ and $d = 2$. In case (ii), prove that $r = 2$ and $d = \sqrt{5}$.

16.17. Prove that the function f defined by

$$f(z) = \sum_{n=0}^{\infty} z^{2^n}$$

is a complete analytic function.

16.16. Strictly speaking, a function defined by a power series is not necessarily analytic, for its region of existence is the set of those points at which the series converges, and that is not always a domain: we have to exclude any points on the circle of convergence. So, by *the analytic function associated with the power series*

$$\sum_{n=0}^{\infty} a_n(z - z_0)^n,$$

whose radius of convergence is r, I mean the function f for which $f(z)$ is equal to the sum of the series if $|z - z_0| < r$, and $f(z)$ does not exist if $|z - z_0| \geqslant r$. By the *singularities of a power series* I mean the singularities of the analytic function associated with it.

EXERCISES

16.18. D_0, D_1 and D_2 are discs, the centres of D_1 and D_2 are on the circumference of D_0, and $D_1 \cap D_2$ is not empty. Prove that $D_0 \cap D_1 \cap D_2$ is not empty.

16.19. The analytic function f is virtually regular at w. Prove that f has an immediate continuation into a disc about w.

16.17. THEOREM 16.4. *Let f_0 be an analytic function whose region of existence is a disc D_0, and suppose that f_0 has no singularity. Then f_0 has an immediate continuation into a disc concentric with D_0 and larger than D_0.*

Proof. Let D_0 be the disc with centre z_0 and radius r_0, and define an aggregate α of discs as follows: $D_0 \in \alpha$, and any other disc D is in α if and only if (i) the centre of D is on the circumference of D_0, and (ii) f_0 has an immediate continuation into D.

Let U be the union of the members of α (see §3.6). Then, by Exercise 3.1, U is open. Let V be the complement of U.

Then, by Theorem 3.2, V is closed. If V is not empty, let r' be the distance of z_0 from V, and if V is empty, let $r' = r_0 + 1$. In either case, let D' be the set of those points z for which $|z - z_0| < r'$. Obviously none of these points is in V, and so

$$D' \subset U. \qquad (4)$$

I shall show that $r' > r_0$. This is trivial if V is empty. Suppose, therefore, that V is not empty. Then, by Exercise 3.10, there is a point w in V such that

$$|z_0 - w| = r'. \qquad (5)$$

Since $D_0 \subset U$, it is impossible that $w \in D_0$. Now suppose that w is a boundary point of D_0. Then, since f_0 has no singularity, it follows from Theorem 16.3 that f_0 is virtually regular at w. Hence, by Exercise 16.19, w is the centre of a disc into which f_0 has an immediate continuation. This disc is a member of α, and so $w \in U$. This is impossible, since $w \in V$. Thus w is neither in D_0 nor on its boundary. This means that $|w - z_0| > r_0$. From this and (5) it follows that $r' > r_0$. Thus D' is a disc concentric with D_0 and larger than D_0, and it only remains to prove that f_0 has an immediate continuation into D'.

We note that f_0 has an immediate continuation into any member of α.

LEMMA. *Let D_1 and D_2 be any members of α, $w \in D_1 \cap D_2$, and let f_1 and f_2 be the immediate continuations of f_0 into D_1 and D_2 respectively. Then $f_1(w) = f_2(w)$.*

Proof. Since $w \in D_1 \cap D_2$, this set is not empty. Hence $D_0 \cap D_1 \cap D_2$ is not empty; for this is trivial if $D_0 = D_1$ or $D_0 = D_2$, and follows from Exercise 16.18 otherwise. Since D_1 and D_2 are open and convex (see §12.6), so is $D_1 \cap D_2$, and it follows that $D_1 \cap D_2$ is a domain. Now let $z \in D_0 \cap D_1 \cap D_2$. Then, since f_1 and f_2 are immediate continuations of f_0, $f_1(z) = f_0(z) = f_2(z)$. Thus $f_1(z) = f_2(z)$ for every point z of the non-empty open sub-set $D_0 \cap D_1 \cap D_2$ of the domain $D_1 \cap D_2$. From this and the corollary to Theorem 15.4 it follows that $f_1(z) = f_2(z)$ for every point z of this domain, and in particular for $z = w$. This proves the lemma.

Now let z be any point of U. Then there is a disc D, such that $z \in D$ and $D \in \alpha$. Hence there is an immediate continuation g of f_0 into a member of α, such that $g(z)$ exists; and it follows from the lemma that $g(z)$ has the same value for all such functions g. Denote this common value by $h(z)$. Then it follows from Exercise 6.6 that h is regular in U, and is trivial that $h(z) = f_0(z)$ for every point z of D_0. It easily follows that the sub-function of h in D', which exists by (4), is an immediate continuation of f_0. This completes the proof of the theorem.

16.18. THEOREM 16.5. *Any power series with a finite radius of convergence has at least one singularity.*

Proof. Let the power series be

$$\sum_{n=0}^{\infty} a_n(z - z_0)^n,$$

r its radius of convergence, and f the analytic function associated with it (see §16.16). Suppose, if possible, that f has no singularity. Then, by Theorem 16.4, there is a number $r' > r$, such that f has an immediate continuation g, say, into the disc $|z - z_0| < r'$. This means that

$$g(z) = f(z) \quad (|z - z_0| < r), \tag{6}$$

and $g(z)$ is regular for $|z - z_0| < r'$. Hence, by Theorem 14.2,

$$g(z) = \sum_{n=0}^{\infty} \frac{g^{(n)}(z_0)}{n!} (z - z_0)^n \quad (|z - z_0| < r'), \tag{7}$$

which implies that the radius of convergence of the last series is at least r'. Now, by the definition of f,

$$f(z) = \sum_{n=0}^{\infty} a_n(z - z_0)^n \quad (|z - z_0| < r). \tag{8}$$

Hence, by Theorem 14.5, $a_n = f^{(n)}(z_0)/n!$, $(n = 0, 1, 2, \ldots)$. From this and (6) it follows that the two series in (7) and (8) are the same. But the radius of convergence of the one is at least r', and that of the other is r, and $r' > r$. This is a contradiction, and so the theorem is proved.

EXERCISE

16.20. The power series

$$\sum_{n=0}^{\infty} a_n(z - z_0)^n \tag{9}$$

has radius of convergence r, the analytic function associated with it is f, and $|z_1 - z_0| = r$. Prove that the radius of convergence of the power series

$$\sum_{n=0}^{\infty} \frac{f^{(n)}\{\frac{1}{2}(z_0 + z_1)\}}{n!} w^n$$

is equal to or greater than $\frac{1}{2}r$ according as z_1 is or is not a singularity of f.

The next theorem is due to Pringsheim.

THEOREM 16.6. *Let* $a_n \geqslant 0$ $(n = 0, 1, 2, \ldots)$, *and let the power series*

$$\sum_{n=0}^{\infty} a_n z^n$$

have radius of convergence r. *Then the point* r *is a singularity of that power series.*

Proof. Let the analytic function associated with the power series be f, and suppose that the point r is not a singularity of f. Then, by Exercise 16.20, the radius of convergence of the power series

$$\sum_{n=0}^{\infty} \frac{f^{(n)}(\frac{1}{2}r)}{n!} w^n$$

is greater than $\frac{1}{2}r$. This implies that there is a number $t > \frac{1}{2}r$ such that

$$\sum_{n=0}^{\infty} \frac{f^{(n)}(\frac{1}{2}r)}{n!} t^n \tag{10}$$

converges. On the other hand, by Theorem 16.5, f has a singularity s, and, by the definition of the term 'singularity' (§16.8), $|s| = r$. By Exercise 16.20, the power series

$$\sum_{n=0}^{\infty} \frac{f^{(n)}(\frac{1}{2}s)}{n!} w^n$$

has radius of convergence $\frac{1}{2}r$. Hence

$$\sum_{n=0}^{\infty} \frac{f^{(n)}(\frac{1}{2}s)}{n!} t^n \tag{11}$$

does not converge. Now

$$f(z) = \sum_{m=0}^{\infty} a_m z^m \quad (|z| < r).$$

Hence, by §14.2,

$$\left| f^{(n)}(\tfrac{1}{2}s) \right| = \left| \sum_{m=n}^{\infty} \frac{m!}{(m-n)!} a_m (\tfrac{1}{2}s)^{m-n} \right| \leqslant \sum_{m=n}^{\infty} \left| \frac{m!}{(m-n)!} a_m (\tfrac{1}{2}s)^{m-n} \right|$$

$$= \sum_{m=n}^{\infty} \frac{m!}{(m-n)!} a_m (\tfrac{1}{2}r)^{m-n} = f^{(n)}(\tfrac{1}{2}r) \quad (n = 0, 1, 2, \ldots).$$

From this and Exercise 2.1 it follows that the convergence of (10) implies that of (11). This is a contradiction, and so the theorem is proved.

For another proof see Landau (3), §17.

16.19. As indicated in the proof of Theorem 16.2, I shall now give an example of an analytic function f with an analytic sub-function g, such that g has an immediate continuation to a singularity of f.

Let f_1 and f be defined as in Exercise 16.16(i). Let g be the sub-function of f in the first quadrant of the plane. Let h be defined by $h(z) = 1/\{f_1(iz) - \tfrac{1}{2}\pi i - \log(-2+i)\}$. Then the point $-2+i$ is a singularity of f, h is an immediate continuation of g, and $h(-2+i)$ exists.

LAURENT'S THEOREM.
ISOLATED SINGULARITIES

17.1. By a *ring in the wider sense* I mean either (i) the set of the points between two concentric circles, or (ii) a disc without its centre, or (iii) the exterior of a circle (excluding the point ∞), or (iv) a set consisting of all finite points except one. In cases (i), (ii) and (iii), the *centre of the ring* is the centre of the circles or disc or circle involved; in case (iv) it is the exceptional point.

17.2. THEOREM 17.1. *Let*

$$0 < r_1 < |w - z_0| < r_2, \tag{1}$$

$$C_m = \mathscr{C}(t; z_0 + r_m e^{it}, 0, 2\pi) \quad (m = 1, 2), \tag{2}$$

and suppose that $f(z)$ is regular for $r_1 \leqslant |z - z_0| \leqslant r_2$. Then

$$2\pi i f(w) = \int_{C_2} \frac{f(z)}{z - w} \, dz - \int_{C_1} \frac{f(z)}{z - w} \, dz. \tag{3}$$

Proof. Let $g(z) = \{f(z) - f(w)\}/(z - w)$ where this exists, and $g(w) = f'(w)$. Then, by Theorems 13.7 and 6.3, $g(z)$ is regular for $r_1 \leqslant |z - z_0| \leqslant r_2$. Hence, by (2) and Theorem 12.4,

$$\int_{C_1} g(z) dz = \int_{C_2} g(z) dz. \tag{4}$$

Now $f(z)/(z - w) = g(z) + f(w)/(z - w)$ for all points z of C_1 and C_2. Hence, by (4) and Theorems 11.3 and 11.2,

$$\int_{C_2} \frac{f(z)}{z - w} \, dz - \int_{C_1} \frac{f(z)}{z - w} \, dz = f(w) \left\{ \int_{C_2} \frac{dz}{z - w} - \int_{C_1} \frac{dz}{z - w} \right\}. \tag{5}$$

It may be left to the reader to deduce from (1) and (2) that $w \in E(C_1)$ and $w \in I(C_2)$ (see §9.16). Hence, by Theorem 11.12,

$$\int_{C_1} \frac{dz}{z - w} = 0,$$

and, by Theorem 11.13 and Exercise 11.12,

$$\int_{C_2} \frac{dz}{z-w} = 2\pi i.$$

From these two equations and (5) we obtain the result stated.

17.3. THEOREM 17.2.   *Let the hypotheses of Theorem 17.1 hold, and let*

$$a_n = \frac{1}{2\pi i} \int_{C_m} f(z)(z-z_0)^{-n-1} dz \tag{6}$$

for every integer n, with $m=2$ or 1 according as $n \geqslant 0$ or $n < 0$. Then

$$f(w) = \sum_{n=-\infty}^{\infty} a_n(w-z_0)^n.$$

Proof.   By (1) and (2),

$$\frac{1}{z-w} = \sum_{n=0}^{\infty} \frac{(w-z_0)^n}{(z-z_0)^{n+1}} \quad (z \in |C_2|). \tag{7}$$

Now, by the corollary to Theorem 4.3, there is a number M such that $|f(z)| \leqslant M$ $(z \in |C_2|)$.   Hence

$$\left| f(z)(w-z_0)^n(z-z_0)^{-n-1} \right| \leqslant M|w-z_0|^n r_2^{-n-1} \quad (z \in |C_2|).$$

The right-hand side of this inequality is independent of z, and, by (1),

$$\sum_{n=0}^{\infty} M|w-z_0|^n r_2^{-n-1}$$

converges.   Hence

$$\sum_{n=0}^{\infty} f(z)(w-z_0)^n(z-z_0)^{-n-1}$$

converges uniformly on C_2.   Using this, (7), Theorems 14.1 and 11.2, and (6), we obtain

$$\int_{C_2} \frac{f(z)}{z-w}\, dz = \int_{C_2} \sum_{n=0}^{\infty} f(z)(w-z_0)^n (z-z_0)^{-n-1} dz$$

$$= \sum_{n=0}^{\infty} (w-z_0)^n \int_{C_2} f(z)(z-z_0)^{-n-1} dz$$

$$= 2\pi i \sum_{n=0}^{\infty} a_n(w-z_0)^n.$$

Similarly, since

$$\frac{1}{w-z} = \sum_{n=1}^{\infty} \frac{(z-z_0)^{n-1}}{(w-z_0)^n} = \sum_{n=-\infty}^{-1} (w-z_0)^n (z-z_0)^{-n-1} \quad (z \in |C_1|),$$

we obtain

$$-\int_{C_1} \frac{f(z)}{z-w}\, dz = 2\pi i \sum_{n=-\infty}^{-1} a_n(w-z_0)^n.$$

Hence the right-hand side of (3) is equal to

$$2\pi i \sum_{n=-\infty}^{\infty} a_n(w-z_0)^n.$$

From this and Theorem 17.1 we obtain the result stated.

17.4. The next theorem is due to Laurent.

THEOREM 17.3. *Let R be a ring in the wider sense, with centre z_0, and suppose the function f is regular in R. Then there are numbers $a_0, a_1, a_2, \ldots$ and $a_{-1}, a_{-2}, \ldots$, such that, for every point w of R, we have*

$$f(w) = \sum_{n=-\infty}^{\infty} a_n(w-z_0)^n.$$

Proof. No matter to which of the four types mentioned in §17.1 the ring R belongs, it has the following property: For every point w of R, there are numbers r_1, r_2, satisfying (1), such that the circles C_1, C_2 defined by (2) are contained in R.

Choose any positive number r so that the circle $C = \mathscr{C}(t; z_0 + re^{it}, 0, 2\pi)$ is contained in R, and let

$$a_n = \frac{1}{2\pi i} \int_C f(z)(z-z_0)^{-n-1} dz \qquad (8)$$

for every integer n.   Now let w be any point of R, and choose r_1, r_2, C_1 and C_2 as indicated in the first paragraph of this proof.   Then, by Theorem 12.4,

$$\int_C f(z)(z-z_0)^{-n-1}dz \;=\; \int_{C_m} f(z)(z-z_0)^{-n-1}dz \quad (m = 1, 2),$$

so that (6) follows from (8), and it is easily seen that all the other hypotheses of Theorem 17.2 are also satisfied.   The result therefore follows from that theorem.

The reader should be aware of the necessity to define a_n before choosing w.

A series like that in Theorem 17.3 is called a Laurent series.

17.5. THEOREM 17.4.   *Let R be a ring in the wider sense with centre z_0, C a circle with the same centre, contained in R and described in the positive sense, and let*

$$f(z) = \sum_{n=-\infty}^{\infty} a_n(z-z_0)^n \tag{9}$$

for every point z of R.   Then

$$a_m = \frac{1}{2\pi i} \int_C f(z)(z-z_0)^{-m-1}dz$$

for every integer m.

Proof.   By (9),

$$\int_C f(z)(z-z_0)^{-m-1}dz = \int_C \sum_{n=-\infty}^{\infty} a_n(z-z_0)^{n-m-1}dz. \tag{10}$$

Here we want to interchange integration and summation.   To justify this, we note that

$$\sum_{n=-\infty}^{\infty} b_n$$

is merely another notation for

$$\sum_{n=0}^{\infty} b_n + \sum_{n=1}^{\infty} b_{-n}.$$

Hence, by (10) and Theorems 11.3, 14.1 and 11.2,

$$\int_C f(z)(z-z_0)^{-m-1}dz$$

$$= \int_C \sum_{n=0}^{\infty} a_n(z-z_0)^{n-m-1}dz + \int_C \sum_{n=1}^{\infty} a_{-n}(z-z_0)^{-n-m-1}dz$$

$$= \sum_{n=0}^{\infty} a_n \int_C (z-z_0)^{n-m-1}dz + \sum_{n=1}^{\infty} a_{-n} \int_C (z-z_0)^{-n-m-1}dz$$

$$= \sum_{n=-\infty}^{\infty} a_n \int_C (z-z_0)^{n-m-1}dz, \tag{11}$$

provided that the two series

$$\sum_{n=0}^{\infty} a_n(z-z_0)^{n-m-1} \tag{12}$$

and

$$\sum_{n=1}^{\infty} a_{-n}(z-z_0)^{-n-m-1} \tag{13}$$

converge uniformly on C.

Now let the radius of C be r. Then there is a number z_1 such that $|z_1-z_0| > r$ and $z_1 \in R$. From this it follows that (9) holds with $z = z_1$, which implies that

$$\sum_{n=0}^{\infty} a_n(z_1-z_0)^n$$

converges. This, in turn, implies that there is a number c, independent of n, such that $|a_n(z_1-z_0)^n| \leqslant c$, $(n = 0, 1, 2, \ldots)$. Hence

$$|a_n(z-z_0)^{n-m-1}| \leqslant cr^{-m-1}(r/|z_1-z_0|)^n \quad (z \in |C|; \; n = 0, 1, 2, \ldots).$$

The right-hand side of this inequality is independent of z, and

$$\sum_{n=0}^{\infty} cr^{-m-1}(r/|z_1-z_0|)^n$$

converges. Hence (12) converges uniformly on C. To deal with (13), we proceed similarly, but use, instead of z_1, a number z_2 such that $|z_2-z_0| < r$ and $z_2 \in R$. This proves (11).

Now, by Exercise 11.3 and Theorem 11.9,

$$\int_C (z-z_0)^{n-m-1}dz = 2\pi i \quad \text{or} \quad 0$$

according as $n=m$ or $n \neq m$. The result therefore follows from (11).

17.6. Theorem 17.4 may be called the *uniqueness theorem for Laurent series*, as it shows that the numbers a_n of Theorem 17.3 are uniquely determined by f and R. The reader will now also easily see that, if R is of the second of the four types mentioned in §17.1, then these numbers are already uniquely determined by f and the *centre* of R. In this case (and only then) the corresponding Laurent series

$$\sum_{n=-\infty}^{\infty} a_n(z-z_0)^n \tag{14}$$

is called the Laurent expansion of $f(z)$ about z_0. Thus (14) is the Laurent expansion of $f(z)$ about z_0 if and only if there is a positive number r, such that the sum of (14) is equal to $f(z)$ for every number z for which $0 < |z-z_0| < r$. Similarly

$$\sum_{n=-\infty}^{\infty} a_n z^n \tag{15}$$

is called the Laurent expansion of $f(z)$ about ∞ if and only if there is a positive number r, such that the sum of (15) is equal to $f(z)$ for every number z for which $|z| > r$.

17.7. The next theorem is called *Cauchy's inequality for the coefficients of a Laurent series*.

THEOREM 17.5. *Let the hypotheses of Theorem 17.4 hold, let r be the radius of C, and let $|f(z)| \leqslant M$ for every point z of C. Then $|a_m| r^m \leqslant M$ for every integer m.*

This follows from Theorems 17.4 and 11.5.

17.8. A point z_0 is called an *isolated singularity* of a function f if and only if (i) there is a positive number r, such that $f(z)$ is regular for $0 < |z-z_0| < r$, and (ii) neither $f(z_0)$ nor $\lim_{z \to z_0} f(z)$ exists.

The point ∞ is called an isolated singularity of f if and only if the point 0 is an isolated singularity of the function g defined by $g(z) = f(1/z)$.

The point z_0 is called a *pole* of f if and only if (i) there is a positive number r, such that $f(z)$ is regular for $0 < |z - z_0| < r$, (ii) $f(z_0)$ does not exist, and (iii) $\lim_{z \to z_0} \{1/f(z)\} = 0$.

The point ∞ is called a pole of f if and only if the point 0 is a pole of the function g defined by $g(z) = f(1/z)$.

An *isolated essential singularity* is defined as an isolated singularity which is not a pole.

The function f is said to be *regular* at ∞ if and only if (i) there is a positive number r such that $f(z)$ is regular for $|z| > r$ (note that z cannot be ∞), and (ii) $\lim_{z \to 0} f(1/z)$ exists.

EXERCISES

17.1. Prove that, if f is an analytic function, then any isolated singularity of f, as defined here, is a singularity of f, as defined in §16.8.

17.2. Prove that any pole, as defined here, is an isolated singularity.

17.3. Prove that a function cannot be regular or have an isolated singularity at a limit point of the set of its isolated singularities.

17.4. Prove that a pole of f cannot be a limit point of the set of the zeros of f, but that an isolated singularity of f can.

17.5. Assuming that the Laurent expansion of $f(z)$ about z_0 is (14), and that $f(z_0)$ does not exist, prove that f has an isolated singularity at z_0 if and only if there is a negative integer n for which $a_n \neq 0$.

17.6. Assuming that the Laurent expansion of $f(z)$ about ∞ is (15), prove that f has an isolated singularity at ∞ if and only if there is a positive integer n for which $a_n \neq 0$.

17.9. If f is regular and has a zero at z_0, but is not identically 0 in any disc about z_0, then there is, by Theorem 14.2, at least one positive integer n for which $f^{(n)}(z_0) \neq 0$. The least such integer n is called the *order* (or *multiplicity*) of the zero.

Now suppose that f has a pole at z_0, and let $g(z) = 1/f(z)$ where this exists, and $g(z_0) = 0$. Then, by §17.8, g is fully continuous at z_0, and there is a disc D about z_0 such that f is regular, and $f(z) \neq 0$, at all points z of D other than z_0. Hence g is regular at all these points, and it follows from Theorem 13.8 that g is regular at z_0. Also g is not identically 0 in any disc about z_0; in fact, z_0 is the only zero of g in D. Thus the zero of g at z_0 has an order. The *order* of the pole of f at z_0 is now defined as the order of the zero of g at z_0.

If f has a pole at ∞, its order is defined as that of the pole at 0 of the function g defined by $g(z) = f(1/z)$.

17.10. THEOREM 17.6.   *Let f have a pole of order k at z_0, and suppose the Laurent expansion of f about z_0 is (14).   Then $a_{-k} \neq 0$, and $a_n = 0$ for every integer $n < -k$.*

Proof.   Let $g(z) = 1/f(z)$ where this exists, and $g(z_0) = 0$. Then, by §17.9, there is a disc D about z_0, such that g is regular in D, and f is regular, and $f(z) \neq 0$, at all points z of D other than z_0.   Hence, by Theorem 14.2,

$$g(z) = \sum_{n=0}^{\infty} \frac{g^{(n)}(z_0)}{n!}(z-z_0)^n \quad (z \in D).$$

Now, again by §17.9, g has a zero of order k at z_0.   This means that $g^{(n)}(z_0) = 0$, $(n = 0, 1, 2, \ldots, k-1)$ and $g^{(k)}(z_0) \neq 0$.   Hence

$$g(z) = \sum_{n=k}^{\infty} \frac{g^{(n)}(z_0)}{n!}(z-z_0)^n = (z-z_0)^k h(z) \quad (z \in D),$$

where

$$h(z) = \sum_{n=k}^{\infty} \frac{g^{(n)}(z_0)}{n!}(z-z_0)^{n-k}.$$

From this and the end of §14.2 it follows that h is regular in D. Also $h(z_0) = g^{(k)}(z_0)/k! \neq 0$, and

$$(z-z_0)^k h(z) f(z) = 1 \quad (z \in D, z \neq z_0). \tag{16}$$

Hence, by Theorem 6.3, $1/h(z)$ is regular in D.   From this and Theorem 14.2 it follows that there are numbers $b_0, b_1, b_2, \ldots$ such that

$$1/h(z) = \sum_{n=0}^{\infty} b_n(z-z_0)^n \quad (z \in D). \tag{17}$$

Hence, by (16),

$$f(z) = \sum_{n=0}^{\infty} b_n(z-z_0)^{n-k} = \sum_{n=-k}^{\infty} b_{n+k}(z-z_0)^n \quad (z \in D, z \neq z_0). \tag{18}$$

Now the Laurent expansion of $f(z)$ about z_0 is (14).   Hence, by (18) and §17.6, $a_n = 0$ $(n < -k)$ and $a_n = b_{n+k}(n \geqslant -k)$.   In particular, $a_{-k} = b_0$, so that, by (17), $a_{-k} = 1/h(z_0) \neq 0$.   This completes the proof.

EXERCISES

17.7. Assuming that $f(z_0)$ does not exist, and that the Laurent expansion of $f(z)$ about z_0 is (14), prove that (i) if k is a positive integer, $a_{-k} \neq 0$, and $a_n = 0$ for every integer $n < -k$, then f has a pole of order k at z_0; and (ii) f has an isolated essential singularity at z_0 if and only if there are infinitely many negative integers n for which $a_n \neq 0$.

17.8. Assuming that the Laurent expansion of $f(z)$ about ∞ is (15), and that k is a positive integer, prove that (i) f has a pole of order k at ∞ if and only if k is the greatest integer n for which $a_n \neq 0$; and (ii) f has an isolated essential singularity at ∞ if and only if there are infinitely many positive integers n for which $a_n \neq 0$.

17.11. The next theorem is due to Weierstrass.

THEOREM 17.7. *Let the function f have an isolated essential singularity at z_0, let $\epsilon > 0$, and let w be any complex number. Then there is a number z such that $|z - z_0| < \epsilon$ and $|f(z) - w| < \epsilon$.*

Proof. Suppose this is not so. Then $|f(z) - w| \geqslant \epsilon$ for every point z for which $|z - z_0| < \epsilon$ and $f(z)$ exists. Now there is a positive number r such that $f(z)$ is regular for $0 < |z - z_0| < r$. Hence

$$|f(z) - w| \geqslant \epsilon \quad (0 < |z - z_0| < r'), \tag{19}$$

where $r' = \min(r, \epsilon)$.

Now let

$$g(z) = 1/\{f(z) - w\}. \tag{20}$$

Then $g(z)$ is regular for $0 < |z - z_0| < r'$, and it follows from (19) that $|g(z)| \leqslant 1/\epsilon$, $(0 < |z - z_0| < r')$, which implies that

$$\lim_{z \to z_0} \{(z - z_0)g(z)\} = 0.$$

Hence, by Theorem 13.9, $\lim_{z \to z_0} g(z)$ exists. Let $\lim_{z \to z_0} g(z) = a$, and suppose, first, that $a \neq 0$. Then, by (20), $\lim_{z \to z_0} f(z) = 1/a + w$, which implies that this limit exists. Hence, by §17.8, z_0 is not an isolated singularity of f. This is a contradiction. Now suppose that $a = 0$, i.e.

$$\lim_{z \to z_0} g(z) = 0. \tag{21}$$

Then, for all points z distinct from z_0 but near enough to z_0, $1 + wg(z) \neq 0$, and hence, by (20), $1/f(z) = g(z)/\{1 + wg(z)\}$. From this and (21) it follows that $\lim_{z \to z_0} \{1/f(z)\} = 0$. Thus, by §17.8, z_0 is a pole of f, and therefore not an isolated essential singularity. This is again a contradiction, and so the theorem is proved.

EXERCISE

17.9. Assuming that f has an isolated essential singularity at ∞, prove that, for every positive number ϵ and every number w, there is a number z such that $|z| > 1/\epsilon$ and $|f(z) - w| < \epsilon$.

17.12. By a *simple* zero or pole, we mean a zero or pole of order 1. Similarly, in this connection, *double* means 'of order 2', and *multiple* means 'not simple'.

It is an accepted convention that zeros and poles are *counted according to their multiplicities*. This means that the phrase 'the number of zeros of f in S' is interpreted as 'the sum of the orders of the zeros of f in S', and the same applies to poles. This agrees with what was said about the zeros of a polynomial in §10.1.

'*Meromorphic* at a point' means 'either regular or having a pole at the point'. 'Meromorphic in S' means 'meromorphic at all points of S'. A *meromorphic function* is defined as a function which is meromorphic at all *finite* points.

17.13. The *principal part* of $f(z)$ about z_0 and the *residue* of f at z_0 exist only if there is a positive number r, such that $f(z)$ is regular for $0 < |z - z_0| < r$. If this condition is satisfied, and the Laurent expansion of $f(z)$ about z_0 is (14), then the said principal part and residue are

$$\sum_{n=-\infty}^{-1} a_n (z - z_0)^n$$

and a_{-1} respectively.

The principal part of $f(z)$ about ∞ exists only if there is a positive number r, such that $f(z)$ is regular for $|z| > r$. If this condition is satisfied, and the Laurent expansion of $f(z)$ about ∞ is (15), then the said principal part is

$$\sum_{n=1}^{\infty} a_n z^n.$$

EXERCISES

17.10. If $g(z)$ is the principal part of $f(z)$ about z_0, prove that g is regular at all points other than z_0, and that $\lim\limits_{z \to z_0} \{f(z) - g(z)\}$ exists.

17.11. If $g(z)$ is the principal part of $f(z)$ about ∞, prove that g is an integral function.

17.14. THEOREM 17.8. *Let C be a closed contour, z_0 a point which is not on C, and let the principal part of $f(z)$ about z_0 and the residue of f at z_0 be $g(z)$ and ρ respectively. Then*

$$\int_C g(z)dz = \rho i \chi(z_0, C).$$

Proof. Let the Laurent expansion of $f(z)$ be (14). Then

$$\rho = a_{-1}, \tag{22}$$

$$g(z) = \sum_{n=-\infty}^{-1} a_n(z-z_0)^n = \sum_{n=1}^{\infty} a_{-n}(z-z_0)^{-n} \quad (z \neq z_0), \tag{23}$$

and there is a positive number r, such that (9) holds for every number z for which $0 < |z - z_0| < r$, which implies that the series in (23) converge for every such number z. Now let d be the distance of z_0 from C, and $b = \frac{1}{2} \min(r, d)$. Then the last series in (23) converges, in particular, for $z = z_0 + b$, i.e.

$$\sum_{n=1}^{\infty} a_{-n} b^{-n}$$

converges. The terms of this series are therefore bounded. This means that there is a number M such that

$$|a_{-n}|b^{-n} \leqslant M \quad (n = 1, 2, 3, \ldots). \tag{24}$$

Also, for any point z of C, $|z - z_0| \geqslant d \geqslant 2b$, and hence, by (24), $|a_{-n}(z-z_0)^{-n}| \leqslant M \cdot 2^{-n}$, $(n = 1, 2, 3, \ldots)$. This shows that the last series in (23) converges uniformly on C. It therefore follows from (23) and Theorems 14.1 and 11.2 that

$$\int_C g(z)dz = \sum_{n=1}^{\infty} a_{-n} \int_C (z-z_0)^{-n}dz. \tag{25}$$

Now, by Theorems 11.12 and 11.9,

$$\int_C (z-z_0)^{-n}dz = \begin{cases} i\chi(z_0, C) & (n = 1) \\ 0 & (n = 2, 3, \ldots). \end{cases}$$

The result therefore follows from (25) and (22).

17.15. The next theorem is called the *theorem of residues*.

THEOREM 17.9.   *Let C be a Jordan contour, described in the positive sense, $z_1, z_2, \ldots, z_k$ (distinct) points within C, f a function regular at all other points within and on C, and r_m the residue of f at z_m $(m = 1, 2, \ldots, k)$.   Then*

$$\int_C f(z)dz = 2\pi i \sum_{m=1}^{k} r_m.$$

Proof.   Let the principal part of $f(z)$ about z_m be $g_m(z)$, and let the function g be defined by

$$g(z) = f(z) - \sum_{m=1}^{k} g_m(z). \qquad (26)$$

Then, by Exercise 17.10 and Theorem 6.3, g is regular at all points, other than $z_1, z_2, \ldots, z_k$, at which f is regular, and $\lim_{z \to z_n} g(z)$ exists for $n = 1, 2, \ldots, k$.   Let $h(z) = g(z)$ for every point z at which g is regular, and $h(z_n) = \lim_{z \to z_n} g(z)$, $(n = 1, 2, \ldots, k)$. Then h is fully continuous at $z_1, z_2, \ldots, z_k$, and regular at all other points within and on C.   From this and Theorem 13.8 it follows that h is regular also at $z_1, z_2, \ldots, z_k$.   Hence, by Theorem 12.9,

$$\int_C h(z)dz = 0. \qquad (27)$$

Now $g(z) = h(z)$ for every point z of C.   Hence, by (27),

$$\int_C g(z)dz = 0.$$

From this, (26), and Theorems 11.3 and 17.8 we obtain

$$\int_C f(z)dz = i \sum_{m=1}^{k} r_m \chi(z_m, C).$$

Now, by §9.23, $\chi(w, C) = 2\pi$ for every point w within C, and the result follows.

EXERCISES

17.12. If f has a zero of order k at z_0, prove that $\lim_{z \to z_0} \{(z - z_0)^{-k} f(z)\}$ exists and differs from 0.

17.13. If f has a pole of order k at z_0, prove that $\lim\limits_{z\to z_0}\{(z-z_0)^k f(z)\}$ exists and differs from 0.

17.14. If $c > 0$, show that, for any $z \neq 0$,

$$\exp\left(z + \frac{c^3}{2z^2}\right) = \sum_{n=-\infty}^{\infty} a_n z^n,$$

where

$$a_n = \frac{e^{-\frac{1}{2}c}}{2\pi c^n} \int_0^{2\pi} e^{c(\cos\theta + \cos^2\theta)} \cos\{c\sin\theta(1-\cos\theta) - n\theta\}d\theta.$$

[London, 1951.]

17.15. A function $f(z)$ is regular inside and on the circle $|z-a| = R$. Prove that, if x is any point inside the circle,

$$f(x) = f(a) + \frac{(x-a)}{1!}f'(a) + \frac{(x-a)^2}{2!}f''(a) + \ldots.$$

Prove that $1/[(z-1)(z-2)]$ can be expanded in the form

$$\sum_{n=0}^{\infty} c_n z^n$$

when $|z| < 1$, and show in any way that $c_n = 1 - 1/2^{n+1}$.

Find also the expansion of the function in the form

$$\sum_{n=0}^{\infty} c_n z^{-n}$$

when $|z| > 2$. [London, 1952.]

Notes. (i) The convention, adopted in this book (see §1.3, footnote), that x is to denote real numbers only, is to be disregarded here.

(ii) The first paragraph is slightly weaker and slightly easier than Theorem 14.2.

(iii) The remainder of the question is trivial, and there is no point in applying the first paragraph to it.

17.16. Show how an integral of the form

$$\int_0^{2\pi} f(\cos\theta, \sin\theta)d\theta,$$

where $f(\cos\theta, \sin\theta)$ is a rational function of $\cos\theta$ and $\sin\theta$, can be evaluated by contour integration.

[Hint: put $g(z) = f\{\frac{1}{2}(z+z^{-1}), -\frac{1}{2}i(z-z^{-1})\}z^{-1}$.]

A function $\phi(z)$ is regular for $|z| \leqslant 1$, and a is a real number such that $-1 < a < 1$. Show that

$$\int_0^{2\pi} \frac{\phi(e^{i\theta})}{1 - 2a\cos\theta + a^2}\, d\theta = \frac{2\pi}{1-a^2}\phi(a).$$

Deduce that, if n is a positive integer and $-1 < a < 1$,

$$\int_0^{2\pi} \frac{\cos n\theta}{1 - 2a \cos \theta + a^2}\, d\theta = \frac{2\pi a^n}{1 - a^2},$$

and, by taking $\phi(z) = \sin z$, show that

$$\int_0^{2\pi} \frac{\sin (\cos \theta) \cosh (\sin \theta)}{1 - 2a \cos \theta + a^2}\, d\theta = \frac{2\pi \sin a}{1 - a^2}.$$

[London, 1952.]

CHAPTER 18

MISCELLANEOUS THEOREMS

18.1. THEOREM 18.1. *Let the function f be regular and have a zero of order k at z_0. Then the function $f'(z)/f(z)$ has a simple pole with residue k at z_0.*

Proof. It follows from §17.9 and Theorem 14.2 that there is a positive number r such that

$$f(z) = \sum_{n=k}^{\infty} a_n(z-z_0)^n \quad (|z-z_0| < r),$$

where $a_n = f^{(n)}(z_0)/n!$ and $a_k \neq 0$. Let

$$g(z) = \sum_{n=k}^{\infty} a_n(z-z_0)^{n-k}.$$

Then

$$f(z) = (z-z_0)^k g(z) \quad (|z-z_0| < r), \tag{1}$$

g is regular at z_0, and $g(z_0) = a_k \neq 0$. Hence $g'(z)/g(z)$ is regular at z_0. From this it follows that there is a positive number $r' \leqslant r$ such that $g'(z)/g(z)$ is regular for $|z-z_0| < r'$. Hence, again by Theorem 14.2, there are numbers $b_0, b_1, b_2, \ldots$ such that

$$\frac{g'(z)}{g(z)} = \sum_{n=0}^{\infty} b_n(z-z_0)^n \quad (|z-z_0| < r').$$

From this and (1) it follows that

$$\frac{f'(z)}{f(z)} = \frac{k}{z-z_0} + \sum_{n=0}^{\infty} b_n(z-z_0)^n \quad (0 < |z-z_0| < r'),$$

which proves the theorem.

THEOREM 18.2. *Let the function f have a pole of order k at z_0. Then the function $f'(z)/f(z)$ has a simple pole with residue $-k$ at z_0.*

This can be deduced from Theorem 17.6 by an argument similar to the one just used. It can also be proved by applying Theorem 18.1 to the function g of the second paragraph of §17.9.

THEOREM 18.3. *Let C be a Jordan contour, and let the function f be meromorphic within and on C, and have no zeros on C. Then f has at most a finite number of zeros and poles within C.*

Proof. Suppose, if possible, that f has infinitely many poles within C, i.e. in $I(C)$. Then, since $I(C)$ is bounded, it follows from Theorem 3.3 that the set of these poles has a limit point z_0, say. Now, since $I'(C)$ is closed (see §9.16), $z_0 \in I'(C)$, so that f is meromorphic at z_0. This is a contradiction (see Exercise 17.3). Now suppose, if possible, that f has infinitely many zeros within C. Then the set of these zeros has a limit point z_0, say, and again $z_0 \in I'(C)$. Hence, by Exercise 17.4, f is regular at z_0, and $f(z_0) = 0$. Thus z_0 cannot be on C, and must, therefore, be within C. Let D be the greatest disc about z_0 which contains no point of C and no pole of f. Then f is regular in D, and there is, on the circumference of D, a point ζ which is either a point of C or a pole of f (or both). It follows that ζ is not a limit point of the set of the zeros of f. On the other hand, by Theorem 15.2, every point of D is a zero of f. Hence ζ is a limit point of that set. This is again a contradiction, and so the theorem is proved.

THEOREM 18.4. *Let C be a Jordan contour, described in the positive sense, and let the function f be meromorphic within and on C, and have neither zeros nor poles on C. Then*

$$\frac{1}{2\pi i} \int_C \frac{f'(z)}{f(z)} \, dz = n_1 - n_2,$$

where n_1 is the number of zeros and n_2 the number of poles of f within C.

Proof. Suppose f has zeros as well as poles within C. Let the former be the (distinct) points $z_1, z_2, \ldots, z_k$, and have orders $h_1, h_2, \ldots, h_k$ respectively, the latter the (distinct) points $w_1, w_2, \ldots, w_l$, with orders $m_1, m_2, \ldots, m_l$ respectively. Then $f'(z)/f(z)$ is regular at all points within and on C except those mentioned. Also, by Theorems 18.1 and 18.2, the residues of

$f'(z)/f(z)$ at z_j and w_j are h_j and $-m_j$ respectively. Hence, by Theorem 17.9,

$$\frac{1}{2\pi i} \int_C \frac{f'(z)}{f(z)} \, dz = \sum_{j=1}^{k} h_j - \sum_{j=1}^{l} m_j.$$

From this and §17.12 we obtain the result stated. A similar argument applies if f has no zeros or no poles within C.

18.2. THEOREM 18.5. *Let C be a Jordan contour, let the functions f and g be regular within and on C, and suppose that $|g(z)-f(z)| < |f(z)|+|g(z)|$ for every point z on C. Then f and g have the same number of zeros within C.*

Proof. We first note that neither $f(z)$ nor $g(z)$ can be 0 if $z \in |C|$. Thus, in virtue of Theorem 18.4, it is sufficient to prove that

$$\int_C \{g'(z)/g(z)-f'(z)/f(z)\}dz = 0. \tag{2}$$

Now $g(z)/f(z)$ is nowhere on C either 0 or real and negative, for this would imply that $|g(z)-f(z)| = |f(z)|+|g(z)|$. Hence $\log\{g(z)/f(z)\}$ is an indefinite integral on C of the integrand in (2). From this and Theorem 11.9 we obtain (2).

The weakened version of Theorem 18.5 obtained by omitting ' $+|g(z)|$ ' is called *Rouché's theorem*.

18.3. The next theorem is a slight refinement of the fundamental theorem of algebra (see §4.8), from which it can be deduced in an elementary way. It is, however, of some interest that it follows almost immediately from Rouché's theorem.

THEOREM 18.6. *Any polynomial of degree n has exactly n zeros.*

Proof. Let the polynomial be

$$g(z) = \sum_{m=0}^{n} a_m z^m.$$

Then $a_n \neq 0$ (see §10.1). Choose the positive number r so large that

$$\sum_{m=0}^{n-1} |a_m| r^{m-n} < |a_n|,$$

let C be the circle $|z| = r$ {i.e. $C \sim \mathscr{C}(t\,;\, re^{it},\, 0,\, 2\pi)$}, and apply Rouché's theorem with $f(z) = a_n z^n$.

18.4. Another almost immediate consequence of Rouché's theorem is the so-called *maximum modulus theorem*, though only in its weakest form. Here it is.

THEOREM 18.7. *Let the function h be regular within and on the Jordan contour C, and let*

$$|h(z)| \leqslant M \qquad (3)$$

for every point z on C. Then (3) *holds also for every point z within C.*

Proof. We have to show that, if $|w| > M$, then there is no point z within C such that $h(z) = w$, i.e. the function g defined by $g(z) = w - h(z)$ has no zero within C. This follows from Rouché's theorem with $f(z) = w$ for every point z.

18.5. The next theorem is called *Schwarz's lemma*.

THEOREM 18.8. *Let $r > 0$, let $f(z)$ be regular for $|z - z_0| \leqslant r$, and let $f(z_0) = 0$ and*

$$|f(z)| \leqslant M \qquad (|z - z_0| = r). \qquad (4)$$

Then $|f(z)| \leqslant Mr^{-1}|z - z_0|$, $(|z - z_0| < r)$.

Proof. Let $g(z) = f(z)/(z - z_0)$ where this exists, and $g(z_0) = f'(z_0)$. Then, by Theorems 6.3 and 13.7, $g(z)$ is regular for $|z - z_0| \leqslant r$. Also, by (4), $|g(z)| \leqslant M/r$, $(|z - z_0| = r)$. Hence, by Theorem 18.7, $|g(z)| \leqslant M/r$, $(|z - z_0| < r)$, and the result follows.

THEOREM 18.9. *Let $f(z)$ be regular for $|z| < 1$, and let $f(0) = 0$ and $|f(z)| \leqslant 1$, $(|z| < 1)$. Then $|f(z)| \leqslant |z|$, $(|z| < 1)$.*

Proof. Let w be any number such that $|w| < 1$. Then we have to prove that $|f(w)| \leqslant |w|$. Now let r be any number such that $|w| < r < 1$. Then $f(z)$ is regular for $|z| \leqslant r$, and $|f(z)| \leqslant 1$, $(|z| = r)$. Hence, by Theorem 18.8 (with $z_0 = 0$ and $M = 1$), $|f(z)| \leqslant r^{-1}|z|$ for every number z for which $|z| < r$. In particular, $|f(w)| \leqslant r^{-1}|w|$. Since this holds for every number r for which $|w| < r < 1$, it follows that $|f(w)| \leqslant |w|$, which was to be proved.

18.6. In dealing with a stronger form of the maximum modulus theorem, I shall use the phrases 'constant in **D**', which occurred already in Exercise 11.7, and 'locally constant at z_0', which means 'constant in some disc about z_0'.

A real function h of a complex variable is said to have a *maximum* at z_0 if and only if there is a disc D about z_0, such that $h(z) \leqslant h(z_0)$ for every point z of D. It follows that, if w is an *interior* point of the set S, and $h(z) \leqslant h(w)$ for every point z of S, then h has a maximum at w.

A *boundary point* of a closed set S is defined as a point of S which is not interior to S.

EXERCISE

18.1. The function f is regular, but not locally constant, at z_0, and k is the least natural number n for which $f^{(n)}(z_0) \neq 0$. Prove that there is a positive number r, such that

$$\left| f(z) - f(z_0) - \frac{f^{(k)}(z_0)}{k!} (z-z_0)^k \right| \leqslant \frac{|f^{(k)}(z_0)|}{2k!} |z-z_0|^k \quad (|z-z_0| \leqslant r).$$

Note. The existence of at least one such number n follows from Exercise 6.1 and Theorem 14.2.

18.7. THEOREM 18.10. *Let f be regular, but not locally constant, at z_0. Then $|f(z)|$ has not a maximum at z_0.*

Proof. Let D be any disc about z_0. Then we have to prove that there is a point z in D such that $|f(z)| > |f(z_0)|$.

Choose k and r in accordance with Exercise 18.1, and let $a = f^{(k)}(z_0)/(2k!)$. Then $a \neq 0$ and

$$\left| f(z) - f(z_0) - 2a(z-z_0)^k \right| \leqslant |a| |z-z_0|^k \quad (|z-z_0| \leqslant r),$$

so that

$$|f(z)| \geqslant |f(z_0) + 2a(z-z_0)^k| - |a| |z-z_0|^k \quad (|z-z_0| \leqslant r). \quad (5)$$

Now let r_1 be the radius of D, $b = \min (r, \frac{1}{2}r_1)$, $\theta = \{\mathrm{am}\, f(z_0) - \mathrm{am}\, a\}/k$ or 0 according as $f(z_0) \neq 0$ or $f(z_0) = 0$, and $z = z_0 + be^{i\theta}$. Then $z \in D$, $|z-z_0| = b \leqslant r$, and $|f(z_0) + 2a(z-z_0)^k| = |f(z_0)| + 2|a|b^k$, and hence, by (5), $|f(z)| \geqslant |f(z_0)| + |a|b^k > |f(z_0)|$. This completes the proof.

EXERCISE

18.2. Prove that, if the function f is regular, but not constant, in the domain D, then f cannot be locally constant at any point of D.

18.8. THEOREM 18.11. *Let S be a non-empty closed bounded set, and suppose that the function f is regular, but not constant, in a domain D containing S, and that $|f(z)| \leqslant M$ for every boundary point z of S. Then $|f(z)| < M$ for every interior point z of S.*

Proof. By Theorem 4.3, there is a point z_0 in S, such that

$$|f(z)| \leqslant |f(z_0)| \quad (z \in S). \tag{6}$$

Now let z_1 be any point of S such that

$$|f(z_1)| = |f(z_0)|, \tag{7}$$

and suppose, if possible, that z_1 is interior to S. Then, by (7), (6) and §18.6, $|f(z)|$ has a maximum at z_1. Now f is regular at z_1 and, by Exercise 18.2, not locally constant at z_1. This contradicts Theorem 18.10. Hence an interior point z_1 of S cannot satisfy (7). From this and (6) it follows that $|f(z)| < |f(z_0)|$ for any interior point z of S. Thus z_0 must be a boundary point of S, which implies that $|f(z_0)| \leqslant M$, and the result follows.

EXERCISE

18.3. Show that the hypotheses of Theorem 18.9 imply that $|f'(0)| \leqslant 1$.

THEOREM 18.12. *Let the hypotheses of Theorem 18.9 hold, and suppose that $|f'(0)| = 1$. Then $f(z) = f'(0)z$, $(|z| < 1)$.*

Proof. Let $g(z) = f(z)/z$, $(0 < |z| < 1)$ and $g(0) = f'(0)$. Then, by Theorems 6.3 and 13.7, g is regular in the unit disc. Also $|g(0)| = 1$, and, by Theorem 18.9, $|g(z)| \leqslant 1$, $(0 < |z| < 1)$. Thus $|g(z)|$ has a maximum at 0. From this and Theorem 18.10 and Exercise 18.2 it follows that g is constant in the unit disc. This means that, for every point z for which $|z| < 1$, we have $g(z) = g(0) = f'(0)$, and the result follows.

EXERCISE

18.4. Assuming that the hypotheses of Theorem 18.9 hold, and that there is a number z for which $0 < |z| < 1$ and $|f(z)| = |z|$, prove that $|f'(0)| = 1$.

18.9. **THEOREM 18.13.** *Let the hypotheses of Exercise 18.1 hold, and let $a = f^{(k)}(z_0)/(2k!)$. Then there is a positive number b, such that, for every number w for which $0 < |w - f(z_0)| < |a|b^k$, there are exactly k numbers z for which $|z - z_0| < b$ and $f(z) = w$.*

Proof. Choose r in accordance with Exercise 18.1. Then $|f(z) - f(z_0) - 2a(z - z_0)^k| \leqslant |a||z - z_0|^k$, $(|z - z_0| \leqslant r)$, which implies that $|f(z) - f(z_0)| \geqslant |a||z - z_0|^k$, $(|z - z_0| \leqslant r)$. By Exercise 6.1, there is a positive number r_1 such that $f(z)$ is regular for $|z-z_0| \leqslant r_1$, and it follows from Theorem 13.6 that $f'(z)$ is also regular for $|z-z_0| \leqslant r_1$. Also, by Exercise 11.7, $f'(z)$ is not identically 0 in any disc about z_0. Hence, by Theorem 15.2, z_0 is not a limit point of the set of the zeros of f'. This means that there is a positive number r_2, such that there is no number z for which $0 < |z-z_0| < r_2$ and $f'(z) = 0$. Let $b = \min(r, r_1, r_2)$. Then $f(z)$ is regular for $|z-z_0| \leqslant b$,

$$|f(z)-f(z_0)| \geqslant |a||z-z_0|^k \quad (|z-z_0| \leqslant b), \tag{8}$$

and

$$f'(z) \neq 0 \quad (0 < |z-z_0| < b). \tag{9}$$

Now let $C = \mathscr{C}(t; z_0 + be^{it}, 0, 2\pi)$. Then, by (8), $|f(z)-f(z_0)| \geqslant |a|b^k$, $(z \in |C|)$. Let w be any number such that $0 < |w-f(z_0)| < |a|b^k$, and let $F(z) = f(z)-f(z_0)$ and $G(z) = f(z)-w$. Then F and G are regular within and on C, and $|G(z)-F(z)| < |F(z)|$, $(z \in |C|)$. Hence, by Rouché's theorem (§18.2), F and G have the same number of zeros within C, the zeros being counted according to their multiplicities. In plain English, however, F has exactly one zero within C, namely at z_0. That it has no others follows from (8). The number k has been so defined as to be the order of the zero of F at z_0. Thus, in the conventional sense, F has exactly k zeros within C, and so has G. Now G has no zero at z_0, and, by (9), $G'(z) \neq 0$ at any other point z within C. Hence the said zeros of G are all of order 1, and so k is also the number of zeros of G within C in the ordinary sense. This proves the theorem.

The terms 'simple in S' and 'simple function' were defined in §7.5. It follows from Theorem 18.13 that, if $k > 1$, then f is not a simple function. Now $k > 1$ if (i) f is regular at z_0, (ii) f is not locally constant at z_0, and (iii) $f'(z_0) = 0$. If f is locally constant at z_0, then k does not exist, but in this case f is not a simple function anyhow. Thus we obtain the following

COROLLARY. *If f is a simple function, then $f'(z_0) \neq 0$ for any point z_0 at which f is regular.*

EXERCISES

18.5. If f and g are regular and have zeros of the same order at z_0, prove that $\lim_{z \to z_0} \{f(z)/g(z)\}$ exists and differs from 0.

18.6. If f and g are regular at z_0, $g(z_0) = 0$, and $g'(z_0) \neq 0$, prove that the residue of $f(z)/g(z)$ at z_0 is $f(z_0)/g'(z_0)$.

18.10. *Example.* Show how Cauchy's theorem may be applied to evaluate

$$\int_0^\infty \frac{\sqrt{t}\,dt}{1+t^2},$$

and find the value of this integral. [London, 1949.]

Solution. In what follows, all square roots are meant to have their principal values.

Let

$$f(z) = \sqrt{(-iz)}/(1+z^2). \qquad (10)$$

Here $\sqrt{(-iz)}$ is used instead of $\sqrt{z}$, because the latter is not regular at any point $z < 0$. Let

$$0 < a < 1 < b, \qquad (11)$$

let C_1 be the upper half of the circle $|z| = a$, described clockwise, C_2 the upper half of the circle $|z| = b$, described counterclockwise, and

$$C = \{-b,\, -a\} + C_1 + \{a,\, b\} + C_2. \qquad (12)$$

Then it is easily seen that C is a Jordan contour, described in the positive sense, that the point i is within C, and that f is regular at all other points within and on C. Also, by Exercise 18.6, the residue of f at i is $1/(2i)$. Hence, by the theorem of residues (Theorem 17.9),

$$\int_C f(z)dz = \pi. \qquad (13)$$

Let

$$J_m = \int_{C_m} f(z)dz. \qquad (14)$$

Then, by (12), (13) and Theorem 11.4,

$$\int_a^b \{f(t) + f(-t)\}dt = \pi - J_1 - J_2. \qquad (15)$$

On C_1, by (10) and (11), $|f(z)| \leqslant \sqrt{a}/(1-a^2)$, and the length of C_1 is πa. Hence, by (14) and Theorem 11.5, $|J_1| \leqslant \pi a^{3/2}/(1-a^2)$.

Similarly $|J_2| \leqslant \pi b^{3/2}/(b^2-1)$. These two inequalities hold for all numbers a, b which satisfy (11). Hence

$$\lim_{a \to 0+} J_1 = \lim_{b \to \infty} J_2 = 0.$$

From this and (15) it follows that

$$\int_0^\infty \{f(t)+f(-t)\} = \pi.$$

Now, by (10), $f(t)+f(-t) = \sqrt{(2t)}/(1+t^2)$, $(t \geqslant 0)$. Hence

$$\int_0^\infty \frac{\sqrt{t}\, dt}{1+t^2} = \frac{\pi}{\sqrt{2}}.$$

By 'Cauchy's theorem' the inventor of the question probably meant the theorem of residues.

EXERCISES

18.7. The function $f(z)$ is regular within and on the closed contour C and such that $|f(z)| > a$ on C, where a is some constant. Show that (i) within the contour C, $f(z)$ assumes every value b, where $|b| \leqslant a$, as many times as $f(z)$ vanishes, and (ii) if $f(z)$ has no zeros within C, then $|f(z)| > a$ throughout the interior of C. Give examples to illustrate both possibilities. [London, 1950.]

Note. The statement '$f(z)$ assumes the value b k times' means that the number of zeros of $f(z) - b$, counted according to their multiplicities (see §17.12), is k.

18.8. If f and g have poles of the same order at z_0, prove that $\lim_{z \to z_0} \{f(z)/g(z)\}$ exists and differs from 0.

18.11. *Example.* Prove that a function which is analytic for all z, including the point at infinity, must be a constant.

A function $\phi(z)$ has a simple pole at infinity, a pole of order 2 at $z = 1$, and is analytic at all other points. It has simple zeros at the points 2, 3, 4, and

$$z^{-1}\phi(z) \to 2 \quad \text{when} \quad |z| \to \infty. \tag{16}$$

Prove that there is only one such function $\phi(z)$, and find it. [London, 1951.]

Note. Here the word 'analytic' apparently means 'regular'.

Solution. Suppose the function f is regular at all points, including ∞. Then, by §17.8, $\lim_{z\to 0} f(1/z)$ exists. Let

$$\lim_{z\to 0} f(1/z) = a.$$

Then there is a positive number δ, such that, for every number z for which $0 < |z| < \delta$, we have $|f(1/z) - a| < 1$, which implies that

$$|f(1/z)| < |a| + 1 \quad (0 < |z| < \delta).$$

This is equivalent to

$$|f(z)| < |a| + 1 \quad (|z| > 1/\delta).$$

Now, by the corollary to Theorem 4.3, $f(z)$ is bounded for $|z| \leqslant 1/\delta$. Hence $f(z)$ is bounded in the whole plane. From this and Liouville's theorem (Theorem 14.7) it follows that $f(z)$ is a constant.

Let

$$f(z) = (z-1)^2 (z-2)^{-1} (z-3)^{-1} (z-4)^{-1} \phi(z) \qquad (17)$$

where this exists. Then it easily follows from Exercises 17.12 and 17.13 that the four limits

$$\lim_{z\to m} f(z) \quad (m = 1, 2, 3, 4)$$

exist. Let

$$f(m) = \lim_{z\to m} f(z) \quad (m = 1, 2, 3, 4).$$

Then it is trivial that f is regular at all finite points other than 1, 2, 3, 4, and it follows from Theorem 13.8 that f is regular also at these four points. Also, by (16) and (17), $f(z) \to 2$ when $|z| \to \infty$, which means that

$$\lim_{z\to 0} f(1/z) = 2. \qquad (18)$$

Hence, by §17.8, f is regular also at ∞. From this and the first part of the question it follows that $f(z)$ is a constant, and, by (18), this constant must be 2. Hence, by (17),

$$\phi(z) = 2(z-1)^{-2}(z-2)(z-3)(z-4).$$

The above argument shows that this is the only function ϕ which possibly has the required properties. That it actually has them is trivial.

CHAPTER 19

EXAMPLES OF THE USE OF CONTOUR INTEGRATION

19.1. Here is a list of things that can be done by means of contour integration:

Certain definite integrals can be evaluated. Certain series can be summed. An analogue to the resolution of a rational function into partial fractions can be obtained for meromorphic functions. Integral functions with infinitely many zeros can be expressed as infinite products, each factor of which has only one zero. For certain functions f and certain sets of points S, the number of zeros of f in S can be obtained.

19.2. *Example.* Evaluate

$$\int_0^\infty \frac{\cos x}{x^2+1}\, dx.$$

Solution. Let $r > 1$. Then

$$\int_0^r \frac{\cos x}{x^2+1}\, dx = \frac{1}{2} \int_0^r \frac{e^{ix}+e^{-ix}}{x^2+1}\, dx$$

$$= \frac{1}{2} \int_0^r \{f(x)+f(-x)\}dx = \frac{1}{2} \int_{-r}^r f(x)dx, \quad (1)$$

where $f(z) = e^{iz}/(z^2+1)$. Now let

$$K(r) = \mathscr{C}(t\,;re^{it},0,\pi) \tag{2}$$

and

$$C(r) = \{-r, r\}+K(r). \tag{3}$$

Then $C(r)$ is a Jordan contour, described in the positive sense, and f is regular within and on $C(r)$, except at the point i. Also, by Exercise 18.6, the residue of f at i is $1/(2ie)$. Hence, by the theorem of residues (Theorem 17.9),

$$\int_{C(r)} f(z)dz = \pi/e.$$

From this and (1) and (3) it follows that

$$\int_0^r \frac{\cos x}{x^2+1}\,dx = \frac{\pi}{2e} - \frac{1}{2}\,J(r), \tag{4}$$

where

$$J(r) = \int_{K(r)} f(z)dz.$$

Now, if z is on $K(r)$, then $|f(z)| = \exp(-\operatorname{im} z)/|z^2+1| \leqslant 1/(r^2-1)$, and the length of $K(r)$ is πr. Hence, by Theorem 11.5, $|J(r)| \leqslant \pi r/(r^2-1)$, which implies that $\lim_{r\to\infty} J(r) = 0$. From this and (4) we obtain

$$\int_0^\infty \frac{\cos x}{x^2+1}\,dx = \frac{\pi}{2e}.$$

19.3. *Example.*   Evaluate

$$\int_0^\infty \frac{\sin x}{x}\,dx.$$

Solution.   Let $r > 0$. Then

$$\int_0^r \frac{\sin x}{x}\,dx = -\frac{1}{2}\,i \int_0^r \frac{e^{ix}-e^{-ix}}{x}\,dx$$

$$= -\frac{1}{2}\,i \int_0^r \{f(x)+f(-x)\}dx = -\frac{1}{2}\,i \int_{-r}^r f(x)dx, \tag{5}$$

where $f(z) = (e^{iz}-1)/z$, $(z \neq 0)$ and $f(0) = i$. It is trivial that f is regular at all finite points other than 0, and follows from Theorem 13.7 that f is regular at 0. Hence, by (5), Theorem 12.6 and §11.5,

$$\int_0^r \frac{\sin x}{x}\,dx = \frac{1}{2}\,i \int_{K(r)} f(z)dz$$

$$= -\frac{1}{2}\,i \int_{K(r)} \frac{dz}{z} + \frac{1}{2}\,i \int_{K(r)} \frac{e^{iz}}{z}\,dz, \tag{6}$$

where $K(r)$ is defined by (2). Now, by Theorem 11.7,

$$\int_{K(r)} \frac{dz}{z} = \int_0^\pi i\,dt = i\pi, \tag{7}$$

and

$$\int_{K(r)} \frac{e^{iz}}{z} \, dz = i \int_0^\pi \exp \, (ire^{it})dt.$$

From this and Exercise 4.2 it follows that

$$\left| \int_{K(r)} \frac{e^{iz}}{z} \, dz \right| \leqslant \int_0^\pi |\exp \, (ire^{it})| dt = \int_0^\pi \exp \, (-r \sin t)dt$$

$$= 2 \int_0^{\frac{1}{2}\pi} \exp \, (-r \sin t)dt$$

$$\leqslant 2 \int_0^{\frac{1}{2}\pi} \exp \, (-2rt/\pi)dt < \pi/r,$$

which implies that

$$\lim_{r \to \infty} \int_{K(r)} \frac{e^{iz}}{z} \, dz = 0.$$

From this and (6) and (7) we obtain

$$\int_0^\infty \frac{\sin x}{x} \, dx = \tfrac{1}{2}\pi.$$

19.4. *Example.* Evaluate

$$\int_0^\infty \frac{x^{a-1}}{1+x} \, dx,$$

where $0 < a < 1$.

Note. This and similar problems are often solved by means of many-valued functions, though the theorems used in the solution are stated and proved only for one-valued functions. In what follows, only one-valued functions are used, and all powers are meant to have their principal values, as defined in §5.3.

Solution. For every positive number r, let $C(r)$ and $K(r)$ be the curves represented by $z = re^{it}$, $0 \leqslant t \leqslant \frac{3}{4}\pi$ and $z = re^{it}$, $\frac{3}{4}\pi \leqslant t \leqslant 2\pi$ respectively, and let $C^*(r)$ and $K^*(r)$ be '$C(r)$ and $K(r)$ described backward'. Let $0 < \rho < 1 < r$,

$$C = C(r) + \{re^{\frac{3}{4}\pi i}, \rho e^{\frac{3}{4}\pi i}\} + C^*(\rho) + \{\rho, r\} \tag{8}$$

(see Fig. 2),

$$K = K(r) + \{r, \rho\} + K^*(\rho) + \{\rho e^{\frac{3}{4}\pi i}, re^{\frac{3}{4}\pi i}\} \tag{9}$$

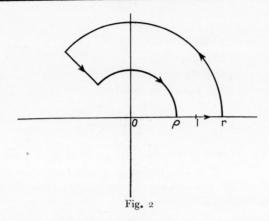

Fig. 2

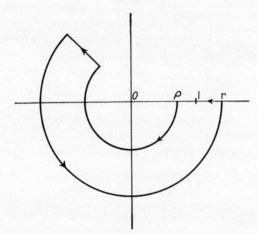

Fig. 3

(see Fig. 3),

$$f_1(z) = z^{a-1}/(1+z), \text{ and } f_2(z) = (iz)^{a-1} \exp\left\{\tfrac{3}{2}\pi i(a-1)\right\}/(1+z).$$

Then C and K are Jordan contours, f_1 is regular within and on C, and f_2 is regular within and on K, except at -1, where it has the residue $(-i)^{a-1} \exp\left\{\tfrac{3}{2}\pi i(a-1)\right\} = \exp\left\{\pi i(a-1)\right\} = -e^{\pi i a}$ (see Exercise 18.6).   Hence

$$\int_C f_1(z)dz + \int_K f_2(z)dz = -2\pi i e^{\pi i a}. \tag{10}$$

Also

$$\int_C f_1(z)dz = J_1 + J_2 + J_3 + J_4, \tag{11}$$

where J_1, J_2, J_3 and J_4 are the integrals of $f_1(z)$, taken along the four parts of C in the order in which they appear in (8), and

$$\int_K f_2(z)dz = J_5 + J_6 + J_7 + J_8, \tag{12}$$

where J_5, J_6, J_7 and J_8 are the integrals of $f_2(z)$, taken along the four parts of K in the order in which they appear in (9). Now, if z is on the line segment $\{re^{\frac{3}{2}\pi i}, \rho e^{\frac{3}{2}\pi i}\}$, then $f_2(z) = f_1(z)$, and if z is real and positive, then $f_2(z) = e^{2\pi i a} f_1(z)$. Hence $J_2 + J_8 = 0$ and

$$J_4 + J_6 = (1 - e^{2\pi i a}) \int_\rho^r f_1(z)dz.$$

From this and (10), (11) and (12) it follows that

$$(e^{2\pi i a} - 1) \int_\rho^r f_1(z)dz = 2\pi i e^{\pi i a} + J_1 + J_3 + J_5 + J_7. \tag{13}$$

Now, if $|z| = r$, then $|f_m(z)| \leqslant r^{a-1}/(r-1)$ $(m = 1, 2)$, and if $|z| = \rho$, then $|f_m(z)| \leqslant \rho^{a-1}/(1-\rho)$. Hence, by Theorem 11.5, $|J_1 + J_5| \leqslant 2\pi r^a/(r-1)$ and $|J_3 + J_7| \leqslant 2\pi \rho^a/(1-\rho)$, so that $\lim_{r \to \infty} (J_1 + J_5) = \lim_{\rho \to 0+} (J_3 + J_7) = 0$. From this and (13) it follows that

$$(e^{2\pi i a} - 1) \int_0^\infty f_1(z)dz = 2\pi i e^{\pi i a}.$$

Hence

$$\int_0^\infty \frac{x^{a-1}}{1+x} \, dx = \frac{2\pi i e^{\pi i a}}{e^{2\pi i a} - 1} = \pi \operatorname{cosec} \pi a.$$

19.5. *Example.* Evaluate

$$\sum_{n=-\infty}^{\infty} (w-n)^{-2}, \tag{14}$$

where w is not an integer.

Solution. Let $h(z) = (w-z)^{-2}\pi \cot \pi z$. Then h is regular at all finite points except w and the integers. Using Exercise

18.6 with $f(z) = (w-z)^{-2}\pi \cos \pi z$ and $g(z) = \sin \pi z$, we find that the residue of h at any integer n is $(w-n)^{-2}$. To find the residue of h at w, we note that there is a positive number r such that $\pi \cot \pi z$ is regular for $|z-w| < r$. From this and Theorem 14.2 it follows that

$$\pi \cot \pi z = \pi \cot \pi w - \pi^2 \operatorname{cosec}^2 \pi w \cdot (z-w)$$
$$+ \sum_{n=2}^{\infty} a_n (z-w)^n \quad (|z-w| < r),$$

where $a_2, a_3, a_4, \ldots$ are suitable numbers independent of z. Hence

$$h(z) = \pi \cot \pi w \cdot (z-w)^{-2} - \pi^2 \operatorname{cosec}^2 \pi w \cdot (z-w)^{-1}$$
$$+ \sum_{m=0}^{\infty} a_{m+2}(z-w)^m \quad (0 < |z-w| < r),$$

which implies that the residue of h at w is $-\pi^2 \operatorname{cosec}^2 \pi w$. Now let m be an integer, greater than $|w|$, and let C_m be the square with corners at $(m+\frac{1}{2})(\pm 1 \pm i)$, described in the positive sense. Then, by the theorem of residues (Theorem 17.9),

$$\frac{1}{2\pi i} \int_{C_m} h(z)dz = \sum_{n=-m}^{m} (w-n)^{-2} - \pi^2 \operatorname{cosec}^2 \pi w. \qquad (15)$$

It follows from Exercise 5.10 that, if z is on C_m, then $|\cot \pi z| \leqslant 2$. Hence

$$|h(z)| \leqslant 2\pi(|z| - |w|)^{-2} \leqslant 2\pi(m + \tfrac{1}{2} - |w|)^{-2} \quad (z \in |C_m|).$$

Now the length of C_m is $8(m+\frac{1}{2})$. Hence, by Theorem 11.5,

$$\left| \int_{C_m} h(z)dz \right| \leqslant 16\pi(m+\tfrac{1}{2})(m+\tfrac{1}{2} - |w|)^{-2}. \qquad (16)$$

Since it is trivial that (14) converges, it follows from (15) and (16) that the value of this sum is $\pi^2 \operatorname{cosec}^2 \pi w$.

EXERCISE

19.1. If z_0 is an isolated singularity of both f and g, and $\lim_{z \to z_0} \{f(z) - g(z)\}$ exists, prove that the residues of f and g at z_0 are equal.

12—C.N.F.

19.6. THEOREM 19.1. *Let the function f be regular at 0, let k be a positive integer, $w \neq 0$, and let $g(z) = w^k z^{-k}(w - z)^{-1} f(z)$ where this exists. Then the residue of g at 0 is*

$$\sum_{n=0}^{k-1} \frac{f^{(n)}(0)}{n!} \, w^n.$$

Proof. By Exercise 6.1 and Theorem 14.2, there is a positive number r such that

$$f(z) = \sum_{n=0}^{\infty} \frac{f^{(n)}(0)}{n!} z^n \quad (|z| < r),$$

and it is trivial that

$$(w - z)^{-1} = \sum_{n=0}^{\infty} w^{-n-1} z^n \quad (|z| < |w|).$$

Both these series converge absolutely for $|z| < r'$, where $r' = \min(r, |w|)$. Hence, by Theorem 2.10, with $a_n = f^{(n)}(0)z^n/n!$, $b_n = w^{-n-1}z^n$ and

$$c_n = z^n \sum_{m=0}^{n} \frac{f^{(m)}(0)}{m!} \, w^{m-n-1},$$

we have

$$f(z)(w - z)^{-1} = \sum_{n=0}^{\infty} c_n' w^{-n-1} z^n \quad (|z| < r'),$$

where

$$c_n = \sum_{m=0}^{n} \frac{f^{(m)}(0)}{m!} \, w^m.$$

Hence

$$g(z) = \sum_{n=0}^{\infty} c_n' w^{k-1-n} z^{n-k} \quad (0 < |z| < r'),$$

which implies that the residue of g at 0 is c_{k-1}', and the result follows.

19.7. THEOREM 19.2. *Let k be a positive integer, $w \neq 0$, $z_0 \neq 0$, and $w \neq z_0$. Let the function h have a pole at z_0, let $f(z)$ be the principal part of $h(z)$ about z_0, and let $G(z) = w^k z^{-k}(w - z)^{-1} h(z)$ where this exists. Then the residue of G at z_0 is*

$$f(w) - \sum_{n=0}^{k-1} \frac{f^{(n)}(0)}{n!} w^n.$$

Proof. Let the order of the pole of h at z_0 be q. Then there are numbers $b_1, b_2, \ldots, b_q$, such that

$$f(z) = \sum_{n=1}^{q} b_n(z-z_0)^{-n} \quad (z \neq z_0).$$

Hence

$$|f(z)| \leqslant M/(|z| - |z_0|) \quad (|z| \geqslant |z_0| + 1), \tag{17}$$

where

$$M = \sum_{n=1}^{q} |b_n|.$$

Let g be defined as in Theorem 19.1. Then g is regular at all points except 0, w and z_0. Let its residues at these three points be ρ_1, ρ_2 and ρ_3 respectively. Then, by Theorem 19.1,

$$\rho_1 = \sum_{n=0}^{k-1} \frac{f^{(n)}(0)}{n!} w^n, \tag{18}$$

and, by Exercise 18.6,

$$\rho_2 = -f(w). \tag{19}$$

Now let $r > 2 \max (|w|, |z_0| + 1)$, and let C be the circle $|z| = r$, described in the positive sense. Then, by (17),

$$|g(z)| \leqslant |w|^k r^{-k} (r - |w|)^{-1} M (r - |z_0|)^{-1} \leqslant 4Mr^{-2} \quad (z \in |C|).$$

Hence, by Theorem 11.5,

$$\left| \int_C g(z)dz \right| \leqslant 8\pi Mr^{-1}.$$

Also, by Theorem 17.9,

$$\int_C g(z)dz = 2\pi i(\rho_1 + \rho_2 + \rho_3).$$

Hence $|\rho_1 + \rho_2 + \rho_3| \leqslant 4Mr^{-1}$. Since this holds for every number $r > 2 \max (|w|, |z_0| + 1)$, we have $\rho_1 + \rho_2 + \rho_3 = 0$, and hence, by (18) and (19),

$$\rho_3 = f(w) - \sum_{n=0}^{k-1} \frac{f^{(n)}(0)}{n!} w^n.$$

It remains to show that ρ_3 is the residue of G at z_0. Now, by Exercise 17.10, $\lim\limits_{z\to z_0}\{h(z)-f(z)\}$ exists. From this and Exercise 19.1 it follows that the residue of G at z_0 is equal to that of g, i.e. to ρ_3. This completes the proof.

EXERCISES

19.2. Show that Theorem 19.2 remains true if the words 'a pole' are replaced by 'an isolated singularity'.

19.3. It is assumed that $w\neq z_0$, that h has an isolated singularity at z_0, and that $f(z)$ is the principal part of $h(z)$ about z_0. Prove that the residue of $h(z)/(w-z)$ at z_0 is $f(w)$.

19.8. The next theorem is somewhat complicated, and I do not advise the reader to learn it by heart.

THEOREM 19.3. *Let the following assumptions be made:*

(i) *h is a meromorphic function with infinitely many poles.*

(ii) *h is regular at 0.*

(iii) *C_n is a Jordan contour of length l_n.*

(iv) *$|C_n| \subset I(C_{n+1})$.*

(v) *$0 \in I(C_n)$.*

(vi) *The distance of the point 0 from C_n is d_n.*

(The last four assumptions are made for every natural number n.)

(vii) *$d_n\to\infty$ as $n\to\infty$.*

(viii) *k is a positive integer.*

(ix) *For every natural number n, h is regular on C_n, and*
$$|h(z)| \leqslant M_n \quad (z\in|C_n|).$$

(x) *$\lim\limits_{n\to\infty}(M_n d_n^{-k-1}l_n)=0.$*

(xi) *The only poles of h within C_1 are $z_{1,1}$, $z_{1,2}$, . . ., z_{1,m_1}, and if $n>1$, then the only poles of h in $I(C_n)\cap E(C_{n-1})$ are $z_{n,1}$, $z_{n,2}$, . . ., z_{n,m_n}.*

(xii) *The principal part of $h(z)$ about any pole $z_{n,m}$ is $f_{n,m}(z)$.*

Then, for any point w at which h is regular,

$$h(w) = \sum_{j=0}^{k-1}\frac{h^{(j)}(0)}{j!}\,w^j + \sum_{n=1}^{\infty}\sum_{m=1}^{m_n}\left\{f_{n,m}(w) - \sum_{j=0}^{k-1}\frac{f_{n,m}^{(j)}(0)}{j!}\,w^j\right\}.$$

Proof. We may assume, without loss of generality, that all the contours C_n are described in the positive sense. The result is trivial for $w=0$. So let w be any point, other than 0, at which h is regular, and let G be defined as in Theorem 19.2. Let ν be a natural number such that

$$d_\nu > 2|w|. \tag{20}$$

This is so, by assumption (vii), if ν is large enough. Then, by assumptions (v), (vi), (iv) and (xi) {and the first parts of (i) and (ix)}, the points 0, w, and $z_{n,m}$, $(n=1, 2, \ldots, \nu;$ $m=1, 2, \ldots, m_n)$ are within C_ν, and G is regular at all other points within and on C_ν. Hence, by Theorem 17.9,

$$\frac{1}{2\pi i}\int_{C_\nu} G(z)dz = r_0 + r + \sum_{n=1}^{\nu} \sum_{m=1}^{m_n} r_{n,m}, \tag{21}$$

where r_0, r and $r_{n,m}$ are the residues of G at 0, w and $z_{n,m}$ respectively.

Now, by assumption (vi), $|z| \geqslant d_\nu$, $(z \in |C_\nu|)$. Hence, by (20), assumption (ix), and the definition of G, $|G(z)| \leqslant 2|w|^k d_\nu^{-k-1} M_\nu$, $(z \in |C_\nu|)$, and hence, by Theorem 11.5 and assumption (iii),

$$\left| \int_{C_\nu} G(z)dz \right| \leqslant 2|w|^k M_\nu d_\nu^{-k-1} l_\nu.$$

Since this holds for every large enough ν, it follows from (21) and assumption (x) that

$$-r = r_0 + \sum_{n=1}^{\infty} \sum_{m=1}^{m_n} r_{n,m}. \tag{22}$$

By Exercise 18.6, $r = -h(w)$. By Theorem 19.1 and assumption (ii),

$$r_0 = \sum_{n=0}^{k-1} \frac{h^{(n)}(0)}{n!} w^n.$$

By Theorem 19.2 and assumption (xii),

$$r_{n,m} = f_{n,m}(w) - \sum_{j=0}^{k-1} \frac{f_{n,m}^{(j)}(0)}{j!} w^j.$$

The result therefore follows from (22).

EXERCISES

19.4. Show that Theorem 19.3 remains true if assumption (v) is omitted.

19.5. Show that Theorem 19.3 remains true if assumptions (ii), (v) and (viii) are omitted, k replaced by 0 in assumption (x), and the formula at the end of the theorem replaced by

$$h(w) = \sum_{n=1}^{\infty} \sum_{m=1}^{m_n} f_{n,m}(w).$$

19.9. *Example.* Prove that, if w is not an integer, then

$$\pi \cot \pi w = \frac{1}{w} + \sum_{n=1}^{\infty} \left(\frac{1}{w-n} + \frac{1}{w+n} \right).$$

Solution. It follows from Theorem 18.1, with $f(z) = \sin \pi z$, that $\pi \cot \pi z$ has a simple pole with residue 1 at the point 0. This means that the principal part of $\pi \cot \pi z$ about 0 is $1/z$. From this and Exercise 17.10 it follows that $\lim_{z \to 0} (\pi \cot \pi z - 1/z)$ exists. Let the function h be defined as follows:

$$h(z) = \pi \cot \pi z - 1/z \quad \text{if } z \text{ is not an integer,} \qquad h(0) = \lim_{z \to 0} h(z)$$

(the existence of this limit has just been proved), and $h(z)$ does not exist if z is an integer other than 0. Then $h(-z) = -h(z)$ for any number z that is not an integer, and it is trivial that the existence of $\lim_{z \to 0} h(z)$ implies that this limit is equal to $\lim_{z \to 0} h(-z)$. Hence

$$h(0) = \tfrac{1}{2} \lim_{z \to 0} h(z) + \tfrac{1}{2} \lim_{z \to 0} h(-z) = \tfrac{1}{2} \lim_{z \to 0} \{h(z) + h(-z)\} = 0.$$

Also, by Theorem 13.8, h is regular at 0, and it is trivial that h is meromorphic at all other finite points, and that it has poles at all integers other than 0. For any natural number n let

$$C_n = \{(n + \tfrac{1}{2})(-1-i), (n + \tfrac{1}{2})(1-i), (n + \tfrac{1}{2})(1+i),$$
$$(n + \tfrac{1}{2})(-1+i), (n + \tfrac{1}{2})(-1-i)\},$$

$d_n = n + \tfrac{1}{2}$, $l_n = 8n + 4$, $M_n = 8$, $m_n = 2$, $z_{n,1} = n$, $z_{n,2} = -n$, $f_{n,1}(z) = 1/(z-n)$, and $f_{n,2}(z) = 1/(z+n)$. Let $k = 1$. Then it is trivial that all the assumptions of Theorem 19.3 are satisfied, except the second part of assumption (ix), and this follows from Exercise 5.10.   Hence, by that theorem, if w is not an integer, then

$$h(w) = h(0) + \sum_{n=1}^{\infty} \sum_{m=1}^{2} \{f_{n,m}(w) - f_{n,m}(0)\} = \sum_{n=1}^{\infty} \left(\frac{1}{w-n} + \frac{1}{w+n} \right),$$

which implies the result stated.

EXERCISES

19.6. Deduce the results of §19.5 and §19.9 from each other.

19.7. Prove that, if w is not an integer, then

$$\pi \operatorname{cosec} \pi w = \sum_{n=-\infty}^{\infty} (-1)^n (w-n)^{-1}.$$

19.8. Explain why the formula

$$\pi \cot \pi w = \sum_{n=-\infty}^{\infty} (w-n)^{-1}$$

is not true for any number w.

19.9. Prove that, if

$$\sum_{n=1}^{\infty} z_n = s, \quad \text{then} \quad \prod_{n=1}^{\infty} e^{z_n} = e^s.$$

19.10. THEOREM 19.4.   *Let D be a domain, and suppose that the functions $f, f_1, f_2, \ldots$ are regular and have no zeros in D, that*

$$\frac{f'(z)}{f(z)} = \sum_{n=1}^{\infty} \frac{f_n'(z)}{f_n(z)} \tag{23}$$

for every point z of D, that the last series converges uniformly in every bounded sub-set of D, and that

$$f(z) = \prod_{n=1}^{\infty} f_n(z) \tag{24}$$

for one point z of D.   Then (24) holds for every point z of D.

Proof.   By hypothesis, there is a point z_0 in D, such that (24) holds for $z = z_0$, i.e.

$$f(z_0) = \prod_{n=1}^{\infty} f_n(z_0). \tag{25}$$

Now let w be any point of D. Then there is a broken line C, contained in D, leading from z_0 to w. By Theorems 11.11 and 13.5,

$$\exp \int_C \frac{f'(z)}{f(z)}\, dz = \frac{f(w)}{f(z_0)} \tag{26}$$

and

$$\exp \int_C \frac{f_n'(z)}{f_n(z)}\, dz = \frac{f_n(w)}{f_n(z_0)}. \tag{27}$$

Also, by hypothesis, the series on the right-hand side of (23) converges uniformly on C. Hence, by (23) and Theorem 14.1,

$$\int_C \frac{f'(z)}{f(z)}\, dz = \sum_{n=1}^\infty \int_C \frac{f_n'(z)}{f_n(z)}\, dz.$$

From this and Exercise 19.9 it follows that

$$\exp \int_C \frac{f'(z)}{f(z)}\, dz = \prod_{n=1}^\infty \exp \int_C \frac{f_n'(z)}{f_n(z)}\, dz.$$

Hence, by (26) and (27),

$$\frac{f(w)}{f(z_0)} = \prod_{n=1}^\infty \frac{f_n(w)}{f_n(z_0)}.$$

and hence, by (25),

$$f(w) = f(z_0) \prod_{n=1}^\infty \frac{f_n(w)}{f_n(z_0)} = \prod_{n=1}^\infty \left\{ f_n(z_0) \frac{f_n(w)}{f_n(z_0)} \right\} = \prod_{n=1}^\infty f_n(w),$$

which proves the theorem.

19.11. *Example.* Prove that

$$\sin \pi z = \pi z \prod_{n=1}^\infty \left(1 - \frac{z^2}{n^2} \right). \tag{28}$$

Solution. Let $f(z) = (\sin \pi z)/(\pi z)$, $(z \neq 0)$ and $f(0) = 1$. Then (28) is equivalent to

$$f(z) = \prod_{n=1}^\infty \left(1 - \frac{z^2}{n^2} \right). \tag{29}$$

Now let the set D consist of 0 and those numbers which are not integers, and let $f_n(z) = 1 - z^2/n^2$, $(n = 1, 2, \ldots)$. Then D is a domain, it follows from §19.9 that (23) holds for every point z of D other than $z = 0$, and it is trivial that the series in (23) converges uniformly in every bounded sub-set of D, that $f_1, f_2, \ldots$ are regular and have no zeros in D, and that f has no zeros in D, and is regular at all points of D other than 0. It is easily seen that f is regular also at 0, and that $f'(0) = 0$. Hence (23) holds also for $z = 0$, and it is trivial that (24) holds for $z = 0$. Thus all the hypotheses of Theorem 19.4 are satisfied, and it follows from that theorem that (24) holds for every number z that is not an integer. This means that (29) holds for every such number z, and it is trivial that (29) holds when z is an integer. This completes the proof.

19.12. *Example.* Prove Stirling's formula

$$\lim_{n \to \infty} (n!e^n n^{-n-\frac{1}{2}}) = \sqrt{(2\pi)}. \tag{30}$$

Solution. For every natural number n, let

$$a_n = \log (n!e^n n^{-n-\frac{1}{2}}). \tag{31}$$

Then

$$a_n = (n+\tfrac{1}{2})\{\log (n+\tfrac{1}{2}) - \log n\} - \tfrac{1}{2} + \sum_{m=1}^{n} \log m - \int_0^{n+\frac{1}{2}} \log x\, dx. \tag{32}$$

Using the identity

$$\int_0^{n+\frac{1}{2}} f(x)dx = \int_0^{\frac{1}{2}} [f(x) + \sum_{m=1}^{n} \{f(m+x) + f(m-x)\}]dx$$

with $f(x) = \log x$, we obtain

$$\int_0^{n+\frac{1}{2}} \log x\, dx - \sum_{m=1}^{n} \log m = \int_0^{\frac{1}{2}} \left\{\log x + \sum_{m=1}^{n} \log \left(1 - \frac{x^2}{m^2}\right)\right\}dx,$$

and

$$\sum_{m=1}^{\infty} \log \left(1 - \frac{x^2}{m^2}\right)$$

converges uniformly for $0 \leqslant x \leqslant \frac{1}{2}$. Hence, by (28),

$$\lim_{n \to \infty} \left(\int_0^{n+\frac{1}{2}} \log x\, dx - \sum_{m=1}^{n} \log m\right) = \int_0^{\frac{1}{2}} \left\{\log x + \sum_{m=1}^{\infty} \log\left(1 - \frac{x^2}{m^2}\right)\right\}dx$$

$$= \int_0^{\frac{1}{2}} \log \sin \pi x\, dx - \tfrac{1}{2} \log \pi. \tag{33}$$

Using the identity

$$\int_0^{\frac{1}{2}} \{f(2x) - \tfrac{1}{2}f(\tfrac{1}{2}+x) - \tfrac{1}{2}f(\tfrac{1}{2}-x)\}dx = 0$$

with $f(x) = \log \sin \pi x$, which implies that $f(x) = f(2x) - \tfrac{1}{2}f(\tfrac{1}{2}+x) - \tfrac{1}{2}f(\tfrac{1}{2}-x) - \log 2$, we obtain

$$\int_0^{\frac{1}{2}} \log \sin \pi x \, dx = -\tfrac{1}{2}\log 2.$$

From this and (32) and (33) it follows that $\lim_{n\to\infty} a_n = \tfrac{1}{2}\log(2\pi)$, which, together with (31), proves (30).

19.13. *Example.* Find the number of zeros of the polynomial $f(z) = z^4 + z + 1$ in the set S of those points z for which $-1 < \operatorname{re} z < 0$ and $0 < \operatorname{im} z < 1$.

Solution. The set S is the interior of the square with sides $C_1 = \{-1, 0\}, C_2 = \{0, i\}, C_3 = \{i, -1+i\}, C_4 = \{-1+i, -1\}$. Let $\operatorname{re} z = x$, $\operatorname{im} z = y$.

If $z \in |C_1|$, then $f(z) > 0$. If $z \in |C_2|$, then $z = iy$ and $\operatorname{im} f(z) = y$. If $z \in |C_3|$, then $z = x+i$, $-1 \leqslant x \leqslant 0$, and hence $\operatorname{im} f(z) = 4x^3 - 4x + 1 > 0$. If $z \in |C_4|$, then $z = -1+iy$, $0 \leqslant y \leqslant 1$, and

$$\operatorname{im} f(-1+iy) = y(4y^2 - 3). \tag{34}$$

Hence the only points z of $C_1 + C_2 + C_3 + C_4$, for which $f(z)$ is real, are the points of C_1, for which $f(z) > 0$, and the point $-1 + \tfrac{1}{2}i\sqrt{3}$, for which $f(z) < 0$. The broken lines $C_5 = \{i, -1+i, -1+\tfrac{1}{2}i\}$ and $C_6 = \{-1+\tfrac{1}{2}i, -1, 0, i\}$, for which

$$C_5 + C_6 = C_3 + C_4 + C_1 + C_2, \tag{35}$$

therefore have the properties that $f(z)$ is nowhere on C_5 positive or 0, and nowhere on C_6 negative or 0. Thus $\log\{-f(z)\}$ and $\log f(z)$ are indefinite integrals of $f'(z)/f(z)$ on C_5 and C_6 respectively. From this and Theorem 11.8 it follows that

$$\int_{C_5} \frac{f'(z)}{f(z)} \, dz = \log\{-f(-1+\tfrac{1}{2}i)\} - \log\{-f(i)\} \tag{36}$$

and

$$\int_{C_6} \frac{f'(z)}{f(z)} \, dz = \log f(i) - \log f(-1+\tfrac{1}{2}i). \tag{37}$$

Let n be the number of zeros in question. By (35) and Exercise 9.36, $S = I(C_5 + C_6)$. Hence, by Theorem 18.4,

$$2\pi i n = \int_{C_5+C_6} \frac{f'(z)}{f(z)}\,dz.$$

From this, Theorem 11.4, (36) and (37) it follows that

$$2\pi i n = \log\{-f(-1+\tfrac{1}{2}i)\} - \log f(-1+\tfrac{1}{2}i)$$
$$+ \log f(i) - \log\{-f(i)\}. \quad (38)$$

Now $\operatorname{im} f(i) > 0$, and, by (34), $\operatorname{im} f(-1+\tfrac{1}{2}i) < 0$. Hence, by (38) and Exercise 5.13, $n = 1$.

EXERCISES

19.10. If $\alpha \geqslant 0$ and $\Gamma(R)$ denotes the semi-circular path in the upper half-plane on $(-R, +R)$ as diameter, show that

$$\lim_{R\to\infty} \int_{\Gamma(R)} \frac{e^{i\alpha z}}{z^2}\,dz = 0.$$

Deduce the value of the limit when $\Gamma(R)$ is replaced by the semi-circular path in the lower half-plane on the same diameter.

Prove that

$$\int_0^\infty \left(\frac{\sin x}{x}\right)^2 dx = \frac{\pi}{2}.$$

[London, 1950.]

[Hint: if the said path in the lower half-plane is $C(R)$, and both paths are described counter-clockwise, then, by Theorem 11.18 with $f(z) = -z$,

$$\int_{\Gamma(R)} \frac{e^{-2iz}}{z^2}\,dz = -\int_{C(R)} \frac{e^{2iz}}{z^2}\,dz\Big].$$

19.11. Evaluate by contour integration the integral

$$\int_0^\infty \frac{\cos x}{(b^2+x^2)^2}\,dx \quad (b > 0).$$

[London, 1951.]

19.14. *Example.* Show that the roots of the equation

$$z^5 - 11z^2 + 13 = 0 \quad\quad (39)$$

all lie between the circles $|z| = 1$ and $|z| = 3$.

Find how many roots lie to the right of the imaginary axis. [London, 1951.]

Solution. It is trivial that, if $|z| \leqslant 1$, then $|z^5 - 11z^2| < 13$, which is incompatible with (39). Hence the equation cannot have any roots on or inside the first circle.

Let

$$f(z) = z^5 - 11z^2 + 13, \qquad g(z) = z^{-5}f(z). \qquad (40)$$

Then

$$|g(z) - 1| = |-11z^{-3} + 13z^{-5}| \leqslant 11 \times 3^{-3} + 13 \times 3^{-5} < 1$$
$$(|z| \geqslant 3). \quad (41)$$

Hence

$$\mathrm{re}\, g(z) > 0 \quad (|z| \geqslant 3), \qquad (42)$$

and hence, by (40),

$$f(z) \neq 0 \quad (|z| \geqslant 3). \qquad (43)$$

This means that (39) has no roots on or outside the second circle. Thus all the roots lie between the two circles.

Let N be the number of roots of (39), i.e. the number of zeros of f, in the right-hand half-plane. Then, since f has no zeros on or outside the second circle, N is also the number of zeros of f inside the Jordan contour

$$C = \Gamma + \{3i, -3i\}, \qquad (44)$$

where Γ is the right-hand half of the circle $|z| = 3$, described counter-clockwise, i.e. from $-3i$ to $3i$. It is easily seen that C is described in the positive sense. Hence, by Theorem 18.4,

$$2\pi i N = \int_C \frac{f'(z)}{f(z)}\, dz, \qquad (45)$$

provided that f has no zeros on C.

Now it follows from (43) that f has no zeros on Γ. As for zeros on $\{3i, -3i\}$, we have, by (40),

$$\mathrm{re}\, f(iy) = 11y^2 + 13 > 0, \qquad (46)$$

which shows that there are none. Thus f has no zeros on C, and (45) holds.

Now, by (40),

$$\frac{f'(z)}{f(z)} = \frac{5}{z} + \frac{g'(z)}{g(z)}$$

whenever $zf(z) \neq 0$.   Hence, by (45), (44) and Theorems 11.4, 11.3 and 11.2,

$$2\pi i N = 5 \int_\Gamma \frac{dz}{z} + \int_\Gamma \frac{g'(z)}{g(z)}\, dz + \int_{\{3i,\,-3i\}} \frac{f'(z)}{f(z)}\, dz. \qquad (47)$$

It is trivial that

$$\int_\Gamma \frac{dz}{z} = \pi i. \qquad (48)$$

By (42), $g(z)$ is not 0 or negative for any point z of Γ.   Hence, by Exercise 11.8(i),

$$\int_\Gamma \frac{g'(z)}{g(z)}\, dz = \log g(3i) - \log g(-3i). \qquad (49)$$

Similarly, by (46) and Exercise 11.8(i),

$$\int_{\{3i,\,-3i\}} \frac{f'(z)}{f(z)}\, dz = \log f(-3i) - \log f(3i). \qquad (50)$$

By (47), (48), (49) and (50),

$$2\pi i N = 5\pi i + \log g(3i) - \log f(3i) + \log f(-3i) - \log g(-3i),$$

and, on equating imaginary parts,

$$2\pi N = 5\pi + \operatorname{am} g(3i) - \operatorname{am} f(3i) + \operatorname{am} f(-3i) - \operatorname{am} g(-3i). \qquad (51)$$

Now, by (40), $f(3i) = 3^5 ig(3i)$.   Also, by (42), $\operatorname{re} g(3i) > 0$. Hence, by Exercise 1.1(i),

$$\operatorname{am} f(3i) = \operatorname{am} \{ig(3i)\} = \operatorname{am} i + \operatorname{am} g(3i) = \tfrac{1}{2}\pi + \operatorname{am} g(3i). \qquad (52)$$

Similarly

$$\operatorname{am} f(-3i) = -\tfrac{1}{2}\pi + \operatorname{am} g(-3i). \qquad (53)$$

By (51), (52) and (53), $N = 2$.

EXERCISES

19.12. If $m > 0$ and Γ denotes the semi-circle in the upper half-plane on $(-R, +R)$ as diameter, and if $f(z)$ is regular in the upper half-plane except at a finite number of poles, while $f(z) \to 0$ uniformly on Γ as $R \to \infty$, prove that

$$\int_{\Gamma} e^{miz} f(z) dz \to 0$$

as $R \to \infty$. [London, 1952.]

Note. The regularity of f is irrelevant. In fact, f need not even be fully continuous anywhere. It is, for instance, sufficient that f should be continuous on Γ whenever R is large enough.

19.13. Prove that

$$\int_0^{\infty} \frac{\cos \pi x}{1 + x^2 + x^4} \, dx = \frac{\pi}{2} \exp\left(-\tfrac{1}{2}\pi\sqrt{3}\right).$$

[London, 1952.]

Note. It would be clumsy to apply the result of Exercise 19.12 to this question.

19.14. By integrating $\cot \pi z / (z^2 + 1)$ round a suitable contour, prove that

$$1 + 2 \sum_{n=1}^{\infty} \frac{1}{n^2 + 1} = \pi \coth \pi.$$

[London, 1952.]

CHAPTER 20

CONFORMAL TRANSFORMATIONS

20.1. A transformation

$$w = f(z) \tag{1}$$

(see §7.1), in so far as it transforms a set S, is said to be smooth if and only if, in the notation of §6.1, the four derivatives $\partial u/\partial x$, $\partial u/\partial y$, $\partial v/\partial x$, $\partial v/\partial y$, considered as functions of (x, y), are continuous at all points of S.

20.2. Before defining the term 'conformal transformation', I have to explain what is meant by a 'signed angle'. If we denote the half-lines from z_0 through z_1 and z_2 (see §9.18) by H_1 and H_2 respectively, then the angle, in the Euclidean sense, between H_1 and H_2 is $|\text{am} \{(z_2 - z_0)/(z_1 - z_0)\}|$, but the *signed angle* between H_1 and H_2 is am $\{(z_2 - z_0)/(z_1 - z_0)\}$. Thus, in general, the signed angle between H_1 and H_2 is minus that between H_2 and H_1.

20.3. The term 'conformal' means, essentially, 'leaving signed angles unchanged'. Since, however, a transformation (even a smooth one) does not usually transform half-lines into half-lines, we have to use the word 'angle' in a more general sense than was done in the last section.

Let the curve C be represented by

$$z = g(t), \quad a \leqslant t \leqslant b. \tag{2}$$

If $g(t) \neq g(a)$, then the half-line from $g(a)$ through $g(t)$ is also the half-line from $g(a)$ through

$$g(a) + \{g(t) - g(a)\}/|g(t) - g(a)|.$$

If

$$\lim_{t \to a+} \frac{g(t) - g(a)}{|g(t) - g(a)|} = l,$$

I call the half-line from $g(a)$ through $g(a) + l$ the *initial half-tangent* of C. If this limit does not exist, I say that C has no initial half-tangent. *The signed angle between two curves with the same first point* is defined as the signed angle between their initial half-tangents.

20.4. The *right-hand derivative* $f'_+(a)$ is defined by the equation

$$f'_+(a) = \lim_{x \to a+} \frac{f(x) - f(a)}{x - a}$$

(see §4.3).

EXERCISE

20.1. Prove that, if $g'_+(a)$ exists and differs from 0, then

$$\lim_{t \to a+} \frac{g(t) - g(a)}{|g(t) - g(a)|} = \frac{g'_+(a)}{|g'_+(a)|}.$$

20.5. A *conformal transformation* is defined as a smooth one-one transformation of an open set S, which conserves every signed angle (as defined in §20.3) between curves contained in S.

20.6. THEOREM 20.1. *Let T be an open set, and let the function f be regular and simple in T. Then the transformation of T given by $w = f(z)$ is conformal.*

Proof. It follows from Theorems 13.5 and 6.1 that the transformation is smooth, and it is one-one by hypothesis. Now let z_0 be any point of T, and let C_1 and C_2 be any curves, contained in T, starting at z_0, and having initial half-tangents. For $m = 1$ and $m = 2$, let $C_m = \mathscr{C}(g_m, a_m, b_m)$. Then, by §11.12, the transformation $w = f(z)$ transforms C_m into

$$\Gamma_m = \mathscr{C}[t; f\{g_m(t)\}, a_m, b_m],$$

and we have to prove that the signed angle between Γ_1 and Γ_2 is equal to that between C_1 and C_2.

By §20.3, the initial half-tangent of C_m is the half-line from z_0 through $z_0 + l_m$, where

$$l_m = \lim_{t \to a_m+} \frac{g_m(t) - z_0}{|g_m(t) - z_0|}. \tag{3}$$

Let α be the signed angle between C_1 and C_2. Then, by §20.3 and §20.2,

$$\alpha = \mathrm{am}\ (l_2/l_1). \tag{4}$$

Now

$$\lim_{z \to z_0} \frac{f(z) - f(z_0)}{z - z_0} = f'(z_0).$$

Also, since the right-hand side of (3) exists, there is a positive number δ such that, for every number t in $(a_m, a_m + \delta)$, we have $g_m(t) \neq z_0$; and $g_m(t) \to z_0$ as $t \to a_m+$. Hence

$$\lim_{t \to a_m+} \frac{f\{g_m(t)\} - f(z_0)}{g_m(t) - z_0} = f'(z_0), \tag{5}$$

which implies that

$$\lim_{t \to a_m+} \frac{|f\{g_m(t)\} - f(z_0)|}{|g_m(t) - z_0|} = |f'(z_0)|. \tag{6}$$

Now, by the corollary to Theorem 18.13 (applied to the sub-function of f in T), $f'(z_0) \neq 0$. From this and (5), (6) and (3) it follows that

$$\lim_{t \to a_m+} \frac{f\{g_m(t)\} - f(z_0)}{|f\{g_m(t)\} - f(z_0)|} = \frac{f'(z_0)}{|f'(z_0)|} l_m = \lambda_m,$$

say, so that $\lambda_2/\lambda_1 = l_2/l_1$. By an argument similar to that which led to (4), the signed angle between Γ_1 and Γ_2 is equal to am (λ_2/λ_1), and the result follows.

20.7. THEOREM 20.2. *Let T be an open set, and let the transformation of T given by $w = f(z)$ be conformal. Then f is regular in T.*

Proof. I note that, by hypothesis, $\partial u/\partial x$, $\partial u/\partial y$, $\partial v/\partial x$ and $\partial v/\partial y$ are continuous. Thus, if the Cauchy-Riemann equations hold at all points of T, it follows from Theorem 6.2 and §6.3 that f is regular in T. It is, therefore, sufficient to prove that the Cauchy-Riemann equations hold at all points of T.

Now let $z_0 = x_0 + iy_0$ be any point of T. Then, since T is open, there is a disc about z_0 contained in T. Let r be a positive number less than the radius of that disc. Then the three line segments $C_m = \{z_0, z_0 + re^{\frac{1}{4}m\pi i}\}$, $(m = 0, 1, 2)$ are contained in T, and the signed angle between C_0 and C_m is $\frac{1}{4}m\pi$. The transformation $w = f(z)$ transforms C_m into the curve Γ_m represented by $w = g_m(t)$, $0 \leqslant t \leqslant r$, where $g_m(t) = f(z_0 + te^{\frac{1}{4}m\pi i})$, which implies that re $g_m(t)$ and im $g_m(t)$ are the values of u

13—C.N.F.

and v respectively, corresponding to $x = x_0 + t \cos \frac{1}{4}m\pi$ and $y = y_0 + t \sin \frac{1}{4}m\pi$. From this and the well-known formula for differentiating a function of two functions (Hardy, §157) it follows that

$$g'_m(t) = (\partial u/\partial x) \cos \tfrac{1}{4}m\pi + (\partial u/\partial y) \sin \tfrac{1}{4}m\pi$$
$$+ i\{(\partial v/\partial x) \cos \tfrac{1}{4}m\pi + (\partial v/\partial y) \sin \tfrac{1}{4}m\pi\},$$

where g'_m is a derivative relative to the real axis (see §4.5). In particular,

$$'_m 0) = u_1 \cos \tfrac{1}{4}m\pi + u_2 \sin \tfrac{1}{4}m\pi + i(v_1 \cos \tfrac{1}{4}m\pi + v_2 \sin \tfrac{1}{4}m\pi), \tag{7}$$

where u_1, u_2, v_1, v_2 are the values of $\partial u/\partial x$, $\partial u/\partial y$, $\partial v/\partial x$, $\partial v/\partial y$ respectively at the point z_0. Formula (7) means that

$$g'_0(0) = u_1 + iv_1, \tag{8}$$

$$\sqrt{2} \cdot g'_1(0) = u_1 + u_2 + i(v_1 + v_2) \tag{9}$$

and

$$g'_2(0) = u_2 + iv_2. \tag{10}$$

Let

$$\lambda_m = \lim_{t\to 0+} \frac{g_m(t) - f(z_0)}{|g_m(t) - f(z_0)|},$$

and suppose that $\lambda_0 = 1$. There is no loss of generality in this, for we may replace $f(z)$ by $\lambda_0^{-1}f(z)$. Then the signed angle between Γ_0 and Γ_m is am λ_m. Hence, by hypothesis,

$$\text{am } \lambda_m = \tfrac{1}{4}\pi m \quad (m = 0, 1, 2). \tag{11}$$

Now, by Exercise 20.1, $\lambda_m = g'_m(0)/|g'_m(0)|$ if $g'_m(0) \neq 0$. Hence, by (11), im $g'_0(0) = 0$, re $g'_1(0) = $ im $g'_1(0)$ and re $g'_2(0) = 0$. From this and (8), (10) and (9) it follows that $v_1 = 0 = -u_2$ and $u_1 + u_2 = v_1 + v_2$. Thus the Cauchy-Riemann equations hold at z_0. This completes the proof.

20.8. THEOREM 20.3. *Let S be a sub-set of the region of existence of f, z_0 an interior point of S, and suppose that f is regular, but not locally constant, at z_0. Then $f(z_0)$ is an interior point of $f(S)$.*

Proof. Let us assume that S is the region of existence of f. (There is no loss of generality in this, for we may replace f by its sub-function in S.) Then $w \in f(S)$ if and only if there is a number z for which $f(z) = w$. Choose k, a and b in accordance with Theorem 18.13, and let D be the disc with centre $f(z_0)$ and radius $|a|b^k$. Then, by Theorem 18.13, every point of D, other than $f(z_0)$, is a point of $f(S)$. Since it is trivial that $f(z_0)$ is also in $f(S)$, it follows that $D \subset f(S)$, which proves the result stated.

THEOREM 20.4. *Suppose the function f is regular in the open set S, and not locally constant at any point of S. Then $f(S)$ is open.*

This follows immediately from Theorem 20.3 and §7.1 and §3.4.

20.9. THEOREM 20.5. *Suppose the function f is regular, but not constant, in the domain D. Then $f(D)$ is a domain.*

Proof. By Exercise 18.2 and Theorem 20.4, $f(D)$ is open, and it is obvious that $f(D)$ is not empty. Thus, in virtue of Exercise 9.25, it is sufficient to prove that every pair of points of $f(D)$ can be joined by a curve contained in $f(D)$.

Let w_1 and w_2 be any two points of $f(D)$. Then there are points z_1, z_2 in D, such that $w_1 = f(z_1)$ and $w_2 = f(z_2)$. By §9.17, there is a broken line C, contained in D, leading from z_1 to z_2. Now $f(C)$ (see §11.12) is a curve, contained in $f(D)$, leading from w_1 to w_2. This completes the proof.

20.10. THEOREM 20.6. *Let f be a simple analytic function with region of existence D, and let g be the inverse function of f. Then g is fully continuous at every point of $f(D)$.*

Proof. Let w_0 be any point of $f(D)$, and let $g(w_0) = z_0$. Then $z_0 \in D$, and $f(z_0) = w_0$. By §16.2, D is a domain. Hence z_0 is interior to D, which means that there is a disc D_0 about z_0, such that $D_0 \subset D$. Let the radius of D_0 be r.

Now let ϵ be any positive number, $\epsilon_1 = \min(\epsilon, r)$, and let S be the disc with centre z_0 and radius ϵ_1. Then the hypotheses of Theorem 20.3 are satisfied, and it follows from that theorem that w_0 is interior to $f(S)$. This means that there is a disc T about w_0, such that $T \subset f(S)$. Let the radius of T be δ.

Now let w be any number such that $|w - w_0| < \delta$. Then $w \in T$, and hence $w \in f(S)$. This is equivalent to $g(w) \in S$, i.e.

to $|g(w)-g(w_0)|<\epsilon_1$, which implies that $|g(w)-g(w_0)|<\epsilon$. Thus, for every positive number ϵ, there is a positive number δ, such that, for every number w for which $|w-w_0|<\delta$, we have $|g(w)-g(w_0)|<\epsilon$. This means that g is fully continuous at w_0.

EXERCISE

20.2. It is assumed that $\delta>0$, $\lim_{w\to w_0} g(w)=z_0$ and $\lim_{z\to z_0} h(z)=l$, and that $g(w)\neq z_0$ for every number w for which $0<|w-w_0|<\delta$. Prove that $\lim_{w\to w_0} h\{g(w)\}=l$.

20.11. THEOREM 20.7.   *On the hypotheses of Theorem 20.6, g is fully differentiable at every point w of $f(D)$, and $g'(w)=1/f'\{g(w)\}$.*

Proof. Let w_0 be any point of $f(D)$, $g(w_0)=z_0$, and let h be defined by $h(z)=\{f(z)-f(z_0)\}/(z-z_0)$. Then $\lim_{z\to z_0} h(z)=f'(z_0)$. Also, by Theorem 20.6, $\lim_{w\to w_0} g(w)=z_0$. Now, by Theorem 20.5, w_0 is interior to $f(D)$. Hence there is a positive number δ, such that, for every number w for which $0<|w-w_0|<\delta$, we have $w\in f(D)$, which implies that $g(w)$ exists. We cannot have $g(w)=z_0$ for any such number w, since this would imply $w=f(z_0)=w_0$. Hence the hypotheses of Exercise 20.2 are satisfied with $l=f'(z_0)$, and hence

$$\lim_{w\to w_0} h\{g(w)\}=f'(z_0). \qquad (12)$$

Now, for every point w of $f(D)$ other than w_0, and in particular for every point w for which $0<|w-w_0|<\delta$, we have

$$h\{g(w)\} = \frac{f\{g(w)\}-f(z_0)}{g(w)-z_0} = \frac{w-w_0}{g(w)-g(w_0)}.$$

Hence, by (12),

$$\lim_{w\to w_0} \frac{w-w_0}{g(w)-g(w_0)} = f'(z_0).$$

Now, by the corollary to Theorem 18.13, $f'(z_0)\neq 0$. Hence

$$\lim_{w\to w_0} \frac{g(w)-g(w_0)}{w-w_0} = \frac{1}{f'(z_0)},$$

which means that g is fully differentiable at w_0, and $g'(w_0)$ $= 1/f'\{g(w_0)\}$.   This proves the theorem.

THEOREM 20.8.   *The inverse function of any simple analytic function is an analytic function.*

This follows immediately from §16.2 and Theorems 20.5 and 20.7.

*20.12. THEOREM 20.9.   *Let D be a simply connected domain, and let the function f be regular and simple in D. Then $f(D)$ is a simply connected domain.*

Proof.   By Theorem 20.5, $f(D)$ is a domain.   Hence, by §9.17, it is sufficient to prove that, if a simple polygon Π is contained in $f(D)$, then the interior of Π is also contained in $f(D)$.

Let Π, then, be any simple polygon, contained in $f(D)$, and let w_0 be any point of $I(\Pi)$.   Then, by Theorem 11.12,

$$\text{im} \int_\Pi \frac{dw}{w - w_0} = \chi(w_0, \Pi),$$

and hence, by §9.16,

$$\int_\Pi \frac{dw}{w - w_0} \neq 0. \tag{13}$$

Now let g be the inverse function of the sub-function of f in D. Then, by Theorem 20.8, Exercise 11.11 and §11.2, $g(\Pi)$ is a smooth curve.   Let $g(\Pi) = C$.   Then $\Pi = f(C)$, and hence, by Theorem 11.18,

$$\int_\Pi \frac{dw}{w - w_0} = \int_C \frac{f'(z)}{f(z) - w_0} \, dz. \tag{14}$$

Suppose, if possible, that w_0 is not in $f(D)$.   This means that $f(z) \neq w_0$ for any point z of D.   Hence the function $f'(z)/\{f(z) - w_0\}$ is regular in D; and it is trivial that C is a closed contour, contained in D.   It therefore follows from Theorem 12.15 that

$$\int_C \frac{f'(z)}{f(z) - w_0} \, dz = 0.$$

This is inconsistent with (13) and (14), and so it is proved that $w_0 \in f(D)$.   Since this holds for every point w_0 of $I(\Pi)$, we have $I(\Pi) \subset f(D)$, which completes the proof of the theorem.

20.13. I say that an open set S is *conformally equivalent* to an open set T if and only if S can be transformed conformally into T, i.e. (see §§20.5–20.7) if and only if there is a function f, regular and simple in S, such that $f(S) = T$.

It may be left to the reader to show that this equivalence is reflexive, symmetrical and transitive (see §9.2).

A theorem of Riemann, which is outside the scope of this book, states that every simply connected domain, other than the whole plane, is conformally equivalent to the unit disc. On the other hand, the whole plane has not this property, and no set other than a simply connected domain has it. The former follows from Liouville's theorem (Theorem 14.7), the latter from Theorem 20.9.

20.14. THEOREM 20.10. *Let U be the unit disc, and suppose that the function f is regular and simple in U, and that $f(U) = U$, $f(0) = 0$ and $f'(0) > 0$. Then $f(z) = z$ for every point z of U.*

Proof. Let g be the inverse function of the sub-function of f in U. Then, by Exercise 18.3 and Theorem 20.7, $|f'(0)| \leqslant 1$, $|g'(0)| \leqslant 1$, and $g'(0) = 1/f'(0)$. Since $f'(0) > 0$, it follows that $f'(0) = 1$. From this and Theorem 18.12 we obtain the result stated.

20.15. THEOREM 20.11. *Let the domain D be conformally equivalent to the unit disc U, and let $z_0 \in D$ and $-\pi < \theta \leqslant \pi$. Then there is one and only one simple analytic function f with region of existence D, such that $f(D) = U$, $f(z_0) = 0$ and $\operatorname{am} f'(z_0) = \theta$.*

Proof. By hypothesis, there is a function f_0, regular and simple in D, such that $f_0(D) = U$. This implies that $f_0(z_0) \in U$, i.e.

$$|f_0(z_0)| < 1. \tag{15}$$

Let f_1 be the sub-function of f_0 in D, and let the functions g and f_2 be defined by

$$g(w) = \frac{w - f_0(z_0)}{\overline{f_0(z_0)}w - 1},$$

where $\overline{f_0(z_0)}$ is the conjugate complex number to $f_0(z_0)$, and $f_2(z) = g\{f_1(z)\}$. Then, by (15) and Theorem 8.6, $g(U) = U$, and it is trivial that g is regular and simple in U. It easily follows that f_2 is a simple analytic function with region of existence D. Also

$$f_2(D) = g\{f_1(D)\} = g\{f_0(D)\} = g(U) = U,$$

and

$$f_2(z_0) = g\{f_1(z_0)\} = g\{f_0(z_0)\} = 0.$$

Now let the function f be defined by $f(z) = \exp\{i\theta - i \text{ am } f_2'(z_0)\}$ $\cdot f_2(z)$, noting that the existence of $\text{am } f_2'(z_0)$ follows from the corollary to Theorem 18.13. Then f has all the properties mentioned in the theorem.

Now suppose the function f_3 also has all these properties. Then we have to prove that $f_3(z) = f(z)$ for every point z of D.

Let h be the inverse function of f, and let the function ϕ be defined by $\phi(w) = f_3\{h(w)\}$. Then $h(U) = D$,

$$\phi(U) = f_3\{h(U)\} = f_3(D) = U, \qquad \phi(0) = f_3\{h(0)\} = f_3(z_0) = 0,$$
$$(16)$$

and, by Theorems 4.1 and 20.7,

$$\phi'(0) = f_3'\{h(0)\}h'(0) = f_3'(z_0)/f'(z_0). \qquad (17)$$

Since $\text{am } f'(z_0) = \theta = \text{am } f_3'(z_0)$, it follows from (17) that $\phi'(0) > 0$. Hence, by (16) and Theorem 20.10, $\phi(w) = w$ for every point w of U. It follows that, for every point z of D, $\phi\{f(z)\} = f(z)$, and hence $f_3(z) = f_3[h\{f(z)\}] = \phi\{f(z)\} = f(z)$, which was to be proved.

20.16. *Example.* The function $f(z)$ is regular within the domain D and is such that its derivative $f'(z)$ does not vanish in D. Prove that the transformation $w = f(z)$ transforms D conformally into a domain in the w-plane. [London, 1949.]

Solution. It follows from Theorem 20.5 that $f(D)$ is a domain, i.e. that the transformation $w = f(z)$ transforms D into a domain.

In the terminology of this example, which differs in this respect from the terminology of this book, a conformal transformation need not be one-one. Therefore we need only show that the transformation in question has the other properties mentioned in §20.5. This can be proved in the same way as Theorem 20.1, except that the reference to the corollary to Theorem 18.13 is now irrelevant.

20.17. *Example.* Show that the transformation $w = z^2$ maps the region $\mathscr{I}z > 0$ conformally on the w-plane, cut along the positive real axis. Find the region in the w-plane corresponding to the interior of the circle $|z - i| = 1$, and the region in the z-plane corresponding to the infinite half-strip $\mathscr{R}w > 0$, $0 < \mathscr{I}w < 1$. [London, 1949.]

Solution. The symbols '$\mathscr{I}$' and '$\mathscr{R}$' mean 'im' and 're' respectively. For the conformality see §20.16. To prove that the transformation maps the upper half-plane on the plane cut along the positive real axis, one can use the method of §7.4.

For the next part of the question, let the required region be T. Then, by §7.1, $w \in T$ if and only if there is a point z such that

$$|z - i| < 1 \tag{18}$$

and

$$w = z^2. \tag{19}$$

Now the point $z = i\sqrt{(-w)}$, where the square root has its principal value, certainly satisfies (19). Hence, if

$$\left| i\sqrt{(-w)} - i \right| < 1,$$

i.e. if

$$\left| \sqrt{(-w)} - 1 \right| < 1, \tag{20}$$

then $w \in T$. Conversely, if (19) is satisfied, then either $z = i\sqrt{(-w)}$ or $z = -i\sqrt{(-w)}$. But the latter point is not in the upper half-plane, and therefore cannot satisfy (18). Thus (19) and (18) imply (20). It follows that (20) and $w \in T$ are equivalent, i.e. T is the set of those points w for which (20) holds.

Now, if $w = 0$, then (20) does not hold, and am $(-w)$ does not exist; and if $w \neq 0$, then $\sqrt{(-w)} = \sqrt{|w|}\, e^{\frac{1}{2}i\,\text{am}\,(-w)}$. Hence (20) is equivalent to

$$\left| \sqrt{|w|}\, e^{\frac{1}{2}i\,\text{am}\,(-w)} - 1 \right| < 1,$$

i.e.

$$\left\{ \sqrt{|w|}\, e^{\frac{1}{2}i\,\text{am}\,(-w)} - 1 \right\}\left\{ \sqrt{|w|}\, e^{-\frac{1}{2}i\,\text{am}\,(-w)} - 1 \right\} < 1,$$

i.e.

$$|w| - 2\sqrt{|w|} \cos\left\{ \tfrac{1}{2}\,\text{am}\,(-w) \right\} < 0,$$

i.e.
$$\sqrt{|w|} \; < \; 2 \cos \{ \tfrac{1}{2} \text{ am } (-w) \},$$
i.e.
$$|w| \; < \; 2(1 - \cos \text{ am } w).$$

This means that T is the interior of the curve whose equation in polar coordinates is usually given in the form

$$r \; = \; 2(1 - \cos \theta).$$

The region in the z-plane corresponding to the infinite half-strip re $w > 0$, $0 < \text{im } w < 1$ is the set of those points z for which re $(z^2) > 0$ and $0 < \text{im } (z^2) < 1$, i.e. those points $x + iy$ for which $x^2 - y^2 > 0$ and $0 < 2xy < 1$. This region therefore consists of those points outside the hyperbola $xy = \tfrac{1}{2}$ which lie in the two acute angles between the x-axis and the line $x = y$.

20.18. *Example.* Examine the conformal representation of the z-plane on the w-plane given by the equation $2w = z + c^2/z$, where c is real and positive.

Show that, for different values of $r(> c)$, the circles $|z| = r$ correspond to confocal ellipses in the w-plane. Also, by writing the transformation in the form

$$\frac{w - c}{w + c} = \left(\frac{z - c}{z + c} \right)^2, \tag{21}$$

or otherwise, show that the part of a circle through the points $z = \pm c$ which lies outside $|z| = c$ corresponds to part of a circle through the points $w = \pm c$. [London, 1951.]

Solution. I do not know what the first paragraph means.

Let $r > c$ and $z = re^{i\theta}$, and let θ run through the interval $[0, 2\pi]$. Then z describes the circle $|z| = r$, and the transformation transforms z into

$$u + iv \; = \; w \; = \; \tfrac{1}{2}z + \tfrac{1}{2}c^2/z \; = \; \tfrac{1}{2}re^{i\theta} + \tfrac{1}{2}c^2r^{-1}e^{-i\theta},$$

i.e. into the point (u, v), where

$$u \; = \; \tfrac{1}{2}(r + c^2r^{-1}) \cos \theta, \qquad v \; = \; \tfrac{1}{2}(r - c^2r^{-1}) \sin \theta.$$

These are the parametric equations of the ellipse referred to its principal axes, with semi-axes $a = \tfrac{1}{2}(r + c^2r^{-1})$ and $b = \tfrac{1}{2}(r - c^2r^{-1})$. The foci of this ellipse have ordinate 0 and abscissae $\pm \sqrt{(a^2 - b^2)}$

$= \pm c$. Since these are independent of r, the ellipses corresponding to different values of r are confocal.

Now suppose S is that part of a circle through the points $z = \pm c$ which lies outside $|z| = c$. Then S is the greater of the two arcs into which these points divide the circle. Hence the line segment $\{-c, c\}$ subtends the same angle α, say, at all points of S. This means that, if $z \in S$, then

$$|\text{am } \{(z-c)/(z+c)\}| = \alpha. \tag{22}$$

Also S is contained in either the upper or the lower half-plane. In the former case,

$$\text{am } \{(z-c)/(z+c)\} > 0 \quad (z \in S),$$

and hence, by (22),

$$\text{am } \{(z-c)/(z+c)\} = \alpha \quad (z \in S). \tag{23}$$

Now let T be the set into which the given transformation transforms S, and let w be any point of T. Then there is a point z in S for which (21) holds. By (21) and (23),

$$\text{am } \{(w-c)/(w+c)\} = 2\alpha, \tag{24}$$

provided that $-\pi < 2\alpha \leqslant \pi$. This condition is, however, satisfied, since α is an acute angle in the Euclidean sense, i.e. $0 < \alpha < \frac{1}{2}\pi$. Thus w is a point in the upper half-plane, at which the line segment $\{-c, c\}$ subtends an angle 2α. The set U of all points w with these two properties is an arc of a circle through the points $w = \pm c$, and it has been shown that $T \subset U$. It is, in fact, easily seen that $T = U$, but this is not needed here. Thus T is part of a circle through the points $w = \pm c$ if S is contained in the upper half-plane, and similarly if S is contained in the lower half-plane.

CHAPTER 21

THE GAMMA FUNCTION

21.1. The *Gamma function* is defined by the formula

$$\Gamma(z) = \lim_{n \to \infty} \frac{n!n^z}{z(z+1)\ldots(z+n)}. \tag{1}$$

Accordingly, $\Gamma(z)$ does not exist if z is 0 or a negative integer. I shall show that it does exist for all other values of z.

21.2. Let D_0 be the set of all (finite) points other than 0 and the negative integers. For any point z of D_0 and any natural number n, let

$$\Gamma_n(z) = \frac{n!n^z}{z(z+1)\ldots(z+n)},$$

$$g_n(z) = \log(n!) + z \log n - \sum_{m=0}^{n} \log(z+m). \tag{2}$$

Then

$$\Gamma_n(z) = \exp g_n(z), \tag{3}$$

and (1) is equivalent to

$$\Gamma(z) = \lim_{n \to \infty} \Gamma_n(z). \tag{4}$$

Let $z \in D_0$. Then, for any natural number n,

$$g_n(z) = g_1(z) + \sum_{m=2}^{n} \{g_m(z) - g_{m-1}(z)\}.$$

The existence of $\lim_{n \to \infty} g_n(z)$ is therefore equivalent to the convergence of

$$\sum_{m=2}^{\infty} \{g_m(z) - g_{m-1}(z)\}. \tag{5}$$

Now, if m is an integer, and $m > \max(1, |z|)$, then

$$g_m(z) - g_{m-1}(z) = \log m + z\{\log m - \log(m-1)\} - \log(z+m)$$

$$= \int_0^1 \frac{z(z+1)t}{(m-t)(m+tz)}\, dt.$$

Hence

$$|g_m(z) - g_{m-1}(z)| \leqslant |z(z+1)|(m-1)^{-1}(m-|z|)^{-1}$$

$$\{m > \max(1, |z|)\}. \quad (6)$$

From this and the comparison test it follows that (5) converges, i.e. that $\lim\limits_{n \to \infty} g_n(z)$ exists. Hence, by (3), so does the right-hand side of (4), which is the same as the right-hand side of (1). This proves that $\Gamma(z)$ exists for all points z of D_0.

EXERCISE

21.1. Prove that, if $z \in D_0$, then $\Gamma(z) \neq 0$.

21.3. I shall now show that Γ is regular in D_0.

Let z_0 be any point of D_0. It is trivial that D_0 is open. Hence there is a disc D about z_0, such that $D \subset D_0$. Let r be the radius of D, m_0 an integer greater than $\max(1, |z_0| + r)$, and

$$g(z) = \sum_{m=m_0+1}^{\infty} \{g_m(z) - g_{m-1}(z)\}. \quad (7)$$

Then, by (6), for any point z in D and any integer $m > m_0$,

$$|g_m(z) - g_{m-1}(z)| \leqslant (|z_0| + r + 1)^2(m-1)^{-1}(m - |z_0| - r)^{-1}.$$

Hence the series in (7) converges uniformly in D. Also each term of this series is regular in D. Hence, by Theorem 14.4, so is g. Now, by (7), (3) and (4), $\Gamma(z) = \Gamma_{m_0}(z) \exp g(z)$, $(z \in D)$. Hence, by Theorems 6.3 and 6.4 and §6.2(i), Γ is regular at z_0. Since this holds for every point z_0 of D_0, it follows that Γ is regular in D_0.

EXERCISES

21.2. Prove that, if $z \in D_0$, then $\Gamma(z+1) = z\Gamma(z)$.

21.3. Prove that, if z is a natural number, then $\Gamma(z) = (z-1)!$.

21.4. Prove that, if z is not an integer, then $\Gamma(z)\Gamma(1-z) = \pi \operatorname{cosec} \pi z$. (Hint: use §19.11.)

21.5. Prove that, if $z \in D_0$, then $\lim\limits_{n \to \infty} \dfrac{n! n^z}{\Gamma(z+n+1)} = 1$.

21.4. The *Beta function* is defined by

$$B(z, w) = \int_0^1 t^{z-1}(1-t)^{w-1}dt. \qquad (8)$$

EXERCISES

21.6. Prove that the right-hand side of (8) exists if and only if re $z > 0$ and re $w > 0$.

21.7. Prove that, if re $z > 0$ and re $w > 0$, then $B(z, w) = B(w, z)$.

21.5. THEOREM 21.1.   *Let* re $z > 0$ *and* re $w > 0$.   *Then*

$$B(z, w+1) = B(z, w)w/(z+w).$$

Proof.   We have

$(z+w)B(z, w+1) - wB(z, w)$

$$= (z+w) \int_0^1 t^{z-1}(1-t)^w dt - w \int_0^1 t^{z-1}(1-t)^{w-1}dt$$

$$= \int_0^1 \{zt^{z-1}(1-t)^w - t^z w(1-t)^{w-1}\}dt = [t^z(1-t)^w]_0^1 = 0,$$

and the result follows.

THEOREM 21.2.   *Let* n *be a natural number, and* re $z > 0$.
Then $\Gamma_n(z) = n^z B(z, n+1)$.

Proof.   By Theorem 21.1,

$$B(z, n+1) = \frac{n}{z+n} B(z, n) = \frac{n}{z+n} \cdot \frac{n-1}{z+n-1} \cdot \ldots \cdot \frac{1}{z+1} B(z, 1).$$

Also, by (8),

$$B(z, 1) = \int_0^1 t^{z-1}dt = 1/z.$$

The result therefore follows from (2).

21.6. From (4) and Theorem 21.2 we obtain

$$\lim_{n \to \infty} \{n^z B(z, n+1)\} = \Gamma(z) \quad (\text{re } z > 0). \qquad (9)$$

THEOREM 21.3.   *Let* re $z > 0$.   *Then*

$$\lim_{n \to \infty} \{n^z B(z, w+n+1)\} = \Gamma(z). \qquad (10)$$

Proof. Suppose, first, that re $w \geqslant 1$. Then, for any natural number n,

$$\left| n^z \mathrm{B}(z,\, w+n+1) - n^z \mathrm{B}(z,\, n+1) \right|$$

$$= n^{\mathrm{re}\, z} \left| \int_0^1 t^{z-1} \{(1-t)^w - 1\}(1-t)^n dt \right|$$

$$\leqslant n^{\mathrm{re}\, z} \int_0^1 t^{\mathrm{re}\, z-1} \left| (1-t)^w - 1 \right| (1-t)^n dt,$$

and

$$\left| (1-t)^w - 1 \right| = \left| \int_0^t w(1-x)^{w-1} dx \right| \leqslant t|w| \quad (0 \leqslant t \leqslant 1).$$

Hence, by (8),

$$\left| n^z \mathrm{B}(z,\, w+n+1) - n^z \mathrm{B}(z,\, n+1) \right| \leqslant |w| n^{\mathrm{re}\, z} \mathrm{B}(\mathrm{re}\, z+1,\, n+1).$$

$$(11)$$

Now, by (9), $\lim_{n\to\infty} \{n^{\mathrm{re}\, z+1} \mathrm{B}(\mathrm{re}\, z+1,\, n+1)\} = \Gamma(\mathrm{re}\, z+1)$. Hence the right-hand side of (11) tends to 0 as $n \to \infty$, and so, therefore, does the left-hand side. This, together with (9), proves (10) subject to the restriction re $w \geqslant 1$.

Now consider z temporarily fixed. Then the left-hand side of (10) is a function of w alone, say $g(w)$, and it is trivial that, if k is any positive integer, then $g(w-k) = g(w)$ whenever $g(w)$ exists. The restriction re $w \geqslant 1$ is therefore unnecessary. This proves the theorem.

21.7. THEOREM 21.4. *Let* re $z > 0$ *and* re $w > 0$. *Then*

$$\mathrm{B}(z,\, w) = \Gamma(z)\Gamma(w)/\Gamma(z+w).$$

Proof. Let $F(w) = \mathrm{B}(z,\, w)\Gamma(z+w)/\Gamma(w)$ (considering z fixed). Then, by Theorem 21.1 and Exercise 21.2, $F(w) = F(w+1)$, and hence $F(w) = F(w+n+1)$ for every natural number n. From this, Theorem 21.3, and Exercise 21.5 we obtain

$$F(w) = \lim_{n\to\infty} F(w+n+1)$$

$$= \lim_{n\to\infty} \left\{ n^z \mathrm{B}(z,\, w+n+1) \frac{\Gamma(z+w+n+1)}{n!\, n^{z+w}} \frac{n!\, n^w}{\Gamma(w+n+1)} \right\} = \Gamma(z),$$

and the result follows.

EXERCISE

21.8. Prove that $\int_0^\infty u^{z-1}e^{-u}\,du$ exists if and only if re $z > 0$.

THEOREM 21.5. *Let* re $z > 0$. *Then* $\Gamma(z) = \int_0^\infty u^{z-1}e^{-u}du$.

Proof. We have

$$e^x \geqslant 1 + x \tag{12}$$

for every real number x. Hence $e^{-x} \geqslant 1 - x$. From this and (12) it follows that

$$1 \geqslant e^x(1-x) \geqslant (1+x)(1-x) = 1 - x^2 \quad (x \leqslant 1). \tag{13}$$

Now let n be a natural number. Then, by (13), if $u \leqslant n$, then

$$1 \geqslant e^{u/n}(1 - u/n) \geqslant (1 - u^2/n^2),$$

and hence

$$1 \geqslant e^u(1 - u/n)^n \geqslant (1 - u^2/n^2)^n \quad (0 \leqslant u \leqslant n). \tag{14}$$

Now $(1-x)^n \geqslant 1 - nx\ (x \leqslant 1)$. Hence, by (14),

$$1 \geqslant e^u(1 - u/n)^n \geqslant 1 - u^2/n \quad (0 \leqslant u \leqslant n),$$

so that

$$0 \leqslant e^{-u} - (1 - u/n)^n \leqslant e^{-u}u^2/n \quad (0 \leqslant u \leqslant n). \tag{15}$$

By (8),

$$n^z \mathrm{B}(z,\, n+1) = \int_0^1 (nt)^{z-1}(1-t)^n n\,dt = \int_0^n u^{z-1}(1 - u/n)^n du.$$

Hence, by Exercise 21.8 and (15),

$$\left| \int_0^\infty u^{z-1}e^{-u}du - n^z \mathrm{B}(z,\, n+1) \right|$$

$$\leqslant \int_0^n u^{\mathrm{re}\, z-1}\{e^{-u} - (1 - u/n)^n\}du + \int_n^\infty u^{\mathrm{re}\, z-1}e^{-u}du$$

$$\leqslant n^{-1} \int_0^\infty u^{\mathrm{re}\, z+1}e^{-u}du.$$

The result therefore follows from (9).

21.8. Let S be an unbounded set of points. Then the formula

$$\lim_{\substack{|z|\to\infty \\ z\in S}} f(z) = l$$

means that, for every positive number ϵ, there is a positive number u, such that, for every number z for which $z \in S$ and $|z| > u$, we have $|f(z) - l| < \epsilon$.

The statement '$f(z) \sim g(z)$ {read "$f(z)$ is *asymptotic* to $g(z)$"} as $|z| \to \infty$ while $z \in S$' means that

$$\lim_{\substack{|z|\to\infty \\ z\in S}} \{f(z)/g(z)\} = 1.$$

21.9. THEOREM 21.6. *Let* $0 < a < \pi$, *and let* S *be the set of those points* z *for which* $-a \leqslant \operatorname{am} z \leqslant a$. *Then*

$$\Gamma(z) \sim \sqrt{(2\pi)} z^{z-\frac{1}{2}} e^{-z} \tag{16}$$

as $|z| \to \infty$ *while* $z \in S$.

(16) is called '*the asymptotic formula for the Gamma function*'. The reader will have no difficulty in deducing this theorem from the next one, which is both more general and more precise.

21.10. The distance (see §3.4) of the point z from the negative real axis is equal to $|z|$ if $\operatorname{re} z \geqslant 0$, and to $|\operatorname{im} z|$ if $\operatorname{re} z < 0$.

THEOREM 21.7. *Let* z *be neither* 0 *nor negative. Then*

$$\left| \Gamma(z)(2\pi)^{-\frac{1}{2}} z^{\frac{1}{2}-z} e^z - 1 \right| \leqslant e^{1/\Delta(z)} - 1,$$

where $\Delta(z)$ *is the distance of* z *from the negative real axis.*

Proof. With $g_n(z)$ defined by (2), let

$$g(z) = \lim_{n\to\infty} g_n(z). \tag{17}$$

The existence of this limit was proved in §21.2. Then, by (3) and (4),

$$\Gamma(z) = \exp g(z). \tag{18}$$

Let

$$\psi(u) = (u - [u])([u] + 1 - u), \tag{19}$$

where $[u]$ is the greatest integer less than or equal to u. Then,

for any integer m and any function f whose second derivative
is continuous in $[m, m+1]$,

$$\int_m^{m+1} f''(u)\psi(u)du = \int_m^{m+1} f''(u)(u-m)(m+1-u)du$$
$$= [f'(u)(u-m)(m+1-u)]_m^{m+1}$$
$$- \int_m^{m+1} f'(u)(2m+1-2u)du$$
$$= -[f(u)(2m+1-2u)]_m^{m+1} - 2\int_m^{m+1} f(u)du$$
$$= f(m) + f(m+1) - 2\int_m^{m+1} f(u)du.$$

Hence, for any natural number n and any function f whose
second derivative is continuous in $[0, n]$,

$$\sum_{m=0}^{n} f(m) = \tfrac{1}{2}f(0) + \tfrac{1}{2}f(n) + \tfrac{1}{2}\sum_{m=0}^{n-1}\{f(m) + f(m+1)\}$$
$$= \tfrac{1}{2}f(0) + \tfrac{1}{2}f(n) + \int_0^n f(u)du + \tfrac{1}{2}\int_0^n f''(u)\psi(u)du.$$

In particular, with $f(u) = \log(z+u)$, we have

$$\sum_{m=0}^{n} \log(z+m) = \tfrac{1}{2}\log z + \tfrac{1}{2}\log(z+n) + \int_0^n \log(z+u)du$$
$$- \tfrac{1}{2}\int_0^n (z+u)^{-2}\psi(u)du$$
$$= (\tfrac{1}{2}-z)\log z + (z+n+\tfrac{1}{2})\log(z+n) - n - \tfrac{1}{2}h_n(z), \tag{20}$$

where

$$h_n(z) = \int_0^n (z+u)^{-2}\psi(u)du. \tag{21}$$

By (2) and (20), with a_n defined as in §19.12 (31),

$$g_n(z) = \log(n!) + z\log n + (z-\tfrac{1}{2})\log z$$
$$- (z+n+\tfrac{1}{2})\log(z+n) + n + \tfrac{1}{2}h_n(z)$$
$$= a_n - (z+n+\tfrac{1}{2})\{\log(z+n) - \log n\} + (z-\tfrac{1}{2})\log z + \tfrac{1}{2}h_n(z). \tag{22}$$

Let

$$h(z) = \int_0^\infty (z+u)^{-2}\psi(u)du. \tag{23}$$

The existence of this integral is trivial since, by (19),

$$0 \leqslant \psi(u) \leqslant \tfrac{1}{4}. \tag{24}$$

By (21) and (23),

$$\lim_{n\to\infty} h_n(z) = h(z). \tag{25}$$

It is also trivial that

$$\lim_{n\to\infty} [(z+n+\tfrac{1}{2})\{\log(z+n)-\log n\}] = z, \tag{26}$$

and the last formula of §19.12 states that

$$\lim_{n\to\infty} a_n = \tfrac{1}{2}\log(2\pi). \tag{27}$$

By (17), (22), (27), (26) and (25),

$$g(z) = \tfrac{1}{2}\log(2\pi)-z+(z-\tfrac{1}{2})\log z+\tfrac{1}{2}h(z). \tag{28}$$

From this and (18) it follows that

$$\left|\Gamma(z)(2\pi)^{-1/2}z^{1/2-z}e^z-1\right| = \left|e^{1/2\,h(z)}-1\right| \leqslant e^{1/2|h(z)|}-1. \tag{29}$$

Now let $z=x+iy$. Then, by (23) and (24),

$$|h(z)| \leqslant \tfrac{1}{4}\int_0^\infty \{(x+u)^2+y^2\}^{-1}du.$$

Hence, if $x \geqslant |y|$, then

$$|h(z)| \leqslant \tfrac{1}{4}\int_0^\infty (x+u)^{-2}du = 1/(4x) < 1/|z| = 1/\Delta(z).$$

If, however, $x < |y|$, then

$$|h(z)| \leqslant \tfrac{1}{4}\int_\infty^\infty \{(x+u)^2+y^2\}^{-1}du = \pi/(4|y|). \tag{30}$$

Therefore, if $0 \leqslant x < |y|$, then

$$|h(z)| \leqslant \pi/(2|z|) < 2/|z| = 2/\Delta(z),$$

and if $x < 0$, then

$$|h(z)| < 1/|y| = 1/\Delta(z).$$

Thus, in all cases, $|h(z)| \leqslant 2/\Delta(z)$. From this and (29) we obtain the result stated.

21.11. *Example.* It is assumed that $z = x + iy$, $x \leqslant 0$, and $|y| \geqslant 1$. Prove that $|\Gamma(z)| \leqslant 4e^{-x-\frac{1}{2}\pi|y|}|y|^{x-\frac{1}{2}}$.

Solution. By (30), $|h(z)| \leqslant \frac{1}{4}\pi < \frac{4}{5}$. Hence, by (28),

$$\operatorname{re} g(z) \leqslant \tfrac{1}{2}\log(2\pi) - x + (x - \tfrac{1}{2})\log|z| - y \operatorname{am} z + \tfrac{2}{5}.$$

Now $\frac{1}{2}\log(2\pi) + \frac{2}{5} < \log 4$, $(x - \frac{1}{2})\log|z| \leqslant (x - \frac{1}{2})\log|y|$, and $y \operatorname{am} z = |y||\operatorname{am} z| \geqslant \frac{1}{2}\pi|y|$. Hence

$$\operatorname{re} g(z) \leqslant \log 4 - x - \tfrac{1}{2}\pi|y| + (x - \tfrac{1}{2})\log|y|,$$

and the result follows from (18).

EXERCISE

21.9. Prove that, if $z = x + iy$, $x \geqslant 0$, and $|y| \geqslant 1$, then

$$|\Gamma(z)| \leqslant 22[x]!e^{-\frac{1}{2}\pi|y|}|y|^{x-\frac{1}{2}},$$

where $[x]$ is the greatest integer less than or equal to x.

21.12. Suppose the function f has the property that the expression

$$\int_{-\infty}^{-r} \lim_{v \to 0-} f(u + iv)du + \int_{-\pi}^{\pi} f(re^{it})ire^{it}dt + \int_{-r}^{-\infty} \lim_{v \to 0+} f(u + iv)du \quad (31)$$

exists, and has the same value, for all positive numbers r. Then this value is denoted by

$$\int_{-\infty}^{(0+)} f(w)dw. \quad (32)$$

21.13. In what follows, w^{-z} is meant to have its principal value (see §5.3).

THEOREM 21.8. *The expression*

$$\int_{-\infty}^{(0+)} e^w w^{-z}dw \quad (33)$$

exists, as defined in §21.12, for every complex number z.

Proof. Let $f(w) = e^w w^{-z}$, and let r be any positive number. Then it is easily seen that the expression (31) exists. To prove that it is independent of r, denote it by $g(r)$.   Then we have to prove that

$$g(r_1) = g(r_2) \quad (0 < r_1 < r_2). \qquad (34)$$

Let $f_1(w) = e^w (iw)^{-z} i^z$ and $f_2(w) = e^w (-iw)^{-z} i^{-z}$, where all powers have their principal values.   Then $f_1(w) = f(w)$ for every point w for which am $(iw) =$ am $i +$ am w, i.e.

$$f_1(w) = f(w) \quad (\text{am } w \leqslant \tfrac{1}{2}\pi). \qquad (35)$$

Similarly

$$f_2(w) = f(w) \quad (\text{am } w > -\tfrac{1}{2}\pi). \qquad (36)$$

Now let

$$C_1(r) = \mathscr{C}(t; re^{it}, -\pi, 0), \qquad C_2(r) = \mathscr{C}(t; re^{it}, 0, \pi), \qquad (37)$$

and let $C_m^*(r)$ be '$C_m(r)$ described backward' $(m = 1, 2)$.   Then it is easily seen that

$$g(r) = \int_{-\infty}^{-r} \{f_1(u) - f_2(u)\} du + \int_{C_1(r)} f_1(w) dw + \int_{C_2(r)} f_2(w) dw. \qquad (38)$$

Let $0 < r_1 < r_2$, $C_3 = C_1(r_2) + \{r_2, r_1\} + C_1^*(r_1) + \{-r_1, -r_2\}$, $C_4 = C_2(r_2) + \{-r_2, -r_1\} + C_2^*(r_1) + \{r_1, r_2\}$, and note that, by (35) and (36), $f_1(u) = f_2(u)$ $(u > 0)$, so that

$$\int_{\{r_2, r_1\}} f_1(w) dw + \int_{\{r_1, r_2\}} f_2(w) dw = 0.$$

Then, by (38) and Theorems 11.4 and 11.6,

$$g(r_2) - g(r_1) = \int_{C_3} f_1(w) dw + \int_{C_4} f_2(w) dw. \qquad (39)$$

Now f_1 is regular in the plane cut along the positive imaginary axis, i.e. the set of all finite points other than the points iy with $y \geqslant 0$.   This is a star domain, and contains the closed contour C_3.   Hence, by Theorem 12.6,

$$\int_{C_3} f_1(w) dw = 0.$$

Similarly

$$\int_{C_4} f_2(w) dw = 0.$$

From these two equations and (39) we obtain (34), which was
to be proved.

21.14. THEOREM 21.9. *The function G, defined by*

$$G(z) = \int_{-\infty}^{(0+)} e^w w^{-z} dw,$$

is an integral function.

Proof. By §21.12 and §21.13,

$$G(z) = \int_{-\infty}^{-1} e^w |w|^{-z} (e^{i\pi z} - e^{-i\pi z}) dw + \int_{-\pi}^{\pi} \exp(e^{it}) e^{-itz} i e^{it} dt$$

$$= 2i \sin \pi z \cdot G_1(z) + i G_2(z), \tag{40}$$

where

$$G_1(z) = \int_1^\infty e^{-t} t^{-z} dt, \qquad G_2(z) = \int_{-\pi}^{\pi} \exp(e^{it} + it - itz) dt.$$

Now let z_0 be any number (temporarily fixed), and let

$$h(z) = \frac{G_1(z) - G_1(z_0)}{z - z_0} + \int_1^\infty e^{-t} t^{-z_0} \log t \, dt.$$

Then, for any number $z \neq z_0$,

$$h(z) = \int_1^\infty e^{-t} t^{-z_0} \left(\frac{t^{z_0 - z} - 1}{z - z_0} + \log t \right) dt.$$

Now

$$\left| \frac{t^{z_0 - z} - 1}{z - z_0} + \log t \right| = \left| \sum_{n=2}^\infty \frac{1}{n!} (z_0 - z)^{n-1} (\log t)^n \right|$$

$$\leqslant |z - z_0| (\log t)^2 \sum_{n=2}^\infty \frac{1}{(n-2)!} (|z - z_0| \log t)^{n-2}$$

$$= |z - z_0| (\log t)^2 t^{|z - z_0|} \quad (z \neq z_0, \, t \geqslant 1).$$

Hence

$$|h(z)| \leqslant c|z - z_0| \quad (0 < |z - z_0| < 1), \tag{41}$$

where

$$c = \int_1^\infty e^{-t} t^{1 - \operatorname{re} z_0} (\log t)^2 dt,$$

which is independent of z. It follows that $h(z) \to 0$ as $z \to z_0$, which means that G_1 is fully differentiable at z_0, and

$$G_1'(z_0) = -\int_1^\infty e^{-t} t^{-z_0} \log t \, dt.$$

By the method which led to (41), we can similarly show that

$$\left| \frac{G_2(z) - G_2(z_0)}{z - z_0} + i \int_{-\pi}^\pi t \exp\left(e^{it} + it - itz_0\right) dt \right|$$
$$\leqslant c' |z - z_0| \quad (0 < |z - z_0| < 1),$$

where $c' = 2\pi^3 \exp\left(\pi + 1 + \pi |z_0|\right)$. Hence G_2 is also fully differentiable at z_0, and it follows from (40) that so is G. Since this holds for every point z_0, G is an integral function.

21.15. THEOREM 21.10. *Let G be defined as in Theorem 21.9, and suppose that z is not a positive integer. Then*

$$G(z) = 2i \sin \pi z \cdot \Gamma(1 - z). \tag{42}$$

Proof. Similarly to (40), we have, for every positive number r,

$$G(z) = 2i \sin \pi z \cdot G_1(z, r) + i r^{1-z} G_2(z, r), \tag{43}$$

where

$$G_1(z, r) = \int_r^\infty e^{-t} t^{-z} dt, \qquad G_2(z, r) = \int_{-\pi}^\pi \exp\left(re^{it} + it - itz\right) dt. \tag{44}$$

Suppose, first, that $\operatorname{re} z < 1$. Then $\lim_{r \to 0+} r^{1-z} = 0$, and, by (44) and Theorem 21.5, $\lim_{r \to 0+} G_1(z, r) = \Gamma(1 - z)$. Also, by (44), if $0 < r < 1$, then $\left|G_2(z, r)\right| \leqslant 2\pi \exp\left(1 + \pi |z|\right)$. Hence the right-hand side of (43) tends to that of (42) as $r \to 0+$. This shows that (42) holds for every point z for which $\operatorname{re} z < 1$. The theorem now follows from the corollary to Theorem 15.4 on observing that both sides of (42) are regular in the domain consisting of all finite points other than the positive integers.

EXERCISE

21.10. Prove that, if z is neither 0 nor a negative integer, then $G(z) = 2\pi i / \Gamma(z)$. (Hint: use Theorem 21.10 and Exercise 21.4.)

21.16. The following formula may be taken as the definition of its left-hand side:

$$\int_{a-i\infty}^{a+i\infty} f(z)dz = \lim_{b\to\infty} \int_{\{a,\,a+ib\}} f(z)dz + \lim_{b\to\infty} \int_{\{a-ib,\,a\}} f(z)dz.$$

EXERCISES

21.11. Prove that, if $a > 0$ and re $z > 0$, then

$$\frac{1}{\Gamma(z)} = \frac{1}{2\pi i} \int_{a-i\infty}^{a+i\infty} e^w w^{-z} dw.$$

21.12. Prove that, if n is 0 or a positive integer, then Γ has a simple pole with residue $(-1)^n/n!$ at $-n$.

21.13. Prove that, if $a > 0$ and re $z > 0$, then

$$e^{-z} = \frac{1}{2\pi i} \int_{a-i\infty}^{a+i\infty} \Gamma(w)z^{-w} dw.$$

(Hint: use Theorem 17.9 and §21.11.)

21.14. Prove that, if z is neither 0 nor a negative integer, then

$$\frac{1}{\Gamma(z)} = e^{\gamma z} z \prod_{n=1}^{\infty} \left\{ \left(1 + \frac{z}{n}\right) e^{-z/n} \right\},$$

where

$$\gamma = \lim_{n\to\infty} \left(\sum_{m=1}^{n} \frac{1}{m} - \log n \right)$$

(Euler's constant).

CHAPTER 22

THE JORDAN CURVE THEOREM

22.1. The Jordan curve theorem, which was stated in §9.17, refers to *simple closed curves*. It is expedient to deal first with its analogue for *simple curves* (see §9.7). This may be stated as follows:

THEOREM 22.1. *The complement of the set of the points of any simple curve is a domain.*

The proof will be given later, but here is an outline of it: Let the curve be denoted by C, and the complement of $|C|$ (see §9.3) by D. It follows from Theorems 9.2 and 3.2 and Exercise 9.2(i) that D is open and not empty. It is therefore sufficient to prove that every pair of points of D can be joined by a broken line contained in D, and it is trivial that we may restrict ourselves to pairs of *distinct* points. Now any such pair is transformed by a suitable linear transformation (see §8.2) into the pair 0, 1. Theorem 22.1 therefore follows at once from

THEOREM 22.2. *Suppose that neither of the points 0, 1 is on the simple curve C. Then there is a broken line, leading from 0 to 1, which does not meet C.*

A stronger result than the one required is sometimes more easily proved. So it is here. Accordingly, after choosing a suitable natural number n, I shall prove the existence of a broken line with not only the two properties stated, but the further property that each of its sides has length $1/n$, and is parallel to either the real or the imaginary axis. For this purpose, I shall consider a dissection of C into arcs $C_1, C_2, \ldots, C_k$ of diameters less than $1/n$, and prove by induction that, for every natural number $m \leqslant k$, there is a broken line, which leads from 0 to 1, has the said further property, and does not meet $C_1 + C_2 + \ldots + C_m$. The result will then be obtained by taking $m = k$. The detailed proof will, however, require several theorems which I have not yet given.

22.2. Let w be any complex number, a any positive number, S the set of those points z for which $|\mathrm{re}\, z - \mathrm{re}\, w| < a$ and $|\mathrm{im}\, z - \mathrm{im}\, w| < a$, and z_1 and z_2 any two distinct boundary points (see §16.7) of S. Then there are exactly two simple broken lines (i.e. broken lines which are simple curves; see §9.7), contained in the boundary of S, leading from z_1 to z_2. For instance, if $z_1 = w - a$ and $z_2 = w - ia$, then these broken lines are $\{z_1, z_1 + ia, w + a + ia, z_2 + a, z_2\}$ and $\{z_1, z_2 - a, z_2\}$. In particular, let z_1 and z_2 be chosen from among the four points $w \pm a$ and $w \pm ia$, let the said broken lines be C_1 and C_2, and let w_1 and w_2 be points of C_1 and C_2 respectively, both distinct from z_1 and z_2. Then there is a point w_0 with the following three properties:

(i) All points of the broken line $\{w_1, w_0, w_2\}$, except w_1 and w_2, are in S.

(ii) The line segment $\{w_1, w_0\}$ does not meet the broken line $\{z_1, w, z_2\}$.

(iii) The line segment $\{w_0, w_2\}$ meets exactly one of the two line segments $\{z_1, w\}$ and $\{w, z_2\}$.

To prove this formally is somewhat tedious, but the reader will easily convince himself that it can be done.

22.3. A line segment C_1 is said to *cross* a line segment C_2 if and only if (i) C_1 and C_2 have at least one point in common, and (ii) no end point of either line segment is a point of the other.

22.4. THEOREM 22.3. *Suppose the line segment $\{z_1, z_2\}$ crosses the line segment $\{w_1, w_2\}$. Then $(w_2 - w_1)/(z_2 - z_1)$ is not real.*

Proof. Let z_0 be a point common to the two line segments. Then z_0 is a point, but not an end point, of $\{z_1, z_2\}$. This means that there is a number u such that

$$0 < u < 1 \tag{1}$$

and

$$z_0 = z_1 + u(z_2 - z_1). \tag{2}$$

Similarly there is a number v such that

$$0 < v < 1 \tag{3}$$

and

$$z_0 = w_1 + v(w_2 - w_1). \tag{4}$$

Let

$$q = (w_2 - w_1)/(z_2 - z_1). \tag{5}$$

Then, by (4) and (2),

$$w_1 + t(w_2 - w_1) = z_0 + (t - v)q(z_2 - z_1) = z_1 + \{u + (t - v)q\}(z_2 - z_1).$$

Hence the point $w_1 + t(w_2 - w_1)$, which is on $\{w_1, w_2\}$ if

$$0 \leqslant t \leqslant 1, \tag{6}$$

is on $\{z_1, z_2\}$ if

$$0 \leqslant u + (t - v)q \leqslant 1. \tag{7}$$

We cannot have $(u - 1)/v \leqslant q \leqslant u/v$; for this would imply that the number $t = 0$ satisfies (7), which means that $w_1 \in |\{z_1, z_2\}|$. We cannot have $q > u/v$; for this would imply that the number $t = v - u/q$ satisfies (6), which means that $z_1 \in |\{w_1, w_2\}|$. We cannot have $q < (u - 1)/v$; for this would imply that the number $t = v + (1 - u)/q$ satisfies (6), which means that $z_2 \in |\{w_1, w_2\}|$. Hence q cannot be real.

EXERCISE

22.1. Prove that, if two line segments cross each other, then they have *only* one point in common.

22.5. THEOREM 22.4. *On the hypothesis of* Theorem 22.3,

$$\chi(w_1, \{z_1, z_2\}) - \chi(w_2, \{z_1, z_2\})$$
$$= \operatorname{am}\{(z_2 - w_1)/(z_2 - w_2)\} - \operatorname{am}\{(z_1 - w_1)/(z_1 - w_2)\} \pm 2\pi.$$

Proof. Let z_0, u, v and q be defined as in the proof of Theorem 22.3, and let

$$(z_2 - w_1)/(z_1 - w_1) = q_1, \qquad (z_2 - w_2)/(z_1 - w_2) = q_2,$$
$$(z_2 - w_1)/(z_2 - w_2) = q_3, \qquad (z_1 - w_1)/(z_1 - w_2) = q_4. \tag{8}$$

Then, by Exercise 9.11 (with $k = 1$),

$$\chi(w_1, \{z_1, z_2\}) = \operatorname{am} q_1, \qquad \chi(w_2, \{z_1, z_2\}) = \operatorname{am} q_2,$$

and what we have to prove is equivalent to

$$\operatorname{am} q_1 - \operatorname{am} q_2 - \operatorname{am} q_3 + \operatorname{am} q_4 = \pm 2\pi. \tag{9}$$

Let the left-hand side of (9) be equal to a. Then

$$e^{ia} = \frac{q_1 q_4}{q_2 q_3} \left| \frac{q_2 q_3}{q_1 q_4} \right|.$$

Now, by (8), $q_1 q_4 = q_2 q_3$. Hence $e^{ia} = 1$, which means that a is a multiple of 2π. Now, by (8), (5), (2) and (4), $q_1 = 1 + (-u+vq)^{-1}$, $q_2 = 1 - \{u + (1-v)q\}^{-1}$, $q_3 = 1 + \{(1-u)q^{-1} - (1-v)\}^{-1}$ and $q_4 = 1 - (uq^{-1} + 1 - v)^{-1}$. Also, if im $w > 0$, then im $(1/w) < 0$, and if im $w < 0$, then im $(1/w) > 0$. Hence, if im $q > 0$, then, by (1) and (3), im $q_1 < 0$, im $q_2 > 0$, im $q_3 > 0$ and im $q_4 < 0$, which means that each of the four terms on the left-hand side of (9) is between $-\pi$ and 0 exclusive, so that $-4\pi < a < 0$. Since a is a multiple of 2π, it follows that, in this case, $a = -2\pi$. Similarly $a = 2\pi$ if im $q < 0$, and the case im $q = 0$ is excluded by (5) and Theorem 22.3. This proves (9), which was to be proved.

22.6. THEOREM 22.5. *Let C be a curve leading from z_1 to z_2, $C' \sim C + \{z_2, z_1\}$, and suppose that neither w_1 nor w_2 is on C', and that the line segment $\{w_1, w_2\}$ meets $\{z_2, z_1\}$, but does not meet C. Then $\chi(w_2, C') - \chi(w_1, C') = \pm 2\pi$.*

Proof. It follows from the hypotheses and §22.3 that $\{z_2, z_1\}$ crosses $\{w_2, w_1\}$. Hence, by Theorem 22.4, with the suffixes 1 and 2 interchanged,

$$\chi(w_2, \{z_2, z_1\}) - \chi(w_1, \{z_2, z_1\})$$
$$= \text{am } \{(z_1 - w_2)/(z_1 - w_1)\} - \text{am } \{(z_2 - w_2)/(z_2 - w_1)\} \pm 2\pi.$$

Also, by Exercise 9.12,

$$\chi(w_2, C) - \chi(w_1, C)$$
$$= \text{am } \{(z_2 - w_2)/(z_2 - w_1)\} - \text{am } \{(z_1 - w_2)/(z_1 - w_1)\}.$$

Also, by Exercise 9.40 and the definition of χ (§9.15),

$$\chi(w_m, C') = \chi(w_m, C) + \chi(w_m, \{z_2, z_1\}) \quad (m = 1, 2);$$

and the result follows.

THEOREM 22.6. *Let C be a polygon, and suppose that neither w_1 nor w_2 is on C, and that the line segment $\{w_1, w_2\}$ meets one and only one of the sides of C. Then $\chi(w_2, C) - \chi(w_1, C) = \pm 2\pi$.*

This follows immediately from Theorem 22.5.

22.7. It is trivial that, if z_1 and z_2 are distinct points of the simple curve C, then there is one and only one arc of C with end points z_1 and z_2.

EXERCISE

22.2. Prove that, if the bounded sets of points U, V have at least one point in common, then the diameter of $U \cup V$ is less than or equal to the sum of the diameters of U and V.

THEOREM 22.7. *Let C be any simple curve, and ϵ any positive number. Then there is a positive number δ, such that, for every pair of distinct points z_1, z_2 of C, for which $|z_1 - z_2| < \delta$, the diameter of the arc of C with end points z_1 and z_2 is less than ϵ.*

Proof. By Theorem 9.10, there are curves $C_1, C_2, \ldots, C_k$, each having a diameter less than $\frac{1}{2}\epsilon$, such that $C = C_1 + C_2 + \ldots + C_k$. Since C is simple, any two of these curves C_m, C_n, where $n \geqslant m + 2$, have no point in common. Hence, by Theorems 3.4 and 9.2 and Exercise 9.2(i), the distance $d(m, n)$ between the curves C_m and C_n is positive. If $k \geqslant 3$, let δ be the least of the numbers $d(m, n)$ corresponding to pairs of integers m, n for which $1 \leqslant m$ and $m + 2 \leqslant n \leqslant k$—there are $\frac{1}{2}(k-1)(k-2)$ such pairs. If $k = 1$ or 2, let δ be any positive number. Now suppose z_1 and z_2 are any two distinct points of C such that $|z_1 - z_2| < \delta$, and let C' be the arc of C with end points z_1 and z_2. Then there are integers m, n such that $1 \leqslant m \leqslant n \leqslant k$, and that one of the points z_1, z_2 lies on C_m, the other on C_n. It follows that $d(m, n) \leqslant |z_1 - z_2| < \delta$. Hence, by the definition of δ, either $n = m$ or $n = m + 1$. In the former case, C' is an arc of C_m, and its diameter is therefore less than or equal to that of C_m, which is less than $\frac{1}{2}\epsilon$. In the latter, C' is an arc of $C_m + C_{m+1}$, whose diameter, by Exercise 22.2, is less than or equal to the sum of those of C_m and C_{m+1}. Hence the diameter of C' is again less than ϵ. This proves the theorem.

22.8. Now suppose the hypothesis of Theorem 22.2 is satisfied. Then the distances of the points 0 and 1 from C are both positive. Denote these distances by ϵ_0 and ϵ_1, let $\epsilon = \min(\epsilon_0, \epsilon_1)$, and choose δ in accordance with Theorem 22.7.

Let n be an integer greater than $\max(4/\delta, 4/\epsilon)$. Having chosen n, I define a *lattice point* as a point whose real and imaginary parts are multiples of $1/n$, i.e. a point $x+iy$ such that nx and ny are integers, a *step* as a line segment of length $1/n$ whose end points are lattice points, and a *staircase* as a broken line whose sides are steps.   I call a staircase $\{z_0, z_1, \ldots, z_k\}$ *simple* if and only if the points $z_0, z_1, \ldots, z_k$ are distinct. It is true, but irrelevant, that a staircase is simple if and only if it is a simple curve as defined in §9.7.

22.9. LEMMA 1.   *Let Γ be a staircase leading from 0 to 1. Then there is a simple staircase Γ', also leading from 0 to 1, such that every side of Γ' is a side of Γ.*

Proof.   From among the staircases which lead from 0 to 1 and consist entirely of sides of Γ, choose one with the least number of sides.   It is easily seen that this staircase is necessarily simple.

LEMMA 2.   *Let T be a set of points whose diameter is less than $1/n$.   Then there is a lattice point w such that, for every point z of T, $|\mathrm{re}\, z-\mathrm{re}\, w| < 1/n$ and $|\mathrm{im}\, z-\mathrm{im}\, w| < 1/n$.*

Proof.   Let u_1 and u_2 be the upper bounds of the real and imaginary parts of the points of T respectively.   Then the point $w=[nu_1]/n+i[nu_2]/n$ (where $[x]$ denotes the greatest integer less than or equal to x) has the required properties. This proves the lemma.

22.10.   Now let

$$C=C_1+C_2+\ldots+C_k,$$

where the diameter of each of the curves $C_1, C_2, \ldots, C_k$ is less than $1/n$.   It follows from Theorem 9.10 that such a dissection of C into arcs exists.   Let

$$C'_m = C_1+C_2+\ldots+C_m \quad (m = 1, 2, \ldots, k),$$

and let C'_0 denote the empty set.

22.11. LEMMA 3.   *Let m be one of the numbers $0, 1, \ldots, k-1$, and suppose there is a simple staircase Γ which leads from 0 to 1 and does not meet C'_m.   Then there is a staircase Γ' which leads from 0 to 1 and does not meet C'_{m+1}.*

Proof.   Let Γ be the staircase $\{z_0, z_1, \ldots, z_h\}$, so that $z_0 = 0$ and $z_h = 1$.   By §22.10 and Lemma 2, there is a lattice point w such that, defining S as the set of those points z for which $|\mathrm{re}\, z-\mathrm{re}\, w| < 1/n$ and $|\mathrm{im}\, z-\mathrm{im}\, w| < 1/n$, we have

$$|C_{m+1}| \subset S. \tag{10}$$

On the other hand, any step of which w is not an end point has no point in common with S. Thus such a step cannot meet C_{m+1}. It follows that, if Γ meets C_{m+1}, then w must be one of the points $z_0, z_1, \ldots, z_h$. If, however, Γ does not meet C_{m+1}, then we may take $\Gamma' = \Gamma$, and there is nothing to prove. Suppose, therefore, that Γ meets C_{m+1}. Then, as we have just seen, there is an integer j such that $0 \leqslant j \leqslant h$ and $w = z_j$. Suppose, if possible, that $j = 0$. Then $w = z_0 = 0$. Hence, for any point z of S,

$$|z| = |z - w| \leqslant |\operatorname{re} z - \operatorname{re} w| + |\operatorname{im} z - \operatorname{im} w| < 2/n.$$

This holds, in particular, by (10), for any point z of C_{m+1}. On the other hand, for any such point z, by §22.8, $|z| \geqslant \epsilon_0 \geqslant \epsilon > 4/n$. This is a contradiction, and so $j \neq 0$. Similarly $j \neq h$, and so $0 < j < h$.

Since Γ is simple, no side of Γ other than $\{z_{j-1}, z_j\}$ and $\{z_j, z_{j+1}\}$ has w for an end point. Hence these two are the only sides of Γ which have points in common with S. Let Γ_1 and Γ_2 be the two simple broken lines, contained in the boundary of S, leading from z_{j-1} to z_{j+1} (see §22.2). Then, by (10), neither Γ_1 nor Γ_2 meets C_{m+1}. Hence, if Γ_1 does not meet C'_m, we may take for Γ' the staircase obtained from Γ by substituting Γ_1 for $\{z_{j-1}, z_j, z_{j+1}\}$, and the result follows. It similarly follows if Γ_2 does not meet C'_m. It is therefore sufficient to prove that C'_m does not meet both Γ_1 and Γ_2.

Suppose, if possible, C'_m meets Γ_1 in w_1 and Γ_2 in w_2. Then there is a point w_0 with the three properties obtained from those stated in §22.2 by substituting z_{j-1} for z_1 and z_{j+1} for z_2. Choose w_0 accordingly, and let C' be the arc of C'_m with end points w_1 and w_2. Now, by the definition of S and §22.8,

$$|w_1 - w_2| \leqslant 2\sqrt{2}/n < 4/n < \delta,$$

and hence, in view of our choice of δ (§22.8), the diameter of C' is less than ϵ. Let $\Gamma_3 = \{1, 1-i, -i, 0\}$ or $\{1, 1+i, i, 0\}$ according as $\operatorname{im} w_1 \geqslant 0$ or $\operatorname{im} w_1 < 0$, and let d be the distance of w_1 from Γ_3. Then $d = \min(|w_1|, |w_1 - 1|)$. Also, by §22.8, $|w_1| \geqslant \epsilon_0$, $|w_1 - 1| \geqslant \epsilon_1$, and hence, again by §22.8,

$$d \geqslant \epsilon > 4/n > 2\sqrt{2}/n.$$

This means that the distance of w_1 from Γ_3 is greater than the distance of w_1 from any point or limit point of S. Thus Γ_3 has no point in common with S or its boundary. Hence $\{z_{j-1}, z_j\}$ and $\{z_j, z_{j+1}\}$ are the only sides with points in S, not only of Γ, but also of the polygon $\Gamma + \Gamma_3$; and neither w_1 nor w_2 is on this polygon. From this and our choice of w_0 it follows that $\{w_1, w_0\}$ does not meet this polygon, and that $\{w_0, w_2\}$ meets exactly one of its sides. Hence, by Exercise 9.15 and Theorem 22.6,

$$\chi(w_1, \Gamma + \Gamma_3) = \chi(w_0, \Gamma + \Gamma_3)$$

and

$$\chi(w_0, \Gamma + \Gamma_3) - \chi(w_2, \Gamma + \Gamma_3) = \pm 2\pi,$$

so that

$$\chi(w_1, \Gamma + \Gamma_3) \neq \chi(w_2, \Gamma + \Gamma_3).$$

On the other hand, since the diameter of C' is less than ϵ and therefore less than d, C' cannot meet Γ_3, and since C' is an arc of C'_m, C' cannot meet Γ. Hence, by Exercise 9.31(ii),

$$\chi(w_1, \Gamma + \Gamma_3) = \chi(w_2, \Gamma + \Gamma_3).$$

This is a contradiction, and so the lemma is proved.

LEMMA 4. *For every integer m from 0 to k, there is a staircase which leads from 0 to 1 and does not meet C'_m.*

This is trivial for $m = 0$, and therefore follows from Lemmas 1 and 3 by induction.

Theorem 22.2 follows from Lemma 4 on noting that $C = C'_k$ (see §22.10). Thus this theorem is proved, and with it, as explained in §22.1, Theorem 22.1.

EXERCISE

22.3. Prove that, if the line segments $\{z_1, z_2\}$ and $\{w_1, w_2\}$ have more than one point in common, and neither w_1 nor w_2 is on $\{z_1, z_2\}$, then $|\{z_1, z_2\}| \subset |\{w_1, w_2\}|$.

22.12. The *Jordan curve theorem* may be stated in the following form:

THEOREM 22.8. *Let C be a simple closed curve. Then $I(C)$ and $E(C)$ are domains.*

Proof. Choose z_1, z_2 and define H_1, H_2 as in §9.21. Then, as stated there, im $z_1 <$ im z_2. Choose b so that

$$\text{im } z_1 \; < \; b \; < \; \text{im } z_2. \tag{11}$$

Then, by Theorem 9.11, there are two distinct points w_1, w_2 of C such that

$$\text{im } w_1 = \text{im } w_2 = b, \tag{12}$$

and that all points of the line segment $\{w_1, w_2\}$, other than its end points, are in $I(C)$. Thus $I(C)$ is not empty, and any two points w, w' of $\{w_1, w_2\}$, distinct from w_1 and w_2, can be joined by a broken line contained in $I(C)$. In fact, except in the trivial case $w = w'$, the line segment $\{w, w'\}$ is such a broken line (see §9.6). Also, by Exercise 9.20, $I(C)$ is open. In order to complete the proof that $I(C)$ is a domain, it is therefore sufficient to prove

LEMMA 1. *Any point of $I(C)$, which is not on $\{w_1, w_2\}$, can be joined to a point of $\{w_1, w_2\}$ by a broken line contained in $I(C)$.*

It follows from Exercise 9.21 that any point of $H_1 \cup H_2$, other than z_1 and z_2, is in $E(C)$, and that any two such points can be joined by a broken line contained in $E(C)$. Thus $E(C)$ is not empty. Also, by Exercise 9.20, $E(C)$ is open. In order to complete the proof that $E(C)$ is a domain, it is therefore sufficient to prove

LEMMA 2. *Any point of $E(C)$, which is not in $H_1 \cup H_2$, can be joined to a point of $H_1 \cup H_2$ by a broken line contained in $E(C)$.*

Proof of Lemma 1. By Exercise 9.41, w_1 and w_2 are the end points of two simple curves C', C'', such that

$$z_1 \in |C'|, \qquad z_2 \in |C''|, \tag{13}$$

and

$$C \sim C' + C''. \tag{14}$$

C' leads either from w_1 to w_2, or from w_2 to w_1. We may suppose the former, without loss of generality. Then, by (14), C'' leads from w_2 to w_1. Hence $C' + \{w_2, w_1\}$ and $C'' + \{w_1, w_2\}$ are closed curves. Let

$$C_1' = C' + \{w_2, w_1\}, \qquad C_1'' = C'' + \{w_1, w_2\}. \tag{15}$$

Now suppose z_0' is a point of $I(C)$ which is not on $\{w_1, w_2\}$. Then, by (14), Exercise 9.40 and the definitions of χ (§9.15) and $I(C)$ (§9.16),

$$\chi(z_0', C') + \chi(z_0', C'') = \chi(z_0', C) \neq 0. \tag{16}$$

Also, by (15) and Exercises 9.10, 9.42 and 9.9,

$$\chi(z_0', C_1') + \chi(z_0', C_1'') = \chi(z_0', C') + \chi(z_0', C'').$$

Hence $\chi(z_0', C_1')$ and $\chi(z_0', C_1'')$ cannot both be 0, and we may suppose, without loss of generality, that

$$\chi(z_0', C_1') \neq 0. \tag{17}$$

Let $w = \frac{1}{2}(w_1 + w_2)$. Then neither z_0' nor w is on C'. Hence, by Theorem 22.1 and §9.17, there is a broken line Γ which leads from z_0' to w and does not meet C'. Let $\Gamma = \{z_0', z_1', \ldots, z_k'\}$, and let S be the set of those natural numbers $n \leqslant k$ for which $\{z_{n-1}', z_n'\}$ meets $\{w_1, w_2\}$. Then $z_k' = w \in |\{w_1, w_2\}|$. Hence $k \in S$, and so S is not empty. Let h be the least member of S. Then (if $h > 1$) the broken line $\{z_0', z_1', \ldots, z_{h-1}'\}$ does not meet $\{w_1, w_2\}$, but the line segment $\{z_{h-1}', z_h'\}$ does (also if $h = 1$), and, by Exercise 22.3, in only one point. Let this point be w', and let $\Gamma' = \{z_0', z_1', \ldots, z_{h-1}', w'\}$ if $h > 1$, and $\Gamma' = \{z_0', w'\}$ if $h = 1$. Then any point z of Γ', other than its end points, can be joined to z_0' by a broken line (an arc of Γ') which does not meet C_1'. Hence, by (17) and Exercise 9.31 (ii),

$$\chi(z, C_1') = \chi(z_0', C_1') \neq 0 \tag{18}$$

for any such point z. On the other hand, by §9.21 and formulae (11)–(15), the half-line H_2 does not meet C_1'. Hence, by Exercise 9.21 and the definition of $E(C)$ (§9.16), $\chi(z_2, C_1') = 0$. Now any point z of C, which is not on C', can be joined to z_2 by a curve which does not meet C_1'. Hence, by Exercise 9.31(ii),

$$\chi(z, C_1') = \chi(z_2, C_1') = 0 \tag{19}$$

for any such point z. Since Γ' does not meet C', and (18) and (19) contradict each other, no point of Γ', other than its end points, can be on C. The end points of Γ', however, are not on C either. Hence Γ' does not meet C. From this, Exercise 9.31(ii), and formula (16) it follows that, for every point z

15—C.N.F.

of Γ', we have $\chi(z, C) = \chi(z_0', C) \neq 0$, which means that $|\Gamma'| \subset I(C)$. Since Γ' is a broken line leading from z_0' to a point of $\{w_1, w_2\}$, the lemma is proved.

Proof of Lemma 2. Let C_1, C_2, ϕ_1 and ϕ_2 have the same meaning as in §9.21, and define S_1, S_2 and x_1 as in §9.22. Then, as stated there, either $x_1 \in S_1$ or $x_1 \in S_2$. Suppose, first, $x_1 \in S_2$. Then, by §9.22, formula (29) and the definitions preceding it, there is a point z (there denoted by w_2) such that $z \in |C_2|$ and $\phi_1(z) = \pi$, and it follows from §9.22, Lemma 1, that the last equation holds for *every* point z of C_2 except $z = z_1$ and $z = z_2$ (for which $\phi_1(z)$ does not exist):

$$\phi_1(z) = \pi \quad (z \in |C_2|, \quad z \neq z_1, \quad z \neq z_2). \tag{20}$$

Also, with w_3 defined as in §9.22, $w_3 \in |C_1|$ and $\phi_2(w_3) = \pi$. The last equation can be proved in the same way as §9.22 (32). Hence, by an argument similar to that which led to (20),

$$\phi_2(z) = \pi \quad (z \in |C_1|, \quad z \neq z_1, \quad z \neq z_2). \tag{21}$$

In the case $x_1 \in S_1$, we have to replace π by $-\pi$ in both (20) and (21). Let us denote the formulae so obtained by (20a) and (21a). The proofs are essentially the same.

Now suppose z_0' is a point of $E(C)$ which is not in $H_1 \cup H_2$. Then, by §9.21 (26) and an argument similar to that which led to (16),

$$\phi_1(z_0') + \phi_2(z_0') = \chi(z_0', C) = 0. \tag{22}$$

Hence $\phi_1(z_0')$ and $\phi_2(z_0')$ cannot both be equal to π; nor can both be equal to $-\pi$. Thus at least one of the following four conditions is satisfied:

 i. (20) and (21) hold, and $\phi_1(z_0') \neq \pi$.
 ii. (20) and (21) hold, and $\phi_2(z_0') \neq \pi$.
 iii. (20a) and (21a) hold, and $\phi_1(z_0') \neq -\pi$.
 iv. (20a) and (21a) hold, and $\phi_2(z_0') \neq -\pi$.

I shall deal only with the first of these four cases, leaving the other three, which are similar, to the reader.

Suppose, then, (20) and (21) hold, and

$$\phi_1(z_0') \neq \pi. \tag{23}$$

Let $w = z_1 - i$ (so that $w \in H_1$). Then neither z_0' nor w is on C_1. Hence, by Theorem 22.1 and §9.17, there is a broken line Γ which leads from z_0' to w and does not meet C_1. Let $\Gamma = \{z_0', z_1', \ldots, z_k'\}$. and let S be the set of those natural numbers $n \leqslant k$ for which $\{z_{n-1}', z_n'\}$ meets $H_1 \cup H_2$. Then, as in the proof of Lemma 1, S is not empty. Define h again as the least member of S. Then (if $h > 1$) the broken line $\{z_0', z_1', \ldots, z_{h-1}'\}$ does not meet $H_1 \cup H_2$, but the line segment $\{z_{h-1}', z_h'\}$ does. One can show that it does so in only one point, but it is not worth while to carry the analogy with the proof of Lemma 1 so far. It is easier to proceed as follows: By Exercise 3.10, there is a point w' in $|\{z_{h-1}', z_h'\}| \cap (H_1 \cup H_2)$, such that the distance of z_{h-1}' from this set is equal to $|z_{h-1}' - w'|$. Choose w' accordingly, and let $\Gamma' = \{z_0', z_1', \ldots, z_{h-1}', w'\}$ or $\{z_0', w'\}$, according as $h > 1$ or $h = 1$. Then any point z of Γ', other than its end points, can be joined to z_0' by a broken line which does not meet $|C_1| \cup H_1 \cup H_2$. Hence, as can be proved in the same way as Lemma 1 of §9.22, $\phi_1(z) = \phi_1(z_0')$ for any such point. From this and (20) and (23) it follows (since Γ does not meet C_1) that no such point can be on C. The remainder of the proof can be obtained from the end of that of Lemma 1 by obvious modifications.

CHAPTER 23

PICARD'S THEOREM

23.1. Picard's theorem states that every integral function, except the constants, assumes every value with at most one exception. I shall prove it by the so-called non-elementary method, but my proof should be elementary enough for those who have followed me so far. It depends on the existence of a function J with the following three properties:

(i) J is regular in the upper half-plane.

(ii) For every number w, there is a point z in the upper half-plane such that $J(z) = w$.

(iii) For any points z, w of the upper half-plane, we have $J(z) = J(w)$ if and only if there are integers a, b, c, d, such that $ad - bc = 1$ and $w = (az + b)/(cz + d)$.

23.2. To construct the function J, I use a theorem which states, roughly, that the sum of an absolutely convergent double series is independent of the order of the terms. More precisely it is as follows:

THEOREM 23.1. *Suppose that*

$$\sum_{m=-\infty}^{\infty} \sum_{n=-\infty}^{\infty} |f(m, n)|$$

converges. For every pair of integers (m, n), *let* $g(m, n)$ *and* $h(m, n)$ *be integers, and suppose that, for every pair of integers* (m', n'), *there is one and only one pair of integers* (m, n), *such that* $g(m, n) = m'$ *and* $h(m, n) = n'$. *Then*

$$\sum_{m=-\infty}^{\infty} \sum_{n=-\infty}^{\infty} f\{g(m, n), h(m, n)\} = \sum_{m=-\infty}^{\infty} \sum_{n=-\infty}^{\infty} f(m, n). \quad (1)$$

The proof of this theorem will be given later.

23.3. If S is a finite set of integers, and its members are $n_1, n_2, \ldots, n_k$, then

$$\sum_{n \in S} f(n)$$

is defined as

$$\sum_{j=1}^{k} f(n_j).$$

If S is the empty set, then

$$\sum_{n \in S} f(n) = 0.$$

If S is a finite set of pairs of integers, and its members are the pairs (m_j, n_j) $(j = 1, 2, \ldots, k)$, then

$$\sum_{\substack{m, n \\ (m, n) \in S}} f(m, n)$$

is defined as

$$\sum_{j=1}^{k} f(m_j, n_j),$$

and (for every integer m)

$$\sum_{\substack{n \\ (m, n) \in S}} f(m, n)$$

is defined as

$$\sum_{n \in S_m} f(m, n),$$

where S_m is the set of those integers n for which $(m, n) \in S$. It follows that, if m' and m'' are respectively the least and the greatest of those integers m for which S_m is not empty, then

$$\sum_{\substack{m, n \\ (m, n) \in S}} f(m, n) = \sum_{m=m'}^{m''} \sum_{\substack{n \\ (m, n) \in S}} f(m, n) = \sum_{m=-\infty}^{\infty} \sum_{\substack{n \\ (m, n) \in S}} f(m, n),$$

provided that $f(m, n)$ exists for every member (m, n) of S.

23.4. THEOREM 23.2. *Suppose the hypotheses of Theorem 23.1 are satisfied, and $f(m, n) \geqslant 0$ for every pair of integers (m, n). Then* (1) *holds.*

Proof. Let

$$\sum_{m'=-\infty}^{\infty} \sum_{n'=-\infty}^{\infty} f(m', n') = s, \tag{2}$$

let m be any integer, k any positive integer, and let S be the set of pairs of integers defined as follows: $(m', n') \in S$ if and only if there is an integer n, such that $|n| \leqslant k$, $g(m, n) = m'$ and $h(m, n) = n'$. This means that S consists of the $2k + 1$ pairs $\{g(m, -k), h(m, -k)\}$, $\{g(m, -k+1), h(m, -k+1)\}$, ..., $\{g(m, k), h(m, k)\}$. Hence, by (2) and §23.3,

$$\sum_{n=-k}^{k} f\{g(m, n), h(m, n)\} = \sum_{\substack{m'\, n' \\ (m', n') \in S}} f(m', n')$$

$$= \sum_{m'=-\infty}^{\infty} \sum_{\substack{n' \\ (m', n') \in S}} f(m', n') \leqslant s.$$

Thus

$$\sum_{n=-k}^{k} f\{g(m, n), h(m, n)\} \leqslant s$$

for every positive integer k, and since $f\{g(m, n), h(m, n)\} \geqslant 0$ for every integer n, it follows that

$$\sum_{n=-\infty}^{\infty} f\{g(m, n), h(m, n)\}$$

converges. This holds for every integer m. Hence

$$\sum_{m=-k'}^{k'} \sum_{n=-\infty}^{\infty} f\{g(m, n), h(m, n)\}$$

$$= \lim_{k \to \infty} \sum_{m=-k'}^{k'} \sum_{n=-k}^{k} f\{g(m, n), h(m, n)\} \quad (3)$$

for every positive integer k'.

Now let k and k' be any positive integers, and let S' be the set of pairs of integers defined as follows: $(m', n') \in S'$ if and only if there are integers m, n, such that $|m| \leqslant k'$, $|n| \leqslant k$, $g(m, n) = m'$ and $h(m, n) = n'$. Then, by (2),

$$\sum_{m=-k'}^{k'} \sum_{n=-k}^{k} f\{g(m, n), h(m, n)\} = \sum_{\substack{m', n' \\ (m', n') \in S'}} f(m', n') \leqslant s.$$

From this and (3) it follows that

$$\sum_{m=-k'}^{k'} \sum_{n=-\infty}^{\infty} f\{g(m, n), h(m, n)\} \leqslant s \quad (4)$$

for every positive integer k'. Arguing as before, we deduce that the series

$$\sum_{m=-\infty}^{\infty} \sum_{n=-\infty}^{\infty} f\{g(m, n), h(m, n)\}$$

converges. Let its sum be s'. Then, by (4),

$$s' \leqslant s. \tag{5}$$

Also, putting

$$f\{g(m, n), h(m, n)\} = f^*(m, n), \tag{6}$$

we have

$$\sum_{m=-\infty}^{\infty} \sum_{n=-\infty}^{\infty} f^*(m, n) = s'. \tag{7}$$

For every pair of integers (m', n'), denote the integers m, n for which $g(m, n) = m'$ and $h(m, n) = n'$ by $g^*(m', n')$ and $h^*(m', n')$ respectively. Then, by (6),

$$f(m', n') = f^*\{g^*(m', n'), h^*(m', n')\}. \tag{8}$$

Now, by the argument which led from (2) to (5), we obtain from (7) that

$$\sum_{m'=-\infty}^{\infty} \sum_{n'=-\infty}^{\infty} f^*\{g^*(m'\ n'), h^*(m', n')\} \leqslant s'.$$

From this and (8) and (2) it follows that $s \leqslant s'$. Hence, by (5), $s' = s$, which proves the theorem.

23.5. *Proof* of Theorem 23.1. By Theorem 23.2,

$$\sum_{m=-\infty}^{\infty} \sum_{n=-\infty}^{\infty} \left| f\{g(m, n), h(m, n)\} \right| = \sum_{m=-\infty}^{\infty} \sum_{n=-\infty}^{\infty} |f(m, n)|. \tag{9}$$

Now let $f_1(m, n) = |f(m, n)| - \operatorname{re} f(m, n)$. Then

$$|f_1(m, n)| \leqslant 2|f(m, n)|.$$

Hence, by the comparison test,

$$\sum_{m=1}^{\infty} \sum_{n=1}^{\infty} |f_1(m, n)|$$

converges.   Also $f_1(m, n) \geqslant 0$.   Hence, by Theorem 23.2,

$$\sum_{m=-\infty}^{\infty} \sum_{n=-\infty}^{\infty} f_1\{g(m, n), h(m, n)\} = \sum_{m=-\infty}^{\infty} \sum_{n=-\infty}^{\infty} f_1(m, n). \quad (10)$$

Now

$$\mathrm{re}\, f(m, n) = |f(m, n)| - f_1(m, n)$$

and

$$\mathrm{re}\, f\{g(m, n), h(m, n)\}$$
$$= |f\{g(m, n), h(m, n)\}| - f_1\{g(m, n), h(m, n)\}.$$

Hence, by (9) and (10),

$$\sum_{m=-\infty}^{\infty} \sum_{n=-\infty}^{\infty} \mathrm{re}\, f\{g(m, n), h(m, n)\} = \sum_{m=-\infty}^{\infty} \sum_{n=-\infty}^{\infty} \mathrm{re}\, f(m, n).$$

Similarly

$$\sum_{m=-\infty}^{\infty} \sum_{n=-\infty}^{\infty} \mathrm{im}\, f\{g(m, n), h(m, n)\} = \sum_{m=-\infty}^{\infty} \sum_{n=-\infty}^{\infty} \mathrm{im}\, f(m, n).$$

From the last two formulae we obtain (1) immediately.

23.6. I define

$$\sideset{}{'}\sum_{m, n} g(m, n)$$

as

$$\sum_{m=-\infty}^{\infty} \sum_{n=-\infty}^{\infty} f(m, n), \quad (11)$$

where $f(m, n) = g(m, n)$ if m and n are not both 0, and $f(0, 0) = 0$.

23.7. THEOREM 23.3.   *Let $k > 2$ and* $\mathrm{im}\, z > 0$.   *Then*

$$\sideset{}{'}\sum_{m, n} |mz + n|^{-k}$$

converges.

Proof. Let $f(m, n) = |mz + n|^{-k}$ if m and n are not both 0, and $f(0, 0) = 0$.   Then we have to prove that (11) converges. Now it is trivial that, for any integer m,

$$\sum_{n=-\infty}^{\infty} f(m, n)$$

converges.   Let its sum be s_m.   Then we have to prove that

$$\sum_{m=-\infty}^{\infty} s_m \tag{12}$$

converges.   Now let $z = x + iy$, and suppose that $m > 0$.   Then

$$s_m = \sum_{n'=-\infty}^{\infty} \left| mx + n' + imy \right|^{-k} = \sum_{n=-\infty}^{\infty} \left| mx - [mx] + n + imy \right|^{-k}$$

$$\leqslant \sum_{n=0}^{\infty} \left| n + imy \right|^{-k} + \sum_{n=-\infty}^{-1} \left| n + 1 + imy \right|^{-k}$$

$$= 2 \sum_{n=0}^{\infty} \left| n + imy \right|^{-k} \leqslant 2^{1+k} \sum_{n=0}^{\infty} (n + my)^{-k}$$

$$\leqslant 2^{1+k} \left\{ (my)^{-k} + \int_{my}^{\infty} u^{-k} du \right\}$$

$$= 2^{1+k} \left\{ (my)^{-k} + (k-1)^{-1} (my)^{1-k} \right\}.$$

Hence, by the comparison test,

$$\sum_{m=1}^{\infty} s_m$$

converges.   Similarly, so does

$$\sum_{m=-\infty}^{-1} s_m.$$

Hence (12) converges, and the theorem is proved.

23.8.   I now define the functions G and H by the equations

$$G(z) = \sideset{}{'}\sum_{m,n} (mz + n)^{-4}, \qquad H(z) = \sideset{}{'}\sum_{m,n} (mz + n)^{-6}. \tag{13}$$

THEOREM 23.4.   *Let* im $z > 0$, *let* a, b, c *and* d *be integers, and let* $ad - bc = 1$.   *Then*

$$G(z) = (cz + d)^{-4} G\{(az + b)/(cz + d)\} \tag{14}$$

and

$$H(z) = (cz + d)^{-6} H\{(az + b)/(cz + d)\} \quad . \tag{15}$$

Proof. By (13) and Theorems 23.1 and 23.3,

$$G(z) = \sideset{}{'}\sum_{m,n} \{(am+cn)z + (bm+dn)\}^{-4}$$

$$= (cz+d)^{-4} \sideset{}{'}\sum_{m,n} \{m(az+b)/(cz+d)+n\}^{-4}$$

$$= (cz+d)^{-4}G\{(az+b)/(cz+d)\}.$$

This proves (14), and the proof of (15) is similar.

EXERCISE

23.1. Prove that $G(\tfrac{1}{2}+\tfrac{1}{2}i\sqrt{3}) = H(i) = 0$. [Hint: use (14) with $a=0$, $b=d=-1$, $c=1$, and (15) with $a=d=0$, $b=-1$, $c=1$.]

23.9. Let $0 < |w| < 1$. Then, by §19.9,

$$\pi w \cot \pi w = 1 - 2 \sum_{n=1}^{\infty} \frac{w^2}{n^2-w^2} = 1 - 2 \sum_{n=1}^{\infty} \sum_{m=1}^{\infty} n^{-2m}w^{2m},$$

and

$$\sum_{n=1}^{\infty} \sum_{m=1}^{\infty} |n^{-2m}w^{2m}|$$

converges.   Hence

$$\pi w \cot \pi w = 1 - 2 \sum_{m=1}^{\infty} \sum_{n=1}^{\infty} n^{-2m}w^{2m} = \sum_{m=0}^{\infty} b_m w^{2m}, \quad (16)$$

where $b_0 = 1$ and

$$b_m = -2 \sum_{n=1}^{\infty} n^{-2m} \quad (m = 1, 2, \ldots). \quad (17)$$

Substituting $\sqrt{z}$ for w in (16), and using Chapter 5, we obtain

$$\sum_{m=0}^{\infty} (-1)^m \frac{\pi^{2m}}{(2m+1)!} z^m \sum_{m=0}^{\infty} b_m z^m$$

$$= \sum_{m=0}^{\infty} (-1)^m \frac{\pi^{2m}}{(2m)!} z^m \quad (|z| < 1). \quad (18)$$

Now, by Theorem 2.10,

$$\sum_{m=0}^{\infty} (-1)^m \frac{\pi^{2m}}{(2m+1)!} z^m \sum_{m=0}^{\infty} b_m z^m = \sum_{m=0}^{\infty} c_m z^m \quad (|z| < 1), \quad (19)$$

where

$$c_m = \sum_{n=0}^{m} (-1)^n \frac{\pi^{2n}}{(2n+1)!} b_{m-n} \quad (m = 0, 1, 2, \ldots). \quad (20)$$

By (18), (19) and Theorem 14.5 (or Hardy, §201),

$$c_m = (-1)^m \pi^{2m}/(2m)! \quad (m = 0, 1, 2, \ldots).$$

Hence, by (20),

$$\sum_{n=0}^{m} (-1)^n \frac{\pi^{2n}}{(2n+1)!} b_{m-n} = (-1)^m \frac{\pi^{2m}}{(2m)!} \quad (m = 0, 1, 2, \ldots).$$
$$(21)$$

In particular,

$$b_0 = 1, \qquad b_1 - \frac{\pi^2}{6} b_0 = -\frac{\pi^2}{2}, \qquad b_2 - \frac{\pi^2}{6} b_1 + \frac{\pi^4}{120} b_0 = \frac{\pi^4}{24},$$

$$b_3 - \frac{\pi^2}{6} b_2 + \frac{\pi^4}{120} b_1 - \frac{\pi^6}{5040} b_0 = -\frac{\pi^6}{720},$$

so that

$$\pi^{-2}b_1 = \frac{1}{6} - \frac{1}{2} = -\frac{1}{3}, \qquad \pi^{-4}b_2 = -\frac{1}{6} \times \frac{1}{3} - \frac{1}{120} + \frac{1}{24} = -\frac{1}{45},$$

$$\pi^{-6}b_3 = -\frac{1}{6} \times \frac{1}{45} + \frac{1}{120} \times \frac{1}{3} + \frac{1}{5040} - \frac{1}{720} = -\frac{2}{945}.$$

From this and (17) it follows that

$$\sum_{n=1}^{\infty} n^{-4} = \frac{\pi^4}{90}, \qquad \sum_{n=1}^{\infty} n^{-6} = \frac{\pi^6}{945}. \quad (22)$$

23.10. Let

$$g(w) = \sum_{n=-\infty}^{\infty} (w+n)^{-2}. \quad (23)$$

Then, by Theorem 14.3,

$$g''(w) = 6 \sum_{n=-\infty}^{\infty} (w+n)^{-4}, \qquad g^{(4)}(w) = 120 \sum_{n=-\infty}^{\infty} (w+n)^{-6} \quad (24)$$

for all numbers w except the integers. Also $g''(-w) = g''(w)$

and $g^{(4)}(-w) = g^{(4)}(w)$ for all such numbers w.   Hence, by (13), §23.6 and (22),

$$G(z) = \frac{\pi^4}{45} + \frac{1}{3} \sum_{m=1}^{\infty} g''(mz),$$

$$H(z) = \frac{2\pi^6}{945} + \frac{1}{60} \sum_{m=1}^{\infty} g^{(4)}(mz) \quad (\text{im } z > 0). \tag{25}$$

Now, by (23) and §19.5 and §5.4,

$$g(w) = \pi^2 \operatorname{cosec}^2 \pi w = -4\pi^2 e^{2\pi i w}(1 - e^{2\pi i w})^{-2}$$

$$= -4\pi^2 \sum_{k=1}^{\infty} k e^{2k\pi i w} \quad (\text{im } w > 0).$$

Hence, by Theorem 14.3,

$$g''(w) = 16\pi^4 \sum_{k=1}^{\infty} k^3 e^{2k\pi i w},$$

$$g^{(4)}(w) = -64\pi^6 \sum_{k=1}^{\infty} k^5 e^{2k\pi i w} \quad (\text{im } w > 0).$$

From this and (25) it follows that

$$45\pi^{-4} G(z) = 1 + 240 \sum_{m=1}^{\infty} \sum_{k=1}^{\infty} k^3 e^{2km\pi i z} \quad (\text{im } z > 0) \tag{26}$$

and

$$\tfrac{1}{2} \times 945\pi^{-6} H(z) = 1 - 504 \sum_{m=1}^{\infty} \sum_{k=1}^{\infty} k^5 e^{2km\pi i z} \quad (\text{im } z > 0). \tag{27}$$

23.11. For any number t, let $\sigma_t(n)$ denote the sum of the tth powers of the positive divisors of n, and let $d(k, n) = 1$ or 0 according as k is or is not a divisor of n.   Then

$$\sum_{m=1}^{\infty} w^{km} = \sum_{n=1}^{\infty} d(k, n)w^n \quad (k = 1, 2, \ldots; |w| < 1),$$

$$\sigma_t(n) = \sum_{k=1}^{n} d(k, n)k^t = \sum_{k=1}^{\infty} d(k, n)k^t \quad (n = 1, 2, \ldots),$$

and

$$\sum_{n=1}^{\infty} \sum_{k=1}^{\infty} |d(k, n)k^t w^n|$$

and

$$\sum_{k=1}^{\infty} \sum_{m=1}^{\infty} |k^t w^{km}|$$

converge if $|w| < 1$. Hence

$$\sum_{n=1}^{\infty} \sigma_t(n) w^n = \sum_{n=1}^{\infty} \sum_{k=1}^{\infty} d(k, n) k^t w^n = \sum_{k=1}^{\infty} \sum_{n=1}^{\infty} d(k, n) k^t w^n$$

$$= \sum_{k=1}^{\infty} \sum_{m=1}^{\infty} k^t w^{km} = \sum_{m=1}^{\infty} \sum_{k=1}^{\infty} k^t w^{km} \quad (|w| < 1).$$

From this and (26) and (27) we obtain

$$45\pi^{-4} G(z) = 1 + 240 \sum_{n=1}^{\infty} \sigma_3(n) e^{2n\pi i z} \quad (\text{im } z > 0) \qquad (28)$$

and

$$\tfrac{1}{2} \times 945\pi^{-6} H(z) = 1 - 504 \sum_{n=1}^{\infty} \sigma_5(n) e^{2n\pi i z} \quad (\text{im } z > 0). \qquad (29)$$

Let

$$K(z) = \{45\pi^{-4} G(z)\}^3 - \{\tfrac{1}{2} \times 945\pi^{-6} H(z)\}^2 \qquad (30)$$

and

$$J(z) = \{45\pi^{-4} G(z)\}^3 / K(z). \qquad (31)$$

I shall prove that the function J has the three properties mentioned in §23.1.

23.12. It follows from (28), (29), Theorem 14.4 and (30) that the functions G, H and K are regular in the upper half-plane. In order to prove that so is J, it is therefore sufficient to show that

$$K(z) \neq 0 \quad (\text{im } z > 0). \qquad (32)$$

The proof of this formula will depend partly on the next two theorems and partly on crude numerical calculations.

THEOREM 23.5. *On the hypotheses of Theorem 23.4,*

$$K(z) = (cz + d)^{-12} K\{(az + b)/(cz + d)\}.$$

This follows from (30) and Theorem 23.4.

I say that two points z, w are *congruent*, and write $z \equiv w$, if and only if there are integers a, b, c, d such that $ad - bc = 1$ and $w = (az + b)/(cz + d)$.

EXERCISES

23.2. Prove that the congruency just defined is reflexive, symmetrical and transitive (see §9.2).

23.3 Prove that, if im $z > 0$ and $z \equiv w$, then im $w > 0$.

23.13. I define the set S_0 as follows: $z \in S_0$ if and only if either (i) $0 \leqslant \mathrm{re}\, z \leqslant \frac{1}{2}$, im $z > 0$ and $|z| \geqslant 1$, or (ii) $-\frac{1}{2} < \mathrm{re}\, z < 0$, im $z > 0$ and $|z| > 1$.

23.14. THEOREM 23.6. *Every point of the upper half-plane is congruent to a point of S_0.*

Proof. Let im $z_0 > 0$. I define the set T as follows: $z \in T$ if and only if there are integers m, n, not both 0, such that $z = mz_0 + n$. Let T_0 be the set of those numbers z for which $z \in T$ and $|z| \leqslant |z_0|$. Then $z_0 \in T_0$, and so T_0 is not empty. Suppose $z \in T_0$. Then $|z| \leqslant |z_0|$, and there are integers m, n such that $z = mz_0 + n$. Hence

$$|m| \leqslant |z_0|/\mathrm{im}\, z_0. \tag{33}$$

Also $|m + n/z_0| \leqslant 1$, and im $(m + n/z_0) = -n\, \mathrm{im}\, z_0 \cdot |z_0|^{-2}$. Hence

$$|n| \leqslant |z_0|^2/\mathrm{im}\, z_0. \tag{34}$$

There are only a finite number of pairs of integers m, n satisfying (33) and (34). Thus T_0 is a finite set, and has, therefore, a numerically least member, i.e. a member z_1 such that $|z| \geqslant |z_1|$ for every member z of T_0. It is trivial that the last inequality holds also for those members z of T which are not in T_0. Thus

$$|z| \geqslant |z_1| \quad (z \in T). \tag{35}$$

Since $z_1 \in T$, there are integers c, d, not both 0, such that $z_1 = cz_0 + d$. Now c and d must be relatively prime; for if they had a common divisor $m > 1$, it would follow that $z_1/m \in T$, and this would contradict (35). Hence there are integers a', b', such that

$$a'd - b'c = 1. \tag{36}$$

Let $z' = (a'z_0 + b')/(cz_0 + d)$, let n be the least integer greater than $-\mathrm{re}\, z' - \frac{1}{2}$, and let $z'' = z' + n$. Then

$$-\tfrac{1}{2} < \mathrm{re}\, z'' \leqslant \tfrac{1}{2} \tag{37}$$

and $z'' = (az_0 + b)/(cz_0 + d)$, where

$$a = a' + nc, \qquad b = b' + nd. \tag{38}$$

By (36) and (38), $ad - bc = 1$. Hence $z_0 \equiv z''$. Also $az_0 + b \in T$, and $z'' = (az_0 + b)/z_1$. Hence, by (35),

$$|z''| \geqslant 1. \tag{39}$$

Finally, by Exercise 23.3,

$$\operatorname{im} z'' > 0. \tag{40}$$

It follows from (37), (39), (40) and §23.13 that either $z'' \in S_0$, in which case there is nothing left to prove, or $-\frac{1}{2} < \operatorname{re} z'' < 0$ and $|z''| = 1$. In this case let $w = -1/z''$. Then it is easily seen that $z_0 \equiv w$ and $w \in S_0$. This completes the proof.

EXERCISES

23.4. Assuming that $z \in S_0$, and that m and n are integers, not both 0, prove that $|mz + n| \geqslant 1$, with equality only in the following cases: (i) $m = 0$, $n = \pm 1$; (ii) $|z| = 1$, $m = \pm 1$, $n = 0$; (iii) $z = \frac{1}{2} + \frac{1}{2} i \sqrt{3}$, $m = -n = \pm 1$.

23.5. Prove that, if $w = (az + b)/(cz + d)$ and $ad - bc = 1$, then $(cz + d)(cw - a) = -1$.

23.6. Prove that, if $z \in S_0$, $w \in S_0$ and $z \equiv w$, then $z = w$. [Hint: use Exercises 23.4 and 23.5.]

23.15. Suppose, throughout this section, that $|z| < 1$. Let

$$\phi_1(z) = \sum_{n=1}^{\infty} \sigma_3(n) z^n, \qquad \phi_2(z) = \sum_{n=1}^{\infty} \sigma_5(n) z^n \tag{41}$$

and

$$\phi(z) = \{1 + 240\phi_1(z)\}^3 - \{1 - 504\phi_2(z)\}^2. \tag{42}$$

Then, by (30), (28) and (29),

$$K(w) = \phi(e^{2\pi i w}) \quad (\operatorname{im} w > 0). \tag{43}$$

Also, by (42),

$$144^{-1}\phi(z) = 5\phi_1(z) + 1200\{\phi_1(z)\}^2$$
$$+ 96000\{\phi_1(z)\}^3 + 7\phi_2(z) - 1764\{\phi_2(z)\}^2. \tag{44}$$

Let

$$a(1, n) = \sum_{m=1}^{n-1} \sigma_3(m)\sigma_3(n-m), \qquad a(2, n) = \sum_{m=1}^{n-1} a(1, m)\sigma_3(n-m),$$

$$a(3, n) = \sum_{m=1}^{n-1} \sigma_5(m)\sigma_5(n-m), \qquad (45)$$

with the usual convention that

$$\sum_{m=1}^{0} f(m) = 0$$

for any function f. Then, by (41) and Theorem 2.10,

$$\{\phi_1(z)\}^2 = \sum_{n=1}^{\infty} a(1, n)z^n, \qquad \{\phi_1(z)\}^3 = \sum_{n=1}^{\infty} a(2, n)z^n,$$

$$\{\phi_2(z)\}^2 = \sum_{n=1}^{\infty} a(3, n)z^n.$$

Hence, by (44) and (41),

$$144^{-1}\phi(z) = \sum_{n=1}^{\infty} a(n)z^n, \qquad (46)$$

where

$$a(n) = 5\sigma_3(n) + 1200a(1, n) + 96000a(2, n) + 7\sigma_5(n) - 1764a(3,n). \qquad (47)$$

Noting that $\sigma_3(1) = \sigma_5(1) = 1$, $\sigma_3(2) = 9$, $\sigma_5(2) = 33$, $\sigma_3(3) = 28$, $\sigma_5(3) = 244$, $\sigma_3(4) = 73$ and $\sigma_5(4) = 1057$, we obtain from (47) and (45) that

$$a(1) = 12,\ a(2) = -288,\ a(3) = 3024,\ a(4) = -17664. \qquad (48)$$

23.16. Now let n be any natural number. Then, by §23.11,

$$\sigma_3(n) = \sum_{m=1}^{n} d(m, n)(n/m)^3 \leqslant n^3 \sum_{m=1}^{\infty} m^{-3},$$

and

$$\sum_{m=1}^{\infty} m^{-3} \leqslant 1 + \int_{1}^{\infty} x^{-3}dx = \tfrac{3}{2}.$$

Hence

$$\sigma_3(n) \leqslant \tfrac{3}{2}n^3, \tag{49}$$

and similarly

$$\sigma_5(n) \leqslant \tfrac{5}{4}n^5. \tag{50}$$

By (45) and (49),

$$a(1, n) \leqslant \tfrac{9}{4} \sum_{m=1}^{n-1} m^3(n-m)^3.$$

Now $m(n-m) = \tfrac{1}{4}n^2 - (\tfrac{1}{2}n - m)^2 \leqslant \tfrac{1}{4}n^2$. Hence

$$a(1, n) \leqslant 9 \times 2^{-8}n^7. \tag{51}$$

Similarly

$$a(3, n) \leqslant 25 \times 2^{-14}n^{11}. \tag{52}$$

Again, by (45) and (49),

$$a(2, n) = \sum_{m=1}^{n-1} \sum_{k=1}^{m-1} \sigma_3(k)\sigma_3(m-k)\sigma_3(n-m)$$

$$\leqslant \frac{27}{8} \sum_{m=1}^{n-1} \sum_{k=1}^{m-1} \{k(m-k)(n-m)\}^3.$$

The geometric mean of any three positive numbers is less than or equal to their arithmetic mean. Hence, if $0 < k < m < n$, then $k(m-k)(n-m) \leqslant (\tfrac{1}{3}n)^3$. It follows that

$$a(2, n) \leqslant 2^{-4}3^{-6}n^{11}. \tag{53}$$

Now let $n \geqslant 5$. Then, by (47), (52), (49), (51), (53) and (50),

$$-1764 \times 25 \times 2^{-14} \leqslant n^{-11}a(n)$$

$$\leqslant \tfrac{3}{2} \times 5^{-7} + 1200 \times 9 \times 2^{-8}5^{-4}$$

$$+ 96000 \times 2^{-4}3^{-6} + 7 \times \tfrac{5}{4} \times 5^{-6}.$$

Hence

$$|a(n)| \leqslant 9n^{11} \quad (n = 5, 6, \ldots). \tag{54}$$

Now $n \leqslant 5 \times (6/5)^{n-5}$, $(n = 5, 6, \ldots)$. Thus, if $0 < u < (5/6)^{11}$, it follows from (54) that

$$\sum_{n=5}^{\infty} |a(n)| u^{n-1} \leqslant 9 \times 5^{11}u^4/(1 - 6^{11}5^{-11}u).$$

In particular,

$$\sum_{n=5}^{\infty} |a(n)| e^{-\sqrt{3\pi(n-1)}} < \tfrac{1}{5}.$$

From this and (48) it follows that

$$\sum_{n=2}^{\infty} |a(n)| e^{-\sqrt{3\pi(n-1)}} < 2. \tag{55}$$

If the right-hand side of this inequality were 12 instead of 2, it would still be good enough.

23.17. I am now in a position to prove (32).

Let im $z > 0$. Then, by Theorem 23.6, there is a point w such that $w \in S_0$ and $z \equiv w$. This means that there are numbers a, b, c, d, such that the hypotheses of Theorem 23.4 are satisfied, and that $w = (az + b)/(cz + d)$. Hence, by Theorem 23.5,

$$K(z) = (cz + d)^{-12} K(w). \tag{56}$$

It easily follows from §23.13 that im $w \geqslant \tfrac{1}{2}\sqrt{3}$. Hence, by (55),

$$\sum_{n=2}^{\infty} |a(n) e^{2\pi i (n-1)w}| < 2. \tag{57}$$

Now, by (43), (46) and the first part of (48),

$$\left| 144^{-1} e^{-2\pi i w} K(w) \right| = \left| \sum_{n=1}^{\infty} a(n) e^{2\pi i (n-1)w} \right|$$

$$\geqslant 12 - \sum_{n=2}^{\infty} |a(n) e^{2\pi i (n-1)w}|.$$

This, together with (56) and (57), proves (32).

EXERCISE

23.7. Prove that, if $0 < |z| < 1$, then $\phi(z) \neq 0$. [Hint: use (43).]

23.18. As pointed out in §23.12, it has now been proved that J is regular in the upper half-plane. I shall show that J has the other two properties mentioned in §23.1.

THEOREM 23.7.   *Let* im $z > 0$ *and* $z \equiv w$. *Then* $J(z) = J(w)$.

This follows from the definition of congruence (§23.12), (31), and Theorems 23.4 and 23.5.

EXERCISE

23.8. The function f is continuous in $[-\frac{1}{2}, \frac{1}{2}]$, $f(-\frac{1}{2})=f(\frac{1}{2})$, and $f(t)>0$ for every number t in $[-\frac{1}{2}, \frac{1}{2}]$. The function g is defined by $g(t)=e^{2\pi i t}f(t)$, and $C=\mathscr{C}(g, -\frac{1}{2}, \frac{1}{2})$. Prove that $I(C)$ consists of the point 0 and those points z for which $0<|z|<f\{\operatorname{am} z/(2\pi)\}$, and that C is a Jordan curve, described in the positive sense.

23.19. By (28) and (41),

$$45\pi^{-4}G(z) = 1+240\phi_1(e^{2\pi i z}) \quad (\operatorname{im} z>0). \tag{58}$$

Let

$$\phi_3(z) = \{1+240\phi_1(z)\}^3/\phi(z). \tag{59}$$

Then, by (31), (58) and (43),

$$J(w) = \phi_3(e^{2\pi i w}) \quad (\operatorname{im} w > 0). \tag{60}$$

THEOREM 23.8. *Let* $|z| < 1$ *and* $|\log z| = 2\pi$. *Then* $\phi_3(z)$ *is real.*

Proof. Let $\bar{z}$ be the conjugate of z (see §1.11). Then it follows from (59), (41) and (42) that $\phi_3(\bar{z})$ is the conjugate of $\phi_3(z)$. Hence it is sufficient to prove that

$$\phi_3(z) = \phi_3(\bar{z}). \tag{61}$$

Let $w=\log z/(2\pi i)$. Then $|w|=1$, which implies that $1/w$ is the conjugate of w. Thus

$$e^{2\pi i w} = z, \qquad e^{-2\pi i/w} = \bar{z}. \tag{62}$$

Now $w \equiv -1/w$ and $\operatorname{im} w>0$. Hence, by Theorem 23.7, $J(w)=J(-1/w)$. Also, by (60) and (62), $J(w)=\phi_3(z)$ and $J(-1/w)=\phi_3(\bar{z})$. This proves (61), and with it the theorem.

23.20. Let $g(t)=\exp[2\pi i\{t+i\sqrt{(1-t^2)}\}]$ and $C_0=\mathscr{C}(g, -\frac{1}{2}, \frac{1}{2})$. Then it follows from Exercise 23.8 that $I(C_0)$ consists of the point 0 and those points z for which $0<|z|<1$ and $|\log z|>2\pi$, and that C_0 is a Jordan curve, described in the positive sense. It is trivial that C_0 is a contour (see §11.1). Also $z \in |C_0|$ if and only if $|z|<1$ and $|\log z|=2\pi$. Hence, by Theorem 23.8, $\phi_3(z)$ is real for every point z of C_0.

THEOREM 23.9. *Let w be any number such that there is no point z on C_0 for which $\phi_3(z)=w$. Then*

$$\int_{C_0} \frac{\phi_3'(z)}{\phi_3(z)-w} \, dz = 0.$$

This follows from what has just been said and the first part of Exercise 11.8, with $f(z) = \phi_3(z) - w$ or $i\phi_3(z) - iw$ according as w is imaginary or real (so that $f(z)$ is not real for any point z of C_0).

EXERCISE

23.9. Draw the unit circle and the curve C_0 to scale. [Hint: use a very large sheet of paper.]

23.21. THEOREM 23.10. *On the hypothesis of Theorem 23.9, there is one and only one point z within C_0 for which $\phi_3(z) = w$.*

Proof. It follows from (41) and (42) that ϕ_1 and ϕ are regular in the unit disc. Also, by (46) and the first part of (48), ϕ has a simple zero at 0, and it follows from Exercise 23.7 that this is the only zero of ϕ in the unit disc. Hence, by (59), $\phi_3(z) - w$ is regular for $0 < |z| < 1$, and it follows from §17.8 and §17.9 (on noting that $\phi_1(0) = 0$) that $\phi_3(z) - w$ has a pole of order 1 at 0. From this and §23.20 and Theorem 18.4 it follows that $\phi_3(z) - w$ has exactly one zero within C_0. This proves the theorem.

THEOREM 23.11. *Let w be any number. Then there is a number z such that $z \in S_0$ and $J(z) = w$. Moreover, if im $w \neq 0$, then there is only one such number z.*

Proof. By Theorem 23.10, there is a point z', either on or within C_0, such that $\phi_3(z') = w$; and since $\phi_3(0)$ does not exist, we have $z' \neq 0$. Hence, by §23.20, $0 < |z'| < 1$ and $|\log z'| \geqslant 2\pi$ (and $|\log z'| = 2\pi$ if and only if $z' \in |C_0|$). Let $z'' = \log z'/(2\pi i)$. Then im $z'' = -\log |z'|/(2\pi) > 0$, $-\frac{1}{2} < $ re $z'' \leqslant \frac{1}{2}$ and $|z''| \geqslant 1$. Hence, by §23.13, either (i) $z'' \in S_0$, or (ii) $-\frac{1}{2} < $ re $z'' < 0$ and $|z''| = 1$. In case (i), let $z = z''$; in case (ii), $z = -1/z''$. Then, in either case, $z \in S_0$ and $z \equiv z''$, so that, by Theorem 23.7, $J(z) = J(z'')$. Also $z' = e^{2\pi i z''}$. Hence, by (60), $J(z) = J(z'') = \phi_3(e^{2\pi i z''}) = \phi_3(z') = w$. This proves the first part of the theorem.

Now suppose that im $w \neq 0$, $z_1 \in S_0$, $z_2 \in S_0$, and

$$J(z_1) = J(z_2) = w. \tag{63}$$

Then we have to prove that

$$z_1 = z_2. \tag{64}$$

In the remainder of this proof, let m be either 1 or 2. Then, by §23.13,

$$-\tfrac{1}{2} < \operatorname{re} z_m \leqslant \tfrac{1}{2}, \qquad \operatorname{im} z_m > 0, \qquad |z_m| \geqslant 1. \tag{65}$$

Let

$$z'_m = e^{2\pi i z_m}. \tag{66}$$

Then, by (60) and (63),

$$\phi_3(z'_m) = w. \tag{67}$$

Now, by (65), $-\pi < \operatorname{im} (2\pi i z_m) \leqslant \pi$. Hence, by (66),

$$2\pi i z_m = \log z'_m. \tag{68}$$

From this and (65) it follows that $|z'_m| < 1$ and $|\log z'_m| \geqslant 2\pi$. Hence, by §23.20, z'_m is within or on C_0. Also, since w is not real, it follows from §23.20 that there is no point z on C_0 for which $\phi_3(z) = w$. Hence, by (67), z'_m is within C_0, and, by Theorem 23.10, there is only one point z within C_0 for which $\phi_3(z) = w$. This means that $z'_1 = z'_2$, which, together with (68), proves (64), and so completes the proof of the theorem.

EXERCISES

23.10. Assuming that $z_0 \in S_0$, prove that, in every disc about z_0, there is a point z' of S_0 for which $J(z')$ is imaginary.

23.11. Prove that, if $-\tfrac{1}{2} < \operatorname{re} z_1 \leqslant \tfrac{1}{2}$ and $|z_1| > 1$, then there is a positive number r, such that, for every number z for which $|z - z_1| < r$, either $z \in S_0$ or $z - 1 \in S_0$.

23.12. Prove that, if $0 \leqslant \operatorname{re} z_1 < \tfrac{1}{2}$ and $|z_1| = 1$, then there is a positive number r, such that, for every number z for which $|z - z_1| < r$, either $z \in S_0$ or $-1/z \in S_0$.

23.22. THEOREM 23.12. *J is simple in S_0.*

Proof. Suppose this is not so. Then there are points z_0, z_1 such that

$$z_0 \in S_0, \qquad z_1 \in S_0, \qquad z_0 \neq z_1, \qquad J(z_0) = J(z_1). \tag{69}$$

Since $z_0 \neq z_1$, we cannot have both $z_0 = \tfrac{1}{2} + \tfrac{1}{2}i\sqrt{3}$ and $z_1 = \tfrac{1}{2} + \tfrac{1}{2}i\sqrt{3}$, and there is no loss of generality in the assumption that

$$z_1 \neq \tfrac{1}{2} + \tfrac{1}{2}i\sqrt{3}. \tag{70}$$

Let us make this assumption. Then, by §23.13, either

$$-\tfrac{1}{2} < \text{re } z_1 \leqslant \tfrac{1}{2}, \quad |z_1| > 1, \tag{71}$$

or

$$0 \leqslant \text{re } z_1 < \tfrac{1}{2}, \quad |z_1| = 1. \tag{72}$$

Let $f(z) = z - 1$ or $-1/z$, according as (71) or (72) holds. Then either $f(z_1) = z_1 = i$, or $f(z_1)$ is not in S_0. In either case, by (69), $z_0 \neq f(z_1)$. Also f is continuous at z_1. From this and Exercises 23.11 and 23.12 it follows that, if the positive number r is small enough, and $|z - z_1| < r$, then

$$|z - z_0| > r, \qquad |f(z) - z_0| > r, \tag{73}$$

and

$$z \in S_0 \quad \text{or} \quad f(z) \in S_0. \tag{74}$$

Choose r accordingly.

By Exercise 18.2, J is not locally constant at z_1. Hence, defining S as the disc with centre z_1 and radius r, we infer from Theorem 20.3 that $J(z_1)$ is an interior point of $J(S)$ (see §7.1). This means that there is a positive number r', such that, for every number w for which $|w - J(z_1)| < r'$, there is a number z for which $|z - z_1| < r$ and $J(z) = w$. Choose r' accordingly. Then, since J is continuous at z_0, there is a positive number r'' such that, for every number z' for which $|z' - z_0| < r''$, we have $|J(z') - J(z_0)| < r'$, and hence, by (69),

$$|J(z') - J(z_1)| < r'. \tag{75}$$

Choose z' so that

$$|z' - z_0| < \min{(r, r'')}, \tag{76}$$

$$z' \in S_0 \tag{77}$$

and

$$\text{im } J(z') \neq 0. \tag{78}$$

This is possible by Exercise 23.10. (76) implies (75). Now, by (75) and what was said a little earlier, used with $w = J(z')$, there is a number z for which

$$|z - z_1| < r \tag{79}$$

and

$$J(z) = J(z').\tag{80}$$

(79) implies that (73) and (74) hold. By (73) and (76),

$$z \neq z', \qquad f(z) \neq z'.\tag{81}$$

Now $z \equiv f(z)$, and it easily follows from (74) that $\operatorname{im} z > 0$. Hence, by Theorem 23.7 and (80),

$$J\{f(z)\} = J(z').\tag{82}$$

By (77), (78) and the last part of Theorem 23.11, z' is the only point ζ of S_0 for which $J(\zeta) = J(z')$. By (74), (80), (82) and (81), however, there is at least one other such point, namely either $\zeta = z$, or $\zeta = f(z)$. This is a contradiction, and so the theorem is proved.

EXERCISE

23.13. Deduce the result of Exercise 23.6 from Theorems 23.7 and 23.12.

23.23. THEOREM 23.13. *Let* $\operatorname{im} z > 0$, $\operatorname{im} w > 0$ *and* $J(z) = J(w)$. *Then* $z \equiv w$.

Proof. By Theorem 23.6, there are points z', w' in S_0 such that $z \equiv z'$ and $w \equiv w'$. Hence, by Theorem 23.7, $J(z) = J(z')$ and $J(w) = J(w')$, and since $J(z) = J(w)$, it follows that $J(z') = J(w')$. From this and Theorem 23.12 we obtain $z' = w'$. The result now follows from Exercise 23.2.

It has now been shown that J has the three properties mentioned in §23.1: the proof of (i) was completed in §23.17, (ii) follows from the first part of Theorem 23.11, and (iii) from Theorems 23.7 and 23.13 and the definition of congruence (§23.12).

23.24. I define S_1 as the set of the interior points of S_0, i.e. the points z for which $-\frac{1}{2} < \operatorname{re} z < \frac{1}{2}$, $\operatorname{im} z > 0$ and $|z| > 1$, S_2 as the set of those points z for which $0 < \operatorname{re} z < 1$, $\operatorname{im} z > 0$, $|z| > 1$ and $|z-1| > 1$, and S_3 as the set of those points z for which $0 < \operatorname{re} z < \frac{1}{2}$, $\operatorname{im} z > 0$ and $|z-1| > 1$.

EXERCISES

23.14. Prove that S_1, S_2 and S_3 are domains.

23.15. Prove that $J(\frac{1}{2} + \frac{1}{2}i\sqrt{3}) = 0$ and $J(i) = 1$. [Hint: use Exercise 23.1.]

23.16. Assuming that $z \in S_0$, prove that (i) $J(z) < 0$ if and only if re $z = \frac{1}{2}$ and $|z| > 1$, (ii) $0 < J(z) < 1$ if and only if $0 < $ re $z < \frac{1}{2}$ and $|z| = 1$, and (iii) $J(z) > 1$ if and only if re $z = 0$ and $|z| > 1$.

23.17. Prove that, if z is in S_2, but not in S_0, then $z - 1$ is in S_0, but not in S_2.

23.18. Prove that, if z is in S_3, but not in S_0, then $-1/z$ is in S_0, but not in S_3.

23.25. THEOREM 23.14. *Let* $z \in S_2$, $w \in S_2$ *and* $z \equiv w$. *Then* $z = w$.

Proof. If z and w are both in S_0, the result follows from Exercise 23.6. If neither of them is, let $z' = z - 1$, $w' = w - 1$. Then $z \equiv z'$ and $w \equiv w'$. Hence, by Exercise 23.2, $z' \equiv w'$. Also, by Exercise 23.17, $z' \in S_0$ and $w' \in S_0$. Hence, by Exercise 23.6, $z' = w'$, i.e. $z - 1 = w - 1$, and the result again follows. If w is in S_0, but z is not, let again $z' = z - 1$. Then, arguing essentially as before, we obtain $z' = w$. Now, by Exercise 23.17, z' is not in S_2, but, by hypothesis, w is. This is a contradiction. Hence this case cannot occur. The same applies, similarly, to the case in which z is in S_0, but w is not. This completes the proof.

THEOREM 23.15. *Let* $z \in S_3$, $w \in S_3$ *and* $z \equiv w$. *Then* $z = w$.

To obtain a proof, take that of Theorem 23.14, and replace 'S_2' by 'S_3', '$z - 1$' by '$-1/z$', '$w - 1$' by '$-1/w$' and '23.17' by '23.18'.

THEOREM 23.16. *J is simple in S_2 and in S_3.*

This follows from the last three theorems.

23.26. For $m = 0, 1, 2, 3$, let J_m be the sub-function of J in S_m (see §16.2), and G_m the inverse function of J_m (see §7.5). This exists in virtue of Theorems 23.12 and 23.16. Since J is regular in the upper half-plane, it follows from Exercise 23.14 and §16.2 that J_1, J_2 and J_3 are analytic functions. Hence, by Theorem 20.8, so are G_1, G_2 and G_3.

It follows from these definitions that, for $m = 0, 1, 2, 3$ and any number w, $G_m(w)$ exists if and only if there is a number z in S_m such that $J(z) = w$, and then $G_m(w)$ is this number z. Now, by the first part of Theorem 23.11, there is always such a number z in S_0; and there are only two points of S_0 which are not in any of the three sets S_1, S_2, S_3, namely $\frac{1}{2} + \frac{1}{2}i\sqrt{3}$ and i. Hence $G_0(w)$ always exists, and if $G_0(w) \neq \frac{1}{2} + \frac{1}{2}i\sqrt{3}$ and $G_0(w) \neq i$, then at least one of the numbers $G_1(w)$, $G_2(w)$, $G_3(w)$ also exists. Now $G_0(w) = \frac{1}{2} + \frac{1}{2}i\sqrt{3}$ only if $J(\frac{1}{2} + \frac{1}{2}i\sqrt{3}) = w$. Hence, by Exercise 23.15, $G_0(w) \neq \frac{1}{2} + \frac{1}{2}i\sqrt{3}$ if $w \neq 0$. Similarly $G_0(w) \neq i$ if $w \neq 1$. Thus, if $w \neq 0$ and $w \neq 1$, then at least one of the three numbers $G_1(w)$, $G_2(w)$, $G_3(w)$ exists.

23.27. Now suppose Picard's theorem (see §23.1) is false. Then there are two distinct numbers a, b and a non-constant integral function f_1, such that f_1 does not assume either of the two values a, b. Let $f_2(z) = \{f_1(z) - a\}/(b - a)$. Then f_2 is a non-constant integral function, and

$$f_2(z) \neq 0, \qquad f_2(z) \neq 1 \tag{83}$$

for any number z.

Choose m from the numbers 1, 2, 3 so that $G_m\{f_2(0)\}$ exists. This is possible by (83) and §23.26. Since G_m is an analytic function, it follows that G_m is regular at $f_2(0)$. Hence, by Theorem 6.4, the function g defined by

$$g(z) = G_m\{f_2(z)\} \tag{84}$$

is regular at 0. From this and Exercise 6.1 it follows that there is a positive number r_1 such that $g(z)$ is regular for $|z| < r_1$. Thus, by Theorem 14.2,

$$g(z) = \sum_{n=0}^{\infty} \frac{g^{(n)}(0)}{n!} z^n \quad (|z| < r_1). \tag{85}$$

If this series converges for every number z, let its sum be denoted by $h(z)$, also for every number z. Otherwise let h be the analytic function associated with this power series, as defined in §16.16. Let D be the region of existence of h (so that D is either the whole plane or a disc about 0). Then

$$g(z) = h(z) \quad (|z| < r_1). \tag{86}$$

By (86), (84) and the definition of G_m (§23.26),

$$J\{h(z)\} = f_2(z) \quad (|z| < r_1). \tag{87}$$

16*

23.28. Let S be the set of those numbers z for which $\operatorname{im} h(z) > 0$. If S were the whole plane, then the function h^* defined by $h^*(z) = 1/\{h(z) + i\}$ would be a bounded integral function, and therefore, by Liouville's theorem (Theorem 14.7), a constant. Hence h would be a constant. From this and (87) it would follow that f_2 is locally constant at 0, which, in view of Exercise 18.2, is impossible. Hence S is not the whole plane, i.e. the complement T of S is not empty. It is trivial that S is open. Hence, by Theorem 3.2, T is closed. Also, by (86), (84) and the definitions of G_m, S_m and S, the disc with centre 0 and radius r_1 is contained in S. This means that, denoting the distance of the point 0 from T by r_2, we have

$$r_2 \geqslant r_1. \tag{88}$$

Let D_1 be the disc with centre 0 and radius r_2. Then it is trivial that

$$D_1 \subset S \subset D. \tag{89}$$

This implies that h is regular in D_1, and

$$\operatorname{im} h(z) > 0 \quad (z \in D_1). \tag{90}$$

From this, the regularity of J in the upper half-plane (§23.18), and Theorem 6.4 it follows that $J\{h(z)\}$ is regular in D_1, i.e. for $|z| < r_2$. Hence, by (87) and the corollary to Theorem 15.4 (since f_2 is an integral function),

$$J\{h(z)\} = f_2(z) \quad (|z| < r_2). \tag{91}$$

Now, by Exercise 3.10, there is a point z_0 such that

$$z_0 \in T \tag{92}$$

and

$$|z_0| = r_2. \tag{93}$$

(92) means that either (i) $\operatorname{im} h(z_0) \leqslant 0$, or (ii) $h(z_0)$ does not exist. In case (i) let $z_1 = z_0$. Then

$$\operatorname{im} h(z_1) \leqslant 0 \tag{94}$$

and

$$z_1 \in D. \tag{95}$$

In case (ii), z_0 is not in D. Hence, by §23.27, D is a disc about 0, and its radius is not greater than $|z_0|$. On the other hand, by (89), this radius is at least that of D_1, i.e. r_2. Hence, by (93),

$$D = D_1, \tag{96}$$

i.e. r_2 is the radius of convergence of the power series in (85). From this and Theorem 16.5 and §16.8 it follows that h has at least one singularity z_1, say, and

$$|z_1| = r_2. \tag{97}$$

This equation holds, by (93), also in case (i).

To obtain a contradiction from the assumption that Picard's theorem is false, I shall show in case (i) that (94) cannot hold, and in case (ii) that z_1 cannot be a singularity of h.

23.29. Choose k from the numbers 1, 2, 3 so that $G_k\{f_2(z_1)\}$ exists. This is possible by (83) and §23.26. Then, by an argument like that used in connection with (84), the function g^* defined by

$$g^*(z) = G_k\{f_2(z)\} \tag{98}$$

is regular in some disc D_2 about z_1, and it follows from (98) and the definition of G_k (§23.26) that

$$g^*(z) \in S_k \quad (z \in D_2) \tag{99}$$

and

$$J\{g^*(z)\} = f_2(z) \quad (z \in D_2). \tag{100}$$

23.30. By (97), z_1 is on the circumference of D_1. Hence $D_1 \cap D_2$ is not empty. So let

$$z_2 \in D_1 \cap D_2. \tag{101}$$

Then, by (91) and (100), $J\{h(z_2)\} = J\{g^*(z_2)\}$. Also, by (90), im $h(z_2) > 0$, and, by (99), im $g^*(z_2) > 0$. Hence, by Theorem 23.13, $h(z_2) \equiv g^*(z_2)$. This (see §23.12) means that there are integers a, b, c, d, such that

$$ad - bc = 1 \tag{102}$$

and

$$g^*(z_2) = \{ah(z_2) + b\}/\{ch(z_2) + d\}. \tag{103}$$

Let
$$F(z) = \{ah(z)+b\}/\{ch(z)+d\}. \tag{104}$$

Then, by (103),
$$g^*(z_2) = F(z_2). \tag{105}$$

Now $D_1 \cap D_2$ and S_k are open, and it follows from (101), (99) and (105) that $z_2 \in D_1 \cap D_2$ and $F(z_2) \in S_k$. Hence z_2 and $F(z_2)$ are interior to $D_1 \cap D_2$ and S_k respectively. Also F is continuous at z_2. Hence there is a disc D_3 about z_2 such that

$$D_3 \subset D_1 \cap D_2 \tag{106}$$

and
$$F(z) \in S_k \quad (z \in D_3). \tag{107}$$

By (104) and §23.12, $h(z) \equiv F(z)$ whenever $h(z)$ exists. Hence, by Theorem 23.7 and (90),

$$J\{h(z)\} = J\{F(z)\} \quad (z \in D_1), \tag{108}$$

and hence, by (91),

$$f_2(z) = J\{F(z)\} \quad (z \in D_1). \tag{109}$$

Now, by the definition of G_k (§23.26), if $w \in S_k$ and $J(w)=w'$, then $w=G_k(w')$. Hence, by (106), (107), (109) and (98),

$$F(z) = G_k\{f_2(z)\} = g^*(z) \quad (z \in D_3). \tag{110}$$

From this and (104) it follows that

$$h(z) = \{dg^*(z)-b\}/\{-cg^*(z)+a\} \quad (z \in D_3). \tag{111}$$

Let the function h_1 be defined by

$$h_1(z) = \{dg^*(z)-b\}/\{-cg^*(z)+a\}. \tag{112}$$

Then, by the remark made in connection with (98), h_1 is regular in D_2. Also, by (111), $h(z)=h_1(z)$, $(z \in D_3)$. Now h and h_1 are regular in $D \cap D_2$, $D \cap D_2$ is a domain, and D_3 is open and not empty. Also, by (106) and (89), $D_3 \subset D \cap D_2$. Hence, by the corollary to Theorem 15.4,

$$h(z) = h_1(z) \quad (z \in D \cap D_2). \tag{113}$$

In case (i) it follows from (113) and (95) (since D_2 is a disc about z_1) that

$$h(z_1) = h_1(z_1). \tag{114}$$

Now, by (112), (102) and §23.12, $g^*(z_1) \equiv h_1(z_1)$. Also, by (98), im $g^*(z_1) > 0$. Hence, by Exercise 23.3 and (114), im $h(z_1) > 0$. This contradicts (94).

In case (ii), let h_2 be the sub-function of h_1 in D_2 (see §16.2). Then, since h_1 is regular in D_2, h_2 is an analytic function. Also, by (113), $h(z) = h_2(z)$, $(z \in D \cap D_2)$. Hence, by §16.3, h_2 is an immediate continuation of h, and since $z_1 \in D_2$, it is an immediate continuation of h to z_1. From this and §§16.7–16.8 it follows that z_1 cannot be a singularity of h. Thus, in view of the last paragraph of §23.28, Picard's theorem is proved.

BIBLIOGRAPHY

AHLFORS, L. V. *Complex Analysis*. New York, 1953.

COURANT, R. *Differential and Integral Calculus*. 2nd edn. London and Glasgow, 1937.

HARDY, G. H. *A Course of Pure Mathematics*. 7th edn. Cambridge, 1938.

KNOPP, K. *Theory of Functions*. 1st American edn. New York, 1945.

LANDAU, E. (1) *Foundations of Analysis*. New York, 1957.

—— (2) *Differential and Integral Calculus*. New York, 1951.

—— (3) *Darstellung und Begründung einiger neuerer Ergebnisse der Funktionentheorie*. 2nd edn. New York, 1946.

TITCHMARSH, E. C. *The Theory of Functions*. 2nd edn. London, 1939.

INDEX OF SPECIAL NOTATIONS

GENERAL INDEX